CAMBRIDGE LIBRARY COLLECTION

Books of enduring scholarly value

Classics

From the Renaissance to the nineteenth century, Latin and Greek were compulsory subjects in almost all European universities, and most early modern scholars published their research and conducted international correspondence in Latin. Latin had continued in use in Western Europe long after the fall of the Roman empire as the lingua franca of the educated classes and of law, diplomacy, religion and university teaching. The flight of Greek scholars to the West after the fall of Constantinople in 1453 gave impetus to the study of ancient Greek literature and the Greek New Testament. Eventually, just as nineteenth-century reforms of university curricula were beginning to erode this ascendancy, developments in textual criticism and linguistic analysis, and new ways of studying ancient societies, especially archaeology, led to renewed enthusiasm for the Classics. This collection offers works of criticism, interpretation and synthesis by the outstanding scholars of the nineteenth century.

Lectures and Essays

Lectures and Essays, edited by F. Haverfield, was first published in 1895. It contains the published articles of Henry Nettleship (1839–93) on Latin literature not included in the collection *Lectures and Essays on Subjects Connected with Latin Literature and Scholarship* (1885), along with one unpublished essay. The volume begins with a memoir written by Nettleship's wife, focusing on his progressive approach towards educational reform and modernisation. The collection includes essays on contemporary scholars such as the Danish philologist Madvig (1804–86); the poet Juvenal; the earliest Latin grammarians; literary criticism in antiquity; and on the state of English education in the nineteenth century, including the influential essay 'On the Present Relations between Classical Research and Classical Education in England'. This collection of lectures and essays is a valuable source representing the work of an eminent Victorian scholar and educational reformer who made a lasting contribution to Latin studies.

T0381834

Cambridge University Press has long been a pioneer in the reissuing of out-of-print titles from its own backlist, producing digital reprints of books that are still sought after by scholars and students but could not be reprinted economically using traditional technology. The Cambridge Library Collection extends this activity to a wider range of books which are still of importance to researchers and professionals, either for the source material they contain, or as landmarks in the history of their academic discipline.

Drawing from the world-renowned collections in the Cambridge University Library, and guided by the advice of experts in each subject area, Cambridge University Press is using state-of-the-art scanning machines in its own Printing House to capture the content of each book selected for inclusion. The files are processed to give a consistently clear, crisp image, and the books finished to the high quality standard for which the Press is recognised around the world. The latest print-on-demand technology ensures that the books will remain available indefinitely, and that orders for single or multiple copies can quickly be supplied.

The Cambridge Library Collection will bring back to life books of enduring scholarly value (including out-of-copyright works originally issued by other publishers) across a wide range of disciplines in the humanities and social sciences and in science and technology.

Lectures and Essays

Second Series

HENRY NETTLESHIP
EDITED BY F. HAVERFIELD

CAMBRIDGE UNIVERSITY PRESS

Cambridge, New York, Melbourne, Madrid, Cape Town, Singapore,
São Paolo, Delhi, Dubai, Tokyo

Published in the United States of America by Cambridge University Press, New York

www.cambridge.org
Information on this title: www.cambridge.org/9781108012461

© in this compilation Cambridge University Press 2010

This edition first published 1895
This digitally printed version 2010

ISBN 978-1-108-01246-1 Paperback

LECTURES AND ESSAYS

II

NETTLESHIP

Henry Nettleship

LECTURES AND ESSAYS

BY

HENRY NETTLESHIP

M.A., D.LITT.

LATE CORPUS PROFESSOR OF LATIN LITERATURE IN
THE UNIVERSITY OF OXFORD

SECOND SERIES

EDITED BY

F. HAVERFIELD, M.A.

STUDENT OF CHRIST CHURCH

WITH PORTRAIT AND MEMOIR

Oxford
AT THE CLARENDON PRESS
1895

PREFACE

Mr. Nettleship's intellectual activity expressed itself in three forms, all marked by fine literary taste and judgement. (1) As a Latin scholar he was concerned peculiarly with Vergil and Latin lexicography, and in dealing with these subjects he paid especial attention to grammarians and glossaries. By tracing the sources and establishing the relations of writers like Festus, Nonius, Servius, Gellius, he hoped to recover the earliest text and interpretation of Vergil and the vocabulary of republican and Augustan Latin. (2) But in pursuing these researches he always kept in view the ultimate literary end, and he devoted many essays and lectures to the appreciation of the *Aeneid*, the *Satura*, and other Latin literature. His most characteristic work was, perhaps, literary criticism, and the fine taste and wide sympathy which went with it led him (3), especially in his later years, to write and lecture on educational or philosophical topics unconnected with Latin scholarship.

The present volume contains all Mr. Nettleship's scattered writings on Latin literature and on general subjects—that is, all that comes under the second and third classes enumerated, so far as these contributions were not included in his former volume of *Lectures and Essays* issued in 1885. The two volumes thus contain all

Mr. Nettleship's literary work in a collected shape, while a bibliography which I have appended to this volume will facilitate reference to his uncollected contributions to technical scholarship, grammarians, glossaries, and the like.

All the articles in the present volume have appeared in print already, except the lecture on Madvig. This lecture and a fragment of an edition of Nonius Marcellus were the only unpublished materials left by Mr. Nettleship in a state ready to be printed as his work. The lecture on Madvig is accordingly printed below: the critical notes on Nonius will appear in the *Journal of Philology*. In editing the papers I have verified all references and quotations, added a few references and half a dozen notes in square brackets: further changes were obviously out of place.

I have to thank Messrs. Rivington & Percival, Messrs. Kegan Paul, Trench & Co., Mr. Walter Scott, and the editors and publishers of the *Journal of Philology*, the *American Journal of Philology*, and the *International Journal of Ethics* for leave to reprint various essays, as indicated at the commencement of each essay.

F. HAVERFIELD.

CONTENTS

₊ Mr. Nettleship's volume of *Lectures and Essays on subjects connected with Latin Literature and Scholarship* (Oxford 1885) has, for the sake of clearness, been referred to in the following pages by the title on its binding, *Essays in Latin Literature.*

MEMOIR

HENRY NETTLESHIP was born at Kettering in Northampton-shire on May 5, 1839. His father, Henry John Nettleship, a solicitor practising in that town, married Isabella Ann, daughter of the Rev. James Hogg, Vicar of Geddington, and master of Kettering Grammar School. They had seven children, of whom five boys lived to maturity. The youngest of these, Richard Lewis, Fellow and Tutor of Balliol College, Oxford, perished in a snowstorm on Mont Blanc, August 25, 1892. Of the other brothers, one became an artist, another an oculist, a third a schoolmaster; while the eldest is the subject of this memoir.

His grandfather, John Nettleship, of Tickhill, Yorkshire, married Ann Hunt (first cousin of George Waddington, Dean of Durham), whose brother, J. H. Hunt, was the editor of the *Critical Review* and the translator of Tasso. John Nettleship's mother, the Mrs. Nettleship of Gainsborough spoken of with admiration by Mr. Mozley in his *Reminiscences of Towns, Villages and Schools*, was a remarkable woman, cultivated and musical, pious and charitable. The mother of the late Prof. George Rolleston was one of her daughters.

His grandmother's connexion with Dean Waddington was the cause of his being eventually sent to school at Durham, and this, by bringing him under the influence of Dr. Elder, the Headmaster, determined his future career as a Scholar.

His feeling for music and poetry seems to have been derived from his father's family, who were all musical, an aunt being an accomplished pianist.

As the eldest, Henry was naturally made much of by his
parents and grandparents, though they were afraid of their par-
tiality being seen, and he retained a recollection of a rather
severe bringing-up, the duty of self-denial being much dwelt
upon. Though he could read well at the age of four, he was
not encouraged to occupy himself in this way. His mother
read aloud to him and his brothers, both verse and prose; and
he remembered enjoying *Paradise Lost* when quite a small
child. He had a naturally retentive memory, and was early
accustomed to recite poetry. As a boy he was 'bright, genial
and sympathetic—a main element of happiness in a happy
home,' while the same simplicity and absence of self-
consciousness were characteristic of him then as in later life.
He early showed a sense of humour, and would amuse himself
by inventing nonsense rhymes to suit different occasions, and
setting them to well-known classical airs, frequently from
Handel's oratorios. Without a natural turn for athletics of
any sort, he had considerable pluck and determination, and
made himself a very fair rider, swimmer and skater. After all
connexion with Kettering had ceased, through his father's death
and his mother's removal, he often returned to visit the place he
loved, recalling the old simple life, which had great charms for
him. There was a strong attachment between all the brothers,
as between the sons and their parents, and this was unaffected,
as time went on, by distance or difference in character and
pursuits.

Henry Nettleship's first school was Mr. Darnell's, at Market
Harborough, in 1848. The next year he went to St. Nicholas
College, Shoreham (or Lancing, as it is often called), where
he gained a scholarship and several prizes. He was much
attached to this school and his masters, and regretted leaving.
His father had been in correspondence about his son with
Dean Waddington, and sent him to Durham in August,
1852, where he gained a King's Scholarship the following
November. The Dean, as was his custom if a kinsman were
elected, paid the money out of his own pocket, to avoid all

suspicion of favouritism—the boy retaining the honourable position of King's Scholar, but the money from the school funds passing on to the next in order of examination. The Dean took steady interest in his progress, writing kind letters to the boy himself, as well as to his father and friends.

Prof. Hales, an old schoolfellow, says : ' I first remember Henry Nettleship in the second "half" of 1852, when I entered the Upper Fourth ; he was then the most distinguished member of the form. I can vividly recall his shy, thoughtful, observant manner. I seem to hear him answering one of the endless questions asked us which were too much for all but Nettleship. . . . But indeed everybody liked him. His cleverness, which we were sharp enough to discover, was so entirely free from conceit or pretence ; and though no great hand at games he was anything but a bookworm, but took a thorough interest in all the affairs of our schoolboy world. . . . But I can recognize now, more clearly of course than I did then, Nettleship's eagerness for the truth, whatever it might be ; his scepticism, in the proper sense of the word ; the absence in him of the blind idolatrous spirit. His sympathies were with the High Churchmen of that date, but he was never a bigot ; he was really interested in other views ; he never dreamt the last word had been said about those matters. . . . It was surely one of Nettleship's distinctions that even in his teens he perceived that the party to which he belonged had not, and could not have, any monopoly of light. . . . Most certainly, for my part, I owed him much—for a sense of tolerance, for broadened notions, for an opened mind. He was a delightful companion, unselfish, well-informed and entertaining, and it was with universal regret we heard he was going to follow Dr. Elder to Charterhouse.'

There is no doubt that he was immensely impressed by Dr. Elder's scholarship and teaching. He always spoke of him as having been in advance of his time in thoroughness and grasp of classical knowledge, and felt he owed him much for fostering in him the love of learning and a high ideal of scholarship. Dr. Elder was indeed the hero of his school life ; and

when he heard of his promotion to the Headmastership of the
Charterhouse, in the summer of 1853, he did not rest until
he had gained his parents' permission to follow him there,
promising to use every endeavour to obtain a scholarship at
the Charterhouse, so that they might not be pecuniarily losers
by the change. Devoted as he was to Durham, with its
picturesque situation, its fine old Cathedral, its beautiful
musical services—all appealing to his intense love of beauty in
its noblest forms—yet his affection for Dr. Elder gained the
day, and, six months later, he entered the Charterhouse, on
January 20, 1854, as an inmate of Dr. Elder's house, which
was then known as 'Saunderites.' In January, 1855, he
was in the Sixth Form, and the best classical scholar in the
school.   Next summer he gained the Senior Scholarship
and passed into 'Gownboys,' where his chief friends
were, Prof. Jebb, for whom he kept always a warm regard;
J. W. Churton, a boy of great promise, who died young;
J. W. Irvine, Rector of St. Mary's, Colchester; R. Brodie,
Headmaster of Archbishop Whitgift's School, Croydon; and
H. C. Malkin, Clerk in the House of Lords. He read a great
deal for himself, devouring history, a schoolfellow says, as other
boys do novels, and being a passionate admirer of Tennyson,
Keats and Shelley. With a peculiarly susceptible nature, he
had an intuitive gift for seizing the highest standard of excellence in those about him; and it was natural that Dr. Elder—
a born teacher and brilliant scholar, with the power of winning
boys' hearts as well as bringing out their faculties—should
have exercised a strong personal influence over him.

He was now allowed to indulge his passion for music by taking
lessons on the piano, and seized every opportunity of hearing
good music, especially delighting in oratorios, copies of which,
bought at that time, are full of marks of boyish admiration of
passages that especially struck him. He enjoyed discussing
their construction and the technical processes by which
different effects were produced, particularly in the choruses.
His desire at this time was to become a musician and composer;

but he felt that his lack of early training stood in the way;
he knew also that he would have to depend on his own
exertions in life, and so put the idea away.

From this time he continued to win scholarships and prizes,
and cost his parents little for his education. He was a good
Greek scholar, his Iambics being a strong point in his work, and
in 1857 he gained the gold medal for Latin verse. He worked
without exceptional effort, moved rather by intellectual interest
than ambition, though he recognized the need for this incentive
in others. What he learnt he made his own. He was already
remarkable for thoroughness, for a certain distinction of mind
and a rare simplicity of character. His gentle and affectionate
disposition endeared him to his friends, and he returned in
abundant measure the sympathy he craved from others. At
Charterhouse he was, as a schoolfellow says, 'a living power
for good in the school.'

In October, 1857, he came up to Oxford, having gained in
the preceding April the first Classical Scholarship at Corpus
Christi College, H. G. Madan and W. A. Giffard being the other
successful candidates. There was a keen competition—it
being the first year the scholarships were thrown open.
Mr. Giffard describes him as being at that time 'rather above
the middle height, with a broad, high brow, significant of the
mind within. He had a slight stoop, which seemed to be mental
as well as physical, for he was a bigger man than he ever
allowed himself to appear. He was modest to a fault, with
serious convictions, but not in the least dogmatic. His nature
was generous, and his praise or admiration, when deserved,
was ungrudging. His laugh was hearty and genuine—he
laughed not only with his lips and eyes, but with his whole
being.' He and his friend used to write weekly essays for
Prof. Jowett, hardly appreciating at the time his unsparing
criticism, though laughing afterwards at the perfection to which
he carried the art of snubbing. They both played a good
deal, especially on Sunday evenings, when other men would
come in and listen. Henry Nettleship took lessons on the

piano at this time from Dr. Elvey of New College and Dr.
Corfe of Christ Church, and always enjoyed relating how the
former once said to him, 'When you can play *pretty* well
—which will be in about ten years' time—you will be able to
finger for yourself.'

The College could boast of a distinguished set of tutors
during his residence :—Mr. Walker, afterwards High Master
of St. Paul's, Mr. H. Furneaux, and Mr. Wilson, Whyte's
Professor of Moral Philosophy and afterwards President.
Prof. Conington's lectures, largely attended, were also given
in college.

Henry Nettleship gained a First Class in Classical Moderations, Michaelmas Term, 1858, the Hertford and Craven
Scholarships, the Gaisford Prize for Greek Prose, and the
Chancellor's Medal for Latin Essay. What he owed as an
undergraduate to Prof. Conington's teaching and influence
will be spoken of below. His tutors remember his promise,
his modesty, his genius for study, and his love of work for the
work's sake, uninfluenced by ambition in the ordinary sense.

He was placed in the Second Class in the Final Classical
Schools, Easter Term, 1861. His failure to gain a higher
class was a disappointment to his tutors and friends, but after
the first he never troubled about it himself; he knew he had
not kept strictly in the examination grooves, but had given himself up to the studies that suited him best, and read widely. He
once told a friend that the passion for philosophical divagations
cost him his First Class. Among the men of his own standing
were J. Bryce, T. H. Green, A. Dicey, E. Caird, I. Bywater,
T. W. Jackson, W Pater, R. Bosworth Smith, G. A. Simcox, and
H. A. Giffard. With the last three, who were of his own college,
he was most intimate at that time, later on with Green and
Bryce. He was elected to a Fellowship at Lincoln College
at the end of the same year, 1861, above other competitors,
all First Class men. In a fellowship examination there was
more scope for individuality, and the examiners might allow
themselves to be guided by signs of future promise in any

special direction. This direction in his case was classical scholarship. He justified the wisdom of the choice and was appointed to a lectureship soon after his election.

I am indebted to Prof. Dill's kindness for a detailed account of his work at that time at Lincoln. ' My first meeting with Mr. Nettleship was on the occasion of his taking us to be matriculated by the Vice-Chancellor. He had a certain shyness of manner which made some men feel a little awkward with him, but I soon felt that it only thinly veiled a warmth of heart and genuine intellectual sympathy as welcome as they were unexpected to a raw freshman. He seemed eagerly anxious to find some common ground from which to bring his ideas to work upon you. We had a most able and enthusiastic staff of tutors, the present Heads of Lincoln and Corpus, and Henry Nettleship, all young and full of energy, and men of marked individuality, admirably supplementing each other. The result was soon seen in the place which Lincoln took, as by a sudden bound, in the Schools and Fellowship examinations. It emerged from a condition of obscurity with a considerable number of idle men, reflecting no credit on the college, into a position of some prominence in the University, and though it would be invidious to apportion the credit for this great change, Henry Nettleship undoubtedly had a very large share in it. Though naturally one of the gentlest of men, he could and did show a cutting contempt for a tone or habits he thought unworthy of an academic society. His own life was a standing rebuke to frivolity, vulgarity, and laziness. No man worked harder with his pupils ; he would give hours to the correction of compositions or critical exercises, sorely trying to his patience and fastidious taste, and then rush to his piano for five minutes' playing to relieve the strain. He was full of ideas on philosophy, art, theology, literary criticism. My own impression was that he had gone more than most of his contemporaries at Oxford, in Classical Scholarship as in other things, to original sources, that he had broken away

from the old conventional habits of thought and inquiry,
and like the two men he most revered and admired, Mark
Pattison and Matthew Arnold, his ideal was the free untram-
melled play of the cultivated intellect, and the best results that
had been reached in the various departments of knowledge.
Philistinism was his *bête noire*, and in those days he had
perhaps a natural but excessive contempt for the peculiarly
English rigidity and imperviousness to new ideas.   He
was never much of a politician, his whole interest was in
scientific scholarship and philosophical views of life—in ideals
"yet very far off." He was the least showy of men, his
lectures did not impress men so much as private work
with them.   Standing with one hand behind his back before
the fire, he would give us in a nervous jerky way a mass of
carefully compiled notes and references on Thucydides or
Vergil.   He would not tolerate slipshod renderings, and was
averse to ready-made translations, yet always felt the
importance of the translator.   He interpreted an author by
means of the author himself, and that I think was the best
lesson he taught us.   There were men accustomed to happy
renderings and cut-and-dried explanations of any difficulty,
who sometimes failed to understand the delicate insight and
the learning which indicated, without pretending to express,
the fugitive charms of style or remote antiquarian allusions.
But even these schoolboy critics recognized his immense
superiority to themselves and to the ordinary tutor.   We
were all proud of him and believed in him.   His work was
characterized by a high moral tone : he was trying to educate
us in the highest sense, and he was not merely a scholar, but
a man sensitive to all influences and ideas that gave a fresher
life and a wider outlook.   His leaving Lincoln for Harrow
was a cause of real sorrow.'

His chief friends at Lincoln were perhaps Archer Clive (who
took his work when he went to Berlin), and Mr. Fowler, now
President of Corpus Christi College.   He belonged to the
'Old Mortality,' an Essay Society originated by Mr. Swinburne,

and at first confined to Balliol, a few men from other colleges being later on admitted as members. Among those of older standing who influenced him were Goldwin Smith, Matthew Arnold (of whom he was to see a good deal at Harrow), and Henry Smith. To the friendship of the latter and his sister he owed much in his early Oxford days, and this was renewed on his return to Oxford. For Mark Pattison and his wife (now Lady Dilke) he had a strong regard, which ripened into an intimacy that continued till the Rector of Lincoln's death, in 1884. To Mark Pattison, perhaps, was due not only the further development of his critical faculty, but wider views of scholarship. To John Conington he was drawn not merely by a sympathy of pursuits but by something similar in their mental attitude towards higher and deeper subjects. He had attended the Professor's lectures, and, being singled out as a promising young scholar, was invited to breakfasts, to walks, and to informal reading parties. The two soon became intimate friends, and in 1864 Conington asked his help in an edition of Vergil originally undertaken in conjunction with Prof. Goldwin Smith, who had been called away by the Oxford Commission in 1854. Henry Nettleship undertook the last six books of the *Aeneid*, but finding he could not keep pace with Conington, it was settled that he should edit only Books X and XII. Towards the end of this year he had conceived the idea, supported by the Rector, of spending some time at a German University, in order to become acquainted with the German method of teaching classical philology. His friend Mr. Clive having undertaken his college work for a term, he left Oxford for Berlin in April, 1865, furnished with introductions from the Rector to Prof. Emil Hübner at Berlin, and Prof. Jacob Bernays at Breslau, and matriculated as an ordinary student at the Berlin University. His letters to the Rector have been preserved, and he describes his first impressions of a German scholar as follows :

'Bernays seems to have not only touched upon but

penetrated every branch of philology, and always brings a clear and comprehensive judgement to bear upon the matter in hand. In his build, manner, and in a certain toughness of mind which one seems to discern in him, he gives one the impression of a thorough Jew.' Hübner he finds 'extremely edifying on intellectual matters.' He describes conversations with Bernays upon Spinoza, Greek scholarship, and scholars in England generally. Then upon 'the English competitive examination fever,' of which Bernays speaks with strong disapprobation, saying that so far as it had been introduced into Germany it was spoiling the character of the young men.

He seems to have found Bernays 'very stimulating, but like all talented men now, rather critical than constructive.' He goes on to say, ' I perceive that in Oxford we have hardly any idea of what is meant by knowledge of a subject either in itself or in relation to its surroundings. This is confirmed since I have begun to attend lectures here.' He describes a lecture of Moritz Haupt's on the Epistles of Horace and one of Hübner's on Roman Inscriptions. 'How splendid it would have been to have lived in Germany thirty or forty years ago ; there seemed such a life in those times compared with anything we have now. I have been looking into a life of Robert Schumann, who was a student at Heidelberg in 1829 ; in what a ferment were men's minds then. He is full of mysticism and rhapsody, now everything is dead, the age of critics has succeeded that of artists and philosophers, we have great players but no composers. . . . Here one has a kind of feeling they have worked through what we are only feeling for in England, and that the " Aufschwung " has ceased and not much is left but the dust and ashes of materialism.' He writes a good deal about the political questions of the time ; of Mommsen's pamphlet on the annexation of Schleswig Holstein, of the debates in the Chambers on the Budget,—'one is astounded at the impudence of the Government and the apparent helplessness of the Opposition, who can only use very strong language.' Again : What you say about the impossibility of applying the notion of progress to philology I now see to be true, unless a more distinct conception, and here and there a better adjustment of a skeleton, can be called progress.' Speaking of religion and men's conception of it, he says: 'We must choose between a ghost and a puppet: when shall we have a new and healthy symbolism? One plunges into art, but that is not enough. . . . We have pretty well succeeded in emptying the old bottles, but where is the new wine? . . . I am so busy adjusting my skeleton that I have no time to look into philosophical books.'

That he derived great delight as well as benefit from this stay in Berlin was evident not only from his letters but from the pleasure with which in later years he always referred to it. He did not make Mommsen's acquaintance at this time, but he heard him lecture, and also speak at the Archaeological Society, and conceived an immense admiration for him. At Hübner's house he became intimate, constantly spending the evenings there in the enjoyment of music and conversation, which ranged, the professor says, over a variety of subjects. He left Berlin in August, 1865, filled with new ideas and enthusiasms, and feeling more strongly how imperfect was the Oxford ideal of that day, and how much lay before him if he ever hoped to accomplish anything worthy to be called *work*. He not only appreciated German methods, but tried to make them the basis of his own. He sometimes spent part of a long vacation on the continent, and the friends who accompanied him have happy recollections of those times, of his fresh enjoyment of everything—his geniality, unfailing good temper, and of his finding a humorous side to everything disagreeable [1].

Intense admiration for beautiful scenery, associated in him with love for music and poetry, at times made him long for

---

[1] Pressure of work has prevented Mr. Bryce from contributing, as he had hoped, some account of his long friendship with my husband. He writes of a summer tour in 1863: 'The days he and I spent together are often present to my mind. I wish I could adequately convey how great was the charm of his companionship.'

the power of adequate expression in melodies which floated in his mind. But this gift, to his great sorrow, was denied him, kept under, perhaps, by the continual pressure of the more practical necessities of life.

In 1868 domestic anxieties were pressing upon him, and he felt he ought to find some post which would enable him to render his family more definite pecuniary assistance. His father's failing health compelled him to give up work: none of his brothers were likely for some time to be in a position to render any substantial help: he therefore turned his thoughts towards a mastership at Harrow, where there was a vacancy. He was concerned lest the Rector should misunderstand his action, or think him neglectful of college interests in taking this step suddenly, and he therefore wrote to him confidentially, explaining his reasons at some length. This and other anxieties had told on his health, and for some months he had been low and depressed, and a sufferer from sleeplessness, but a month in the Harz mountains with his great friend, Mr. Willingham F. Rawnsley, did much to restore him, and he went to Harrow in September, 1868. He first took a low form in the school, then shared the sixth-form composition with Mr. Westcott (now Bishop of Durham), and the Rev. E. M. Young (now Canon of Salisbury), and later on took a pupil-room. He was most conscientious in his school-work, sparing no trouble over any boy who showed the least desire for learning, and trying to implant in his pupils a love for classics. Yet school-work was always more or less distasteful to him, and he disliked the prevailing worship of athletics. He was certainly not cut out for a schoolmaster, though he endeared himself to many of his pupils by his kindness and helpfulness, and was on terms of the friendliest intimacy with his colleagues.

Shy and retiring in manner, and not shining in general conversation, he was an original and delightful companion in a *tête à tête* or with one or two friends. He would plunge with startling abruptness into the subject uppermost in his own thoughts, and our first acquaintance began in this way at a dinner-party. Music was the subject, and I was struck with the clear and decisive opinion he had formed for himself of Beethoven's songs, differing much from that of the ordinary amateur. Conscious of his own defects of *technique*, he with characteristic determination put himself into Mr. John Farmer's hands, and set to work on a new system of piano-playing from the beginning.

Henry Nettleship and my father were attracted to each other by similarity of opinions, each having a love of knowledge for its own sake, a width of intellectual outlook, and a certain impatience of the narrowing influences of a schoolmaster's life. This friendship deepened into warmer regard as time went on, and on our marriage in December, 1870, my husband became a real son of the house, sharing in all our joys and sorrows. It is an often-recurring expression in my father's letters to us both, 'I don't know anything that makes me happier to dwell on than the thought of your happiness.'

The year before he had suffered a severe blow in the sudden death of Prof. Conington, and it was some months before his mind recovered its usual tone. He writes to the Rector of Lincoln on Oct. 25: 'To me the loss is far more than I can at present estimate. It was not merely that he had taken a minute interest in everything concerning me, and that I had in return the deepest wish for his fuller development, but he and I saw (I think), without confessing it to each other, deeper into each other's souls than it is given to most friends to do : hence my desire to have been with him, or at least within call, during his last hours. I am at least glad to think that we recently exchanged confidences which indirectly concerned eternal interests ; but I had not seen him for two or three months. It is difficult at first in such a shock to keep one's hold on things here, and to remember that the mere space of fifty years or so is the utmost barrier that one can with any certainty count on as keeping one from the Great Presence into which one would almost fain follow at once a beloved soul.'

Again, he speaks of Conington's intense craving for human sympathy as an impulse which materially injured his mental development, and diverted his powers from objects more worthy of them. 'Our last conversation and serious correspondence were upon this subject. . . . I had urged him to undertake some really great work—not that I had any right to speak *a loco superiore* : it was the feeling of the same thing in myself which gave me some insight into his character.'

Soon after we were married he said to me, 'I wonder if you know what a difference it makes in my work to feel there is some one who understands, to whom I can say everything : the old haunting feelings of uncertainty and distrust are gone : I can put my whole self into my work now.' And again, ' I am so glad you are not ambitious : ambition would have paralyzed me : I should never do any good in my own line unless I were working for the work's sake.'

In August, 1871, while he was engaged on the first edition of Conington's *Persius*, we went to Bonn, for the Beethoven festival held there that year. We spent the mornings chiefly in the University Library, he working, and I helping him to verify references, Prof. Bernays frequently coming in for half an hour's talk. The concerts were an intense enjoyment, and I well remember my husband's pleasure at finding some of our musical German friends sharing in his admiration of Charles Hallé's playing. Beethoven's Ninth Symphony had quite a fascination for him, and for some years we never missed an opportunity of hearing it in England : each time he used to feel some part or other become clearer to him—it was impossible to take it all in at once. He read aloud a great deal at this period—the whole of Carlyle's *Frederick the Great* among other books.

In 1871 he brought out the first edition of Conington's *Vergil*, vol. iii, containing his own notes on *Aeneid*, Books X and XII. In 1873 he edited Books V and VI of the *Aeneid* for an abridged edition (Bell & Sons).

In the spring of 1873 the late President, Mr. Wilson, came

to Harrow, to invite him to return to Corpus Christi College as Fellow and Tutor, in place of Mr. Hicks, who had married and taken a living. By arrangement with the Dean of Christ Church, his lectures and tutorial assistance were to be open to undergraduates at Christ Church who were reading for honours in Classical Moderations. He hesitated at first, as the prospect of succeeding eventually to a house mastership at Harrow of course offered greater pecuniary advantages. But there was no doubt as to which position was more congenial, as he could never hope for leisure for independent study at Harrow, so the offer was accepted, and neither of us ever repented of the decision. We came up to Oxford in October, 1873, and I think the next five years were, as far as work was concerned, perhaps the happiest of his life. He enjoyed the personal intercourse with responsive pupils, and they fully appreciated his help, as well as his never-failing sympathy.

One says, 'His method of teaching was a revelation : he had an unequalled power of interesting his pupils. He made me realize for the first time that Vergil and Horace were literature like Shelley and Byron. One felt he knew ancient literature as a whole, and in its relation with English and all modern literature. He was essentially inspiring, and put heart and soul into the things he taught : he was a real teacher, without the shadow of a trace of the pedant or pedagogue.' Another says, 'No one else ever taught me any scholarship.' Others speak of the influence of his private intercourse with his pupils, of the pains he took to help them before going in either for University scholarships or Moderations. He would get a man to his rooms, and finding out his weak points, make things clear to him, giving him lunch and playing on the piano after, till it was time to return to the Schools, refreshed physically and mentally ; or he would let men come to him for half an hour a week for consultation and advice as to their work. 'He was always full of the most interesting information, of striking and original suggestions. The inspiring effect of these interviews was not easily to be forgotten.' One of his former pupils has an affectionate recollection of a walking tour at the Lakes, 'of talks on Vergil and Beethoven, then of the future, and the question of ordination, a never-to-be-forgotten help and influence.' Others of Sunday walks and talks at Oxford, of wise and friendly counsel, elder-brotherly interest in younger men, of happy healthful influence at a critical period of their lives. 'His manner in lecturing was quiet and reserved, and at first was not felt to be impressive, but attention was soon compelled by the suggestiveness and originality of his remarks, and he acquired a deep and lasting hold over the minds of the more receptive portion of his audience. He seemed to have at his command a storehouse of clear and scholarly comment and illustration. Notes preserved on lectures of philology at that time show how sound and clearly intelligible was the teaching given. In his Vergil lectures, doubtless the most interesting, in addition to a minute criticism of the text, one day a week was given to a general review of the character and significance of the Vergilian epic.' Another pupil says, 'Mr. Nettleship's wide and exhaustive knowledge, his enthusiasm for classical studies, his sympathetic insight and brilliant fancy, contributed to render this description of Vergil and his times a model of literary criticism and exposition. Men found their standard of what should be done rose as their opinion of their own work was brought down. This was not the effect of scathing sarcasm or even playful irony, but by the contrast of exact and accurate work with what they had themselves done.' He is reported occasionally to have indulged in quiet sarcasm, as for instance to a man who was trying to translate Vergil without having looked at it beforehand : 'Don't you find Vergil rather hard at sight. Mr.——? I do.'

At Harrow he had little time for literary work, beyond adding material to new editions of Conington's works and writing reviews in the *Academy*, started in 1869. When he came to Oxford he began to put into shape some of his Vergil studies, and after seeing through the press the second

edition of Conington's *Persius,* as well as vol. iii. of his
Vergil, he published *Suggestions Introductory to a Study of
the Aeneid* (1875). His reading had been 'wide,' as recommended by Prof. Bernays, and now he was seeking some
direction for future labours. An opening came in an invita-
tion to prepare for the Clarendon Press a new Latin-English
Dictionary, of about the same compass as the Greek Lexicon
of Liddell and Scott. The idea approved itself to him, and
he finally accepted the proposal, having first, as he thought,
secured the co-operation of Prof. J. E. B. Mayor, and having
reasonable expectation of assistance from younger scholars in
Oxford. He had given a good deal of consideration to the
question, and had taken the opinion of my father, and also
of Prof. H. A. J. Munro, who was one of the friends with
whom he was most in touch at this time. Mr. Munro was
a frequent correspondent up to the time of his death in 1885,
and always took great interest in the progress of the Dictionary. The book was to be completed by June, 1887, and
in June, 1875, my husband set to work at it definitely. His
aim, as expressed by himself in a letter to a friend, was not
to revise or correct existing dictionaries, but to produce an
entirely new work by fresh reading of the ancient texts and
authorities, and moreover to arrange the references chrono-
logically, so that the historical development might be clearly
perceived. Had he fully foreseen at this time the difficulties of
the work, and its complicated and laborious nature, he would
not have undertaken it without at all events requiring a longer
time for its completion. In 1878 he published an *Essay on the
Roman Satura*; and in June of the same year was elected to
the Corpus Professorship of Latin Literature. It had been
suggested to him after Conington's death that he should
become a candidate for the vacant chair, but he had then
declined to put himself in competition with Mr. Edwin Palmer
(now Archdeacon of Oxford).

Among the letters of congratulation that now poured in is
one from Mark Pattison, who writes: 'Much more may

I congratulate ourselves on having got a philological professor whose mind enshrines the ideal of complete knowledge and progressive science. The longer I live the more clearly I seem to see that, without the inspiration of this ideal, neither great knowledge of the subject nor the most finished scholarship can contribute to true learning.'

In spite of his pleasure at the appointment, and at the prospect of increased leisure for 'making a hole in the Dictionary,' he was sorry to give up his tutorial work, and to miss opportunities of personal intercourse with the undergraduates. 'I have been very happy in my college work,' he writes, 'and feel in some respects it may not be so easy to be directly useful.' And again, 'When one thinks of what a Professor ought to be! and how little even the strongest men seem to get done towards accomplishing their ideal!' His ideal was high, and his disappointment was proportionately great, as he began to realize that, as Professor, he must not expect the large audiences which he had been accustomed to address as Tutor, unless his lectures were framed for the purposes of the Schools. The conditions of the examination system made it impossible for lecturers out of the ordinary beat to obtain many listeners : the mass of compulsory work being so great, an undergraduate had no time to follow his own initiative. But my husband was so genuinely fond of teaching, and felt he had so much to say, that he found it hard to reconcile himself to this state of things. Writing was not sufficient : he wanted a responsive audience to whom he could unfold new ideas as they occurred to him in the course of his own studies.

He gave public lectures on 'Ancient Lives of Vergil,' on 'Textual Criticism in Latin Antiquity,' ' Development of Poetical Expression in Latin,' 'Appreciation of Beauties of Nature in Classical Latin Poetry,' ' History of Latin Literature,' ' Recent Advances in Latin Scholarship,' 'Studies on the Latin Grammarians,' and others, some since printed.

I pass over various publications in the next few years, as

they appear in the Bibliography at the end of this volume, merely noting that in the Memoir of my father, the Rev. T. H. Steel (1882), he clearly expresses his own views upon classical education in schools.

During the summer of 1882 he had an illness which, though slight in itself, might have developed into something more serious, and from the effects of which he did not recover for many months. It was then found that he suffered from a disease of the heart, and this accounted for much of the depression and fatigue he had at times experienced, for which there had seemed no apparent cause. This discovery could not be concealed from him, and at first naturally tended to increase the depression, against which, however, he strove so successfully, that beyond his immediate relatives and the medical men he consulted, no one was aware of the feeling or its cause. His great powers of physical and mental endurance were, however, heavily taxed, and companionship and sympathy became more than ever a necessity to him. He writes during a short absence from home: 'When I am alone, I can't help my brain working, and thinking out difficulties in scholarship or metaphysics, and I get *so* tired.' Sir W. Gull confirmed the opinion that the affection of the heart might not prove fatal or indeed increase, provided he was careful to avoid overtaxing his physical or mental powers, and recommended him to think about it as little as possible, which advice after a time he partially succeeded in following. He had unwillingly to abjure lawn-tennis (any sudden exertion being dangerous), and also climbing, a favourite form of amusement, though he never had a very steady head. He taught his children to row, and took to this form of exercise again himself.

For a short time he seriously contemplated giving up the projected Dictionary, and asking the Press to cancel the agreement, feeling the close consecutive strain too much for him. But in itself it interested him much, and he was always hopeful of obtaining further assistance: in the autumn there-

fore he again set to work, meaning to devote himself entirely
to it. But sustained mental effort in the evenings gave him
sleepless nights, which unfitted him for the next day. He
had never been able to work late: the morning he always
felt to be his best and most productive time. He began
half an hour before an eight o'clock breakfast, and at nine set
to work again. Intervals between lectures were spent at the
Bodleian at work on the Dictionary, part of the afternoon
was given to lectures for the Women Students, and then he
read at home till dinner-time. Of course he got most done
in the vacations. He was with difficulty induced to take
a few days' holiday at Christmas or Easter: in the long
vacation he gave himself a month's rest, but even then his
mornings were occupied with extra work which he could not
fit in while at home.

During the next few years he brought out new editions of
the *Vergil*, adding much valuable matter in the shape of extra
notes, besides several essays. He also published a collection
of his own *Lectures and Essays* (Oxford, 1885), and a book on
Latin Prose Composition (London, 1887).

This kind of work he did in the evenings, or at times when
a 'buzzing in the head,' as he expressed it, warned him he must
break off a while from the Dictionary. He was proud of the
faculty—acquired, he said, at Charterhouse, where separate
studies were luxuries confined to the Sixth Form—of so concentrating his mind on his work that he was regardless of
anything going on around him: so, preferring companionship
to solitude, he would bring his work into the drawing-room and
correct proofs, prepare lectures, and write reviews, without being
disturbed by talking or even music. As relaxation he would
read aloud, getting through all Dickens in this way, and he
played a good deal on the piano, especially directly after
dinner. At the beginning of 1884 the Dictionary was growing
into greater magnitude than even he proposed to himself, and
at the same time hopes of expected aid were vanishing. Prof.
Mayor was absorbed in other work, and he sought in vain

for the help needed, though he received some assistance from Oxford scholars, as he states in the preface to his *Contributions.*

He had set before himself a singularly high ideal; he did not care to aim at anything less than a complete lexicon of the whole Latin language. He did not wish to give it up; his own inclination was to continue working at Latin lexicography, but it seemed quite clear that one man, practically unaided, could not accomplish such an undertaking in the time specified, and he had no reasonable hope of bringing it to a conclusion sooner than twelve years after the time originally agreed on. The Delegates, however, did not see their way to accepting this proposed extension of time, and he therefore continued working till June, 1887, when he sent to the Press all he had been able to accomplish, amounting to a tenth part of the entire book, viz. the whole of the letter A, and a number of articles under other letters.

If he could have put all other work aside and given himself entirely to the Dictionary, his progress would have been much quicker. But one of the symptoms of the heart affection from which he suffered was restlessness and inability to remain long in any one position or at one form of work ; and to the few who knew how careful he had to be in husbanding the resources of his bodily health, and in avoiding prolonged mental strain, such concentration was known to be impossible, as the only result would have been a complete breakdown. He now and again made the attempt, with the result that no more was accomplished in a given time than when he varied it with other work. At times of great depression and discouragement, the only remedy was to divert his thoughts and energies into another channel. Could he have found a *collaborateur* all would have gone well. Then, again, he had begun to realize the uncertainty of his own life, and he was disturbed by the thought that for his children's sake he ought to have undertaken work more directly remunerative. This idea required all my influence to combat, for I knew that the Dictionary work was congenial, that he had devoted his best powers to it, and that if he once persuaded himself he ought to work merely to make money, he would not produce what was worthy of himself or the position he occupied. His disappointment was so great at the failure of the undertaking, and the apparent waste of twelve of the best and most productive years of his life (as the idea was not then suggested of publishing any part of his labours), that his health seemed likely to suffer without complete rest and change. He at first thought of spending six months on the Continent, attacking some fresh subject; but when the time came he could not bring himself to remain so long away from Oxford and his work. He took, therefore, eight or nine weeks' real holiday in Germany, Switzerland, and Italy—a time of great enjoyment to us all. On this occasion he first saw two pictures, which made on him, he said, the greatest impression of his life—The Descent from the Cross, at Antwerp, and The Last Supper, at Milan. He enjoyed everything with the freshness of a boy, and even made a fairly high ascent without any ill effects.

Returning to Oxford thoroughly recruited in health and spirits, he undertook, at the suggestion of the Delegates of the Press, to publish a portion of his labours (*Contributions to Latin Lexicography*, 1889). He was much pleased with the German reviews of this book, and especially with letters from Mommsen and Wölfflin, who had realized the amount of labour and research bestowed upon it.

In 1890 he had drawn up a scheme for a projected *History of Latin Literature*, for which he had much material prepared. He felt bound, however, to put this aside, and accede to the request of the Delegates of the Press to complete the Nonius left unfinished by the death of Mr. J. H. Onions, his old pupil and friend—a subject for which his studies among the Latin grammarians peculiarly fitted him. He began with an exhaustive examination of all the printed editions by Renaissance and post-Renaissance scholars; and two articles contributed to the *Journal of Philology* (one printed after his death) show the careful and elaborate manner in which he proposed to deal with his author. Further work in this direction, however, had to be postponed for a year in consequence of a third edition of the *Persius* being required. In January, 1892, a bad attack of influenza must have affected his heart, and he never entirely recovered from it. He found the next two terms unusually exhausting ; and determined to pass the autumn at Berlin, where he had decided to send his son to study music. He spent a week at Dublin first, during the celebration of the Trinity College Tercentenary, when he was granted the honorary degree of Doctor of Letters. In August we went to Switzerland, and he began to feel better, when, just as we were leaving, we received the terrible news of his brother Lewis's death on Mont Blanc. The awful shock, the long trying journey back to Chamounix, and the harrowing formalities to be gone through there, told fearfully on his health and spirits ; and the effect was plainly visible afterwards in his altered appearance.

It is impossible to describe adequately the kindness and hospitality shown us by friends, old and new, in Berlin. My husband's intimate knowledge of the German language and modes of thought gave him facilities he would not otherwise have enjoyed of discussion on various subjects, and of acquiring information on those which most interested him— philology, literature, politics and music. He renewed his old friendship with Prof. Hübner, and during this visit his acquaintance with Prof. Mommsen grew into friendship. The latter wrote after his death expressing his personal regret, and adding, 'It leaves a gap in the good relations between your country and ours. I have never met an Englishman so able, and so willing to acknowledge the good and noble qualities of our people, and so equitable and kind in judging its many shortcomings.'

His appreciation of the German character, of their intellectual freedom, of their methods as well as of their power of work, may be gathered from his letters to friends at home and, after his return, to friends in Germany : ' An Englishman may be grateful to Germany if he learns from her the old true lesson of high thinking and serious work. . . . What every open-minded Englishman feels when he comes abroad and uses his eyes is, that England is the land of limitations, " das enge Land," I say, when, as often happens, I think in German. . . . To a highly cultivated German the love of truth, the intellectual conscience, is a stronger force and motive, as a rule, than to an Englishman of equal force and ability. . . . In Germany knowledge and culture are more honoured on their own merits than with us.'

During his stay in Berlin he was working at Latin glossaries, writing one or two reviews, and revising the final proof-sheets of the *Persius*.

He went back to Oxford on January 20, 1893, leaving us in Berlin, and proposing to return at Easter. He wished to spend Hilary term with his mother, hoping in some measure to fill up the blank caused by his brother's death. He was not really strong, and needed a longer rest, and I was also most unwilling for him to return alone ; but he could not bear to have it thought that he was neglecting his work, fancied himself quite fit to resume it, and would not listen to the suggestion of remaining abroad till Easter. Circumstances compelled my return to England a month later, when I found him looking and feeling far from well ; but he struggled on till the end of term, which happened to be a peculiarly busy one for him. Then he went to Malvern, where he broke down altogether with what was ascertained a week or two later, on his return to Oxford, to be an attack of typhoid fever. This was slight in itself, but it affected his heart, which had already been much weakened by the illness and trouble of the previous year and the hard work of the term, from the strain of which, had he been in his usual health, he would, however, soon have recovered.

His patience and fortitude never deserted him during the long and trying weeks of illness that followed. At first, though he

could not bear the effort of listening when read to, he read
a great deal to himself—works of fiction ; and later on, strangely
enough, more serious books, one of the last he attempted being
the latest volume of Frederick the Great's correspondence in
French and German.   He enjoyed Balfour's *Essays*, and Prof.
Dicey's *Leap in the Dark*, and was full of suggestions of arguments for the latter's use in the Unionist campaign then going
on.   The *Persius* had just come out, and he looked through
this and directed me to send copies to friends at home and
abroad.   His sense of humour helped him through many
of the wearisome details of an invalid's life when his mind
was clear.   I think he was never conscious of his own danger,
as he made plans for lectures in the autumn, or, failing that,
for the following term.   If a shadow of anxiety crossed his mind
it was dismissed with the assurance of his perfect trust in me.
He made every effort for his own recovery, following all direc-
tions implicitly, but, in spite of slight occasional gleams of
hope, he grew gradually weaker ; his heart could not support
the strain, and he had no strength to rally.

In the last week he was carried out daily into the garden he
was so fond of, and enjoyed the air, the singing of the birds,
and the sunlight on the trees.   But the end came sooner than
was anticipated, and on the morning of July 10, 1893, he passed
peacefully away.

Henry Nettleship's death was a personal loss to very many
beyond his family and friends.   First, perhaps, among these
may be counted the women students, for whom he had done so
much.   He had always taken interest in women's education,
and as early as 1865 lectured on Latin to a class of ladies in
Oxford, formed under the organization of Miss Smith ; lectures
on other subjects being given by Mark Pattison, Mr. William
Sidgwick, and others.   In 1873, on his return to Oxford, he
lectured on Greek and Latin under a different scheme ; and
in 1878 he assisted in organizing the ' Association for the Higher
Education of Women,' being elected on the first committee.
From that time onward he had the chief share in teaching

Latin to the Association students, who have expressed their
warm appreciation of his unvarying kindness and interest in their
work, of his efforts to inspire them with his own earnestness and
zeal for study, as well as with an enthusiasm for, and compre-
hension of, the wider and more scientific view of scholarship.
It was a general feeling that in some ways his place as a teacher
could not be filled up.

We had often talked in early days of how specializing might
narrow and cramp the intellect; and he was aware of this
danger, for in a letter to Mark Pattison in 1883 he writes: ' Your
book (on Milton's sonnets) is a real refreshment to one who
like myself lives in daily terror of being absorbed by philological details.' As he grew older his interests widened; and
it was surprising how he found time and energy to bestow on so
many outside interests and to read so much of general literature,
while apparently absorbed in the details of his own philological
studies and research. But whatever he undertook he did
well and thoroughly, whether in relation to his own work—
for instance, as secretary to the Philological Society—or in an
administrative capacity, as chairman to the East Oxford
British School, where he never failed, unless prevented by
illness, to attend committee-meetings, or take his turn as visitor
for the month, hearing the lessons given and observing the
discipline maintained.

He had bestowed much reflection on the various labour
questions of the day, the subject of Trades Unionism having
attracted his attention as long ago as 1867 as a means of
raising the standard of work and wages. One of the first
called upon to assist in forming a small Women's Trades
Union in Oxford, he acted for several years as trustee of that
Society. He was always ready to render assistance in any way
by speaking or lecturing, or playing the piano at the winter
social gatherings, or giving advice on any questions that arose
concerning the management of the Society. ' He was never
happier,' writes the vicar of one of the neediest parishes in
Oxford, ' than when engaged in some effort for the uplifting and

advancement of the poor.' He was a member of the Teachers' Guild, and often spoke at the meetings. His last lecture, on February 17, 1893, was delivered to the Guild ; it was entitled 'Three Months' Impressions of Berlin,' and he had given it at Toynbee Hall a few weeks before. To my great regret I have been unable to find the notes from which he spoke, I know they contained a *résumé* of his observations on the social, political, and educational life of Berlin.

For some years he was treasurer as well as one of the vice-presidents of the Oxford Philharmonic Society ; and took part as accompanist at the weekly evening practices, under Dr. James Taylor's conductorship.

His feeling for music was a great part of his life. From the time that he could play at all, it was his refuge from all trouble or brain irritation. His enjoyment of great musical works was sometimes too keen to be unalloyed pleasure, the fatigue of trying to understand being too great. His chief favourites were Bach, Handel, Beethoven, and Mozart. Dr. Taylor writes : ' His musical ability was very remarkable, and the attitude of his mind towards music was unique ; he appeared to be always search-ing for the expression of *truth* in music, rather than the mere recreative pleasure which generally satisfies amateur musicians. His steady consistent study of the works of John Sebastian Bach, and his strong though quiet expression of dislike to everything in music that did not reach the highest ideal standard of truth, will long be remembered by all those who knew him well.'

His attitude towards Wagner may be best shown by quoting from a letter to a friend : ' Wagner tries to make music do what it cannot do without degrading itself—namely, paint out in very loud colours certain definite feelings as they arise before the composer. The older musicians seem to me to aim rather at suggesting feeling than at actually exhibiting it, as it were, in the flesh. I think much of Wagner would vitiate my taste ; but perhaps my head is too full of the older music to take in strains to which my nerves are not attuned.'

Mr. G. A. Simcox says : 'He was the most "musical" man I ever knew—always in tune, with an instinctive dislike of everything far-fetched and over-laboured. It was a pleasure to see him at the piano, though the music said little to me, for the sake of the light that played over his face.'

I am indebted to Mr. L. R. Farnell for the following account of the part my husband took in questions affecting the welfare of his University.

'He was always warmly in sympathy with the movement towards a wider academic organization for education and research ; but it was more in the latter years of his life that he took a prominent part in practical measures of reform.

'On his return to Oxford in 1873, an inter-collegiate scheme of lectures had already been established, and seemed likely to produce important results ; but though the organization of teaching was improved, the University, in respect of its higher studies and functions, was still far from attaining that academic ideal to which he was devoted, and in his conception of which he had no doubt been assisted by his residence at a German university, and by his intimate acquaintance with Mark Pattison's views on the subject.

'He was desirous of perfect freedom for the study of every branch of science, and assisted by vote or speech the vital interests of physical science, when opposition was threatened by anti-vivisectionists, or advocates of the older classical *régime.* He aspired to see the professoriate become, as in Germany, a vehicle for the best teaching in each faculty.

'He was anxious that the University should organize and encourage original work, and in his statement before the University Commission he says :

' " There is always a large amount of outlying work to be done in philology as, doubtless, in other subjects, which is not done because there is no direction to men to do it. The only encouragement for independent study is in the prizes, which are useless for the purpose. What is required is a permanent scientific committee with special departments,

whose business it should be to keep an eye on the work to
be done, and to look out for men to do it. Has a MS. to
be collated for a new edition, an inscription or unpublished
document to be edited, an obscure piece of history or usage
to be elucidated ? It should be in the power of those engaged
in philological research to recommend to the committee a fit
person to do the work at a certain sum."

' The principle contained in these suggestions was also urged
by others, and accepted by the commissioners; but if something more nearly approaching the organization of authoritative
supervision of research than the Common University Fund
had been established, a new stimulus would have been given
to the teaching activity of the professoriate.

' He also pleaded the cause of the Non-Collegiate Students
before the Commission, proposing better arrangements for their
tuition, and showing his sympathy with their needs, and desire
for a freer University system than the Collegiate. The reform
suggested was shortly after carried out.

' The chief public questions in which he took a leading part
were concerning the administration of the Bodleian, and the
establishment of a School of Modern Language and Literature.
With regard to the former, he advocated a more concerted
action between the Bodleian and other Oxford libraries, and
urged the importance of remembering that the Bodleian was
a learned library, and should be administered as such. The
part he took in the debates on the subject was prompted by
a scholar's profound interest in a great institution. With regard
to the Modern Language and Literature School, he was the
first to moot the proposal in a suggestion offered to the commissioners—that the chair of Anglo-Saxon might be profitably
connected with a chair of Teutonic language and literature.
In 1886 he was one of those who memorialized Council in
favour of the proposal brought finally before Congregation.
In the debate that followed he delivered a telling speech,
in behalf of a School of Modern Languages that should give
equal weight to philology and literature. He went so far as

to maintain that the rejection of the measure would be
" a national calamity." The votes were equal ; therefore the
measure was lost.

'In a pamphlet published shortly afterwards he pleaded
more effectually still for a University curriculum of the study
of Modern European Languages and Literatures. It contains,
perhaps, the most brilliant exposition that appeared, in the
course of a long controversy, of the reasons in favour of the
reform ; and it gives a clear illustration of his liberal and
practical ideal of study. It triumphantly refutes the objection
that the study of Greek and Latin literature would seriously
suffer : " What has done harm to ' classics '—always in danger,
but never destroyed—is the narrow conception of their scope
sometimes entertained, and the supercilious attitude sometimes
adopted, by their own champions ; the notion that a sound
acquaintance with a score of good Greek and Latin books,
and the trick of writing good composition, are enough to
make a scholar : the notion that scholarship as limited as
this, and nothing else, gives its possessor the key of culture—
as though culture were not rather a habit of mind than the
possession of a certain amount of valuable knowledge."

'Still more weighty is its exposure of the shallow fallacy,
that the cultivation of philology would be prejudicial to the
study of literature. In conclusion, he expresses his belief,
that though a larger scheme might be more adequate to the
proper requirements of a University, " what the nation most
pressingly feels, is the need of a School of the English Language
and Literature." And he could find no argument that supplied
" a justification for our refusing to grant what it is not too
much to call a well-founded national demand."

' He would have rejoiced, had he lived, to see the successful
accomplishment of one at least of the schemes he had so
much at heart.'

Whatever he undertook he carried through with the
same thoroughness and grasp of detail that characterized
his own work. He could do nothing half-heartedly. ' He had an

extraordinarily high standard of work,' writes Mr. W. A. Price an intimate friend, though many years his junior; 'what was worth doing must be done well or not at all; no labour was too great to bestow on good work; no work was good if the workman could have done better. He strongly condemned shallowness and charlatanism, though I can scarcely recall his speaking severely of any one; and he often objected to criticisms of other people, on the ground that it was difficult to put yourself in their place.' Mark Pattison he described as one of the few men in Oxford at that time who understood the meaning of hard work and firstrate workmanship.

He was singularly unassuming as regarded his own claims to distinction as a scholar, though he was as far removed from the affectation of humility, as from conceit or vanity. He had the strange opportunity of reading for himself what was said of him in the newspapers, under the impression that it was he, and not his brother Lewis, who had perished on Mont Blanc, on August 25, 1892. His only comment was, I think I have been overrated. I could have given a truer account of myself; I know the exact extent of my own powers.'

He was now and again haunted by a dread that the physical weakness which at times oppressed him, might show itself in a diminution of his powers of thought or expression. But it was not so. Those best able to judge saw the maturer years bringing ripeness, not only in judgement but in work; and in his last illness he was cheered by the thought that the specimen just printed of the work he had undertaken on Nonius showed no falling off from his own scholarly ideal.

He might have published more had he not been so fastidious. He wished to be absolutely sure of every detail, and shirked no toil, however dry or irksome, that would exhaust all that had been said or written on any particular subject; thus making others feel 'the dignity belonging to the specialist and the beauty of doing work thoroughly.' But he never allowed himself to become absorbed in dry technicalities. His lexicographical studies were all means to an end, and made subservient to higher aims and objects as throwing light on history and literature. For many years he had made a special study of the Latin grammarians. This, and his researches into Glossaries were originally undertaken with a view to a History of the Latin Language.

It was a matter of regret to many that he had not chosen philosophy rather than classics for his object in life. One speaks of 'learning more from conversations with him on difficult philosophical problems, that was instructive and valuable, than from those who made philosophy their study.'

He always retained a certain directness of speech, and in meeting even a casual acquaintance would plunge at once probably into what was uppermost in his own thoughts or into some subject likely to interest his companion.

He was not latterly a great letter-writer, but would at times express himself to close friends with clearness and conviction on subjects occupying his own mind.

An intimate friend relates that one day conversing unreservedly on the difficulty of reconciling the evil and suffering in the world, with a belief in the government of it by a perfectly good and benevolent Spirit, while rejecting the current commonplace solutions of the problem, he yet expressed his unshaken belief in God's goodness, quoting the words, 'Though He slay me, yet will I trust in Him.'

He had a constitutional dislike to dogma, and was strongly opposed to tests, desiring perfect freedom of thought and inquiry in all matters of religion. ' He once,' says Mr. Price, 'expressed his opinion that he would sooner trust the scientific men than the ecclesiastics, if it were necessary to confide the custody of the accepted ideas of morality or ethics to any one body of men, on the ground that truth is only safe in the hands of those whose business it is to examine and verify it, and who are free from any formal profession of faith.'

Yet he had a deep religious vein in his nature, and a strong belief in the superior power of good over evil, and he could not tolerate the persistent upholding of the opposite theory by some of the realistic writers of the day. In a lecture on 'Ideals,' he declares : '"You cannot escape the devil and the beast that is in you, a compound of selfishness, cruelty, and lust," say pessimism and the novel of Zola ; "you cannot escape the better part, the angel within yourself," replies the sane wisdom which in the long run governs the course of the world.' Of this same lecture, delivered at Toynbee Hall, Oct. 17, 1891, Mr. Price says, 'It greatly impressed the audience by its originality and individuality. After pointing out that even the most elevated ideals are not necessarily unattainable, he showed that in mechanics and literature, for instance, ideals might be realized, giving examples. And then he went on to argue that ideals of conduct could also be attained, that the Sermon on the Mount was a set of severely practical rules, and that some men and women did actually lead lives in which only themselves could find the flaws. In art, on the other hand, or in any pursuit where the standard aimed at was not erected solely by human intelligence, but by natural causes, the ideal was not generally to be attained.'

Henry Nettleship's own life may be said to have been consistently true to its early promise. The love of truth showed itself not only in the most scrupulous exactness in every detail of life, but in his 'anxiety before all things to learn the completest truth at whatever cost, and in his eagerness to save those whom he taught from the tolerance of any unreality.'

As a youth he gave the impression of being reserved rather than shy, of possessing much latent force, of holding back his opinions and gathering those of others about him not from any conceit or self-consciousness, but as if waiting to be sure of his own powers. Years brought an increase of self-confidence, and in his complete forgetfulness of self, and desire to put other people at their ease, the shy reserve of the young man developed into the genial cordiality now remembered as his characteristic manner. 'The warm grasp of the hand, the hearty tone of the greeting, made one always feel at home again in Oxford.' It was the same thing in his own house. 'It was impossible to be shy or stiff: he would tell some ridiculous story that made one feel at home in a moment.'

His sense of humour was keen and delicate, and often, by some witty remark, he would give an unexpected turn to a conversation that threatened to become too serious. He told anecdotes well, having a retentive memory, and a knack of reproducing other people's gestures and intonation. His naturally buoyant elastic temperament, which showed itself in a certain childlike lightheartedness, enabled him quickly to throw off depression or fatigue, and then he would invent rhymes or pour out a torrent of puns and jokes, till every one was infected with his high spirits. He wrote a good many parodies and *jeux d'esprit* in prose and verse, some of which were privately printed, but the secret of their authorship never divulged.

It is difficult to write of his devotion to his own home, which he so seldom cared to leave, of which he was the very life and centre, or of the wealth of affection he lavished on his children. He was their playfellow and friend from their earliest years, sharing in every feeling of joy or sorrow, entering into the simplest pleasures with the keenest enjoyment, and putting spirit into every undertaking. He was gifted with that rare unselfishness, which, while preferring the needs of others, made it appear that he was gratifying his own. His clear moral perception and directness of purpose made his advice valuable ; and his intense power of sympathy gave him an instinctive insight into the troubles and perplexities of others.

In the words of his old pupil, colleague, and friend, Prof. Dill:—'After all, the Nettleship one loves to remember is not so much the great scholar, the man of delicate literary tastes, the idealist, as the generous and tolerant friend, the delightful companion, who so readily recognized what was good in others, who had the most critical and fastidious intellect, combined with a profound reverence for noble character or great gifts, who saw the littleness of ordinary life without contempt, and realized the possibilities of the future with untroubled faith.'

M. NETTLESHIP.

I.

JOHAN NICOLAI MADVIG [1].

(PUBLIC LECTURE, MAY 21, 1887.)

THE death of a great master in scholarship is an event which invites those whose calling imposes upon them the duty of following, at however great a distance, along the path of advance in which he has led the way, to pause and recall with gratitude his tokens of command. A remarkably long life, passed, to all appearance, in good health and even fortune, and during the greater part of it with every circumstance to favour the vigorous development of his great gifts,— such was Madvig's allotted course, ending in a peaceful death on December 12, 1886. So long a career bridges over the interval between the learning of the beginning and that of the end of the nineteenth century. The two periods have different characteristics. Madvig's mind was, if ever there was one, a mind independent of its surroundings. But in examining the character of his work we shall probably be led to confess that he belonged on the whole to the earlier rather than to the late period; that his strength lay rather in power of combination, in massive penetrating intelligence, and

---

[1] [In a preliminary paragraph, here omitted, Mr. Nettleship acknowledged obligations to articles on Madvig contributed to the *Berliner Philologische Wochenschrift* (Feb. 5 and 12, 1887) by M. C. Gertz, formerly pupil of Madvig and now Professor of Classics at Copenhagen, and to the late Mr. Vigfusson, Reader in Icelandic, who was personally acquainted with Madvig.]

inexorable logical acumen, than in the patient inexhaustible industry, spending itself on the collection of facts, with which we are familiar as the main literary feature of our own time.

Johan Nicolai Madvig was born at the little town of Svaneke in the island of Bornholm, on August 7, 1804. Mr. Vigfusson tells me that in speaking he never lost his Bornholm accent. His father, like his grandfather and great-grandfather, was clerk to the court of the town and district. The profits of the office were small, and the child had to work for his living. From his eleventh year he used to help his father with the law-books. It is curious that, in the case both of Madvig and of Mommsen, a certain amount—in Mommsen's case a considerable amount—of legal study should have been the introduction to an illustrious philological career. The influence of this study on Mommsen, who carried it a great way, is, I need hardly say, strongly marked. It must have early implanted that belief, which it is his signal merit to have justified and enforced, that to understand a nation's history you must have mastered its law. It must have encouraged him to form his characteristic method of basing Roman institutions upon logically developed legal ideas. It would be absurd to say that the solidity and clearness of Madvig s understanding was the offspring of his boyish familiarity with law : but that it was nourished by it—for he was a very precocious boy—there can be little doubt. And Prof. Gertz remarks that Madvig always retained a strong interest in law, besides exhibiting in his writings, and still more in practical life, a good deal of legal acumen.

His father's wish had been that Johan should succeed him in his office, and the education of the child for this purpose had begun, when his father died in 1816. He was then, by the assistance of private friends, sent to the school of Fried-riksborg in Seeland, where he soon outstripped his companions. In 1820, at the age of sixteen, he went up to the University of Copenhagen, and took his degree in 1825. A month after-wards there appeared an edition of Garatoni's notes on the orations of Cicero, edited by five students of Copenhagen. One of these was Madvig, two others, his friends Henrichsen and Elberling. Cicero was his early love. In the following year (1826) he published, as a dissertation for the degree of M.A., emendations in the text of the *De Legibus* and the *Academica*.

About this time Thorlacius, the *professor eloquentiae* (or I suppose of classical philology) left Copenhagen on a two years' leave of absence, and Madvig was appointed to fill his place. That there should have been no older man eligible for such a post is significant as to the then condition of learning at Copenhagen. Madvig was not long in justifying his appointment. In 1828 he wrote his celebrated *Epistola Critica ad Orellium* (Orelli was at that time the great authority upon Cicero) on restoring the text of the last two Verrine Orations. He also produced a dissertation for the doctor's degree on Asconius and the other ancient Commentators on Cicero. Finally in 1829 (aetat. twenty-five) he was, on Thorlacius's death, advanced to the chair of *professor eloquentiae* in the University of Copenhagen. From this time onward, for fifty years, his life was almost entirely devoted to academical work : almost entirely I say, for he was elected to the Danish Parliament in 1839, and from November 1848 till July 1851 he was Minister of Public Worship under the National Liberal Government. He was also for many years librarian of the University, and from 1848–1874 Inspector of Schools. To these peaceful and, I shall suppose, not exhausting occupations he added some political activity. From 1848-1874 he was a member of the Danish diet, and from 1856–1863 President of the Reichsrath (Council).

For some ten years Madvig confined his studies almost entirely to Latin. His position as *professor eloquentiae* imposed on him the duty of writing a number of short papers as academical programmes. Two volumes of these dissertations he published in 1834 and 1842 under the title of *Opuscula Academica*. Among these an essay on the Roman colonies has perhaps made the most permanent mark, though others are more interesting as showing the young man's brilliant critical talent. A text of twelve select orations of Cicero, published in 1830, has gone through seven editions. At the same time he contributed a good deal to his friend Henrichsen's edition of the *De Oratore*. In 1835 he edited the *De Senectute* and *Laelius* : in 1839 the *De Finibus* : and in 1840 came the first edition of the *Latin Grammar*.

A period now follows during which Greek takes the place of Latin. In 1846 appeared his *Greek Syntax,* enlarged in 1847 by *Remarks on some points of Greek syntactical construction.* After 1851, when he retired from the Ministry of Public Worship, he returned with ardour to his study of Livy, and in 1860 published the great work on which, with the *De Finibus*, his fame rests and will rest, the *Emendationes Livianae.* Then followed (1861–1866) the edition of Livy undertaken jointly with Ussing. In 1871 he published, under the title of *Adversaria Critica*, the first volume of a collection of his scattered notes, prefaced by a general introduction on the causes of corruption in Greek and Latin manuscripts, and on the ascertained rules of critical method. The first volume contains emendations on Greek texts. The second, with emendations on Latin texts, appeared two years later, and a third volume in 1884. In 1875 he brought out a small volume of short philological essays of miscellaneous contents, written in German. From this time onwards he worked under the heavy affliction of almost total blindness. This did not, however, hinder him from completing his two volumes on the Constitution and Administration of the Roman Empire (1881–1882).

Whatever faults may be found in Madvig's work, and it has undoubtedly faults, it has always the characteristic of a sound humanity. The whole man is there : it is not a fragment of a mind, or a half-grown mind, which we see active before us. This fact is no doubt mainly attributable to the genius of the man, independently of circumstances ; but there are one or two facts to be noticed which may have assisted the development of this genius. Madvig, having lost his father young, was thus early thrown on his own resources; and his teachers at the University seem to have been men of little mark[1]. He told Professor John Mayor[2], when the two scholars met at Leyden in 1875, that he was self-taught. To this fact may partly be due a certain simplicity and wholesome independence which is never lacking in Madvig's writings. Again, not merely had he no great teacher, but, like all scholars in this century out of Germany. he was uninfluenced by any definite philological tradition.

The absence of such a tradition, of a discipline embodying the principles by which historical and philological evidence must be weighed, has been responsible for much waste of labour in the countries which have suffered from it, notably in our own. Even Madvig, as we shall see, did not altogether escape its bad influence. But to a mind like his it perhaps did as much good as harm. He had a natural eye for the lie of the country; the instinctive grasp of the features of the region to be explored. This free gift of genius was perhaps, by being left free, more robustly developed.

He was soon to give brilliant evidence of its existence. There is no greater test of genius in a scholar than the power of discerning at a glance between what is ancient and what is not. In 1828 Madvig once and for ever distinguished between the genuine commentaries of Asconius and those of the Pseudo-Asconius, which belong to the fourth century, on Cicero, and gave an account, almost exhaustive, of the history of these commentaries from the time when Pogio first brought them to light. In his twenty-sixth year (1829) he availed himself of a chance which had offered itself three years before (1826).

It had been known that a short Latin Treatise on Ortho-graphy bearing the name of Apuleius was in existence some-where in the libraries of Europe. Quotations from a Caecilius Minutianus Apuleius *De Orthographia* had been given by

---

[1] His contemporaries, Lachmann, Ritschl, and Haupt, all came more or less under the influence of Godfrey Hermann. Mommsen, like Madvig, seems never to have been influenced by any great scholar.

[2] *Classical Review*, I. 124.

Caelius Rhodiginus in his *Antiquae Lectiones*.   Achilles Statius
had given one on Catullus, and the book had also been used
by other scholars, as Gyraldus, Ursinus, and Carrio [1].   Cardinal
Mai, then librarian of the Vatican, set about to find the
original from which these quotations were taken.   He discovered, in the Riccardian library at Florence, and also in the
Vatican, copies of a meagre work on orthography in two books,
bearing the simple name of Apuleius.   Afterwards, in the
Vallicellian library at Rome, he found fragments, written in the
hand of Achilles Statius, of three books bearing the name of
Lucius Caecilius Minutianus Apuleius.   In these fragments he
found the citations used by Caelius Rhodiginus, or rather some
of them.   Mai jumped to the conclusion that in these fragments he had found the true Apuleius, and that the smaller
book was a false Apuleius.

In 1823, accordingly, he edited these fragments, with parts
of Symmachus, Julius Victor, and the fragments of ante-
Justinian law.   The so-called Apuleius was edited again, three
years later, by Osann, a professor at Giessen, who agreed with
Mai in thinking that the shorter Apuleius was a mere extract
from the larger, and that the author of the latter lived not long
after Cassiodorus, at the end of the sixth century A. D.

The book imposed upon Grotefend, and upon Baehr the
historian of Roman Literature.   Madvig was the first to point
out (1) that the work must have been written some centuries
after Cassiodorus, mainly because it gives rules for spelling
such names as Heinrich and Humbert, Guazzo and Guido.
(2) That it mentions an extraordinary farrago of Greek and
Latin authors, some of whom had never before been heard of,
and some works entirely new to the history of Latin literature,
as the *Bellum Punicum* of Varro Atacinus, Latin scholia on
Aristophanes and Pindar, and other such miraculous phenomena : notably a line of Calvus about the verses of Vergil.

[1] The dates are Statius' *Catullus*, 1566 ; Ricchieri of Rovigo (Rhodiginus),
1453–1525 ; Giraldi, 1479–1552 ; Orsini, 1530–1600 ; Carrion, 1547–1595 ;
Mai, 1782–1854.

(3) That of the names of Latin poets mentioned, twenty-three
are identical with those found in a list of twenty-seven given
by Ovid in the sixteenth epistle of the fourth book *Ex Ponto*,
while they are no more than names to the Pseudo-Apuleius.
These and other facts of a similar kind led Madvig to pronounce
the book a forgery, or perhaps a *jeu d'esprit*, of the Italian renaissance, produced (say) between 1430 and 1500. The title,
he thinks, was simply borrowed and enlarged from the smaller
(and genuine) Apuleius.

This little paper, now printed as the first of Madvig's
Opuscula Academica, blew the structure of Mai and Osann to
atoms. It was quite sufficient to place its author in the first
rank of philologists ; and will still be read with enjoyment by
scholars who like sound argument, and who wish to appreciate
the acquaintance, extraordinary in so young a scholar, which
Madvig showed with all the facts essential to a successful
exploration of this obscure corner of literary history.

I mentioned above that in 1830 he edited a text of twelve
select orations of Cicero. The preface to this book, which
showed extraordinary tact in dealing with manuscripts, even
when their readings and mutual relation were partially or
imperfectly known to him, is now printed, with other papers
on the orations of Cicero, in the *Opuscula*. The touch of the
master you feel everywhere, as well as his consciousness of his
power and position.

I learn from Mr. Vigfusson that Madvig was always poor,
his salary being small and his books bringing him but very
little profit. Hence he never travelled, and had far less
opportunity than many scholars of seeing MSS. with his own
eyes. Many then of his emendations are based on an inspec-
tion of printed reports of MSS. This fact must enhance
the admiration with which his skill in dealing with texts is
universally regarded.

It was his edition of the *De Finibus* (1839, 1869) that was
to bring out his genius in its full light before the eyes of the
learned world. To understand the full importance of the

step taken by Madvig, we must go back fifty years, and realize what was then the position of critical scholarship. I need hardly say that no competent scholar would now undertake to edit a classical author without first forming a clear notion what manuscript material he had to deal with, and what was the relation of his manuscripts one to the other. He would try to determine approximately the nature of the original or originals from which they were derived, and their comparative excellence as adequately or inadequately representing that original. He would unhesitatingly reject the evidence of all which were proved to be mere copies of a better copy still in existence. He would, in short, sift his evidence, relying only on what was primary, and rejecting what was secondary and dependent. Some one has said that, after Ritschl, any cook's boy could learn philological method. I am not sure of that, but undoubtedly things which we have now come to think obvious were not obvious in 1839. In 1824 Peyron had pointed out the true way in his edition of the palimpsest fragments of some of Cicero's speeches. The torch was handed on to Madvig, Lachmann, and Ritschl. Madvig's way of putting the matter, in the preface to his *De Finibus*, is as follows :

' If a judge, in hearing a number of witnesses giving evidence on the same fact, had reason to believe that the testimony of one or more of them was derived from that of any of the others, his first endeavour would be to separate the first hand from the second hand evidence, which he would reject as immaterial. Or, if he had before him several copies of a will, the original of which was lost, he would try to find out whether any of these copies were copied from one of the rest. This is very much what the scholar has to do in dealing with manuscripts : to determine, among a number of copies, which (if any) are copied from the rest, and what was the original or originals of all.'

The text of the *De Finibus* was in confusion. Neither had the manuscripts been rightly quoted, nor had any attempt been made to determine their relative value. The most recent edition, that of Goerenz (1831) had made confusion worse confounded by false reports of the manuscript readings, and careless and incompetent work of all kinds. The first thing Madvig did was to classify the manuscripts and ascertain the readings of their archetype : the second, to make such conjectural emendations as seemed certainly called for by the requirements of Latin usage : the third, to write a sound explanatory comment. The three parts of this difficult task were performed in a manner which made the edition a classical one, both as an introduction to critical method and as a store-house of information upon Cicero, as a stylist and as a philosopher: not to speak of the numerous incidental lights thrown upon important points of Latin usage.

Madvig's defect as a writer both in Latin and German is cumbrousness. But he has a merit that more than counterbalances this fault of style. This is his power of placing clearly before the reader, in a short space, a statement of the problems with which he has to deal in their general and special bearings. His own method of emendation, so brilliantly successful in the case of Cicero and Livy, is, for instance, thus expounded in the preface to the *De Finibus* (pp. xlvii–l). 'The first thing to be asked in the case of a conjectural correction is whether it is necessary : A fault must be proved to demonstration before a remedy is attempted. A fault can be proved to exist either by the evidence of good manuscripts, or by the exigencies of the construction, and of the sense, or by all of these. In exacting these conditions, I endeavour to restore not necessarily what is absolutely right, but what Cicero might (whether correctly and elegantly or not) have written, and what the evidence and the reason of the thing show that he did write. Scholars are too strict in requiring that the construction shall always be absolutely correct. They adhere too closely to their grammatical manuals, and forget the general nature and conditions of human language. In this general nature and conditions,

ancient languages do not differ from modern.   It is a mistake
to suppose that an ancient writer was never careless or
ambiguous.   When the question is raised of the correctness of
an expression, or of its existence at a particular time, we shall
have to consider what degrees of transition there may have
been between the expression and ordinary usage.   If it is
a case of license or carelessness, attention must be paid to the
occasion for such license which may have been offered by
legitimate usage.   In following up these points, I have come
to regard some hitherto accepted expressions as doing
intolerable violence to Latin forms, and therefore impossible ;
while I have defended some carelessness of expression as
possible in Cicero.   For it is mere superstition to imagine
that he always wrote at the highest pitch of perfection . . .
Keeping these considerations in mind, a scholar may proceed
to the work of restoring the text : that is, to restoring the
readings pointed to by the evidence of the manuscripts and
the requirements of meaning and construction.   A prudent
critic will see that in some cases the restoration of the words
is possible, in others, that the general sense, but not the words,
may be recovered, in others, that nothing can be done.   The
scholar who follows in this line will be able to correct corrupt
texts with confidence.   Before making a conjecture, he will
remember that moderation is, in scientific work, a sign of
wisdom.   I say this by way of protest, on the one hand
against the habit of throwing out groundless conjectures, on
the other hand against the silly superstition which holds that
manuscripts are infallible.'

In 1840 appeared the first edition of the work by which
Madvig is still, I suppose, most commonly known, his Latin
Grammar.   This work has passed through many editions and
has been translated into several languages.   For a long time,
indeed, it was the standard school Latin Grammar in Europe
and America.   The period treated is, on the whole, that of
classical Latin.   The great merits of the book are its clearness
and grasp of the subject within the limits which the writer set

himself; its power of analysis, and its command of classical usage. In the present state of knowledge it seems to me very doubtful whether so good a book could be written in so short a compass. As in every other study, so in that of grammar, the historical method now holds the field ; we work inevitably by the theory of evolution. Usages must be traced from their source downwards : from the oldest monuments to the time when the language decays and dies. Forms must be analysed in the light of comparative philology. And, as if all this were not enough, the peculiarities of separate authors must be mastered and embodied. No one has as yet succeeded in producing a Latin Grammar which satisfactorily fulfils all these conditions, though it is tolerably certain that, sooner or later, the task will be accomplished. That it should even have been conceived in 1839 is hardly possible. The task which Madvig set himself, to give a clear and logical account of the usages of the best Latin authors, he performed admirably, and threw much new light on several difficult questions. Though his point of view is superseded, no scientific student of grammar can yet afford to neglect him.

For some years, as the *Opuscula* amply testify, Madvig had been studying Livy, and in 1834 had read through all the remains of that author. From 1848 to 1851 he had been taken from his studies—unfortunately, as I gather from Mr. Vigfusson, for all concerned—to the Ministry of Public Worship. In 1851, when he returned to his books, a combination of circumstances, partly accidental, determined him to try what he could do for the whole of Livy's remains. He had already received a complete collation of the Vienna MS., the only MS. of the last five books. In four years—and working only in leisure hours—he had ready a set of notes on the whole text. His friends urged him to put these together and publish them in a collected form. Others wished him to go further and edit the text, embodying not only his own emendations, but such old readings as he thought had been wrongly rejected by recent editors. From this task he at present shrank, partly owing to its magnitude, partly because Alschefsky had already begun, and Weissenborn already completed, a text of Livy; partly because he wished and hoped to turn to what he thought more important studies. How often has a scholar to do this : instead of dashing at the mountain for his own pleasure, to make a road for posterity over the marshes and boulders at the foot. The philosopher says that he has no power of thinking, and the literary man, that his mind is absorbed with details.

The lighter work, however, of collecting and publishing his own emendations,—some of which, as was natural, had been anticipated by Kreyssig and Weissenborn,—he undertook ; and the result was the first edition of the *Emendationes Livianae* in 1860, the second in 1877. In the preface to this work he goes much nearer than he had done in the *De Finibus* towards giving a general account of the more obvious causes of corruption in Latin manuscripts which meet the scholar in his attempt to restore a text. His problem indeed was somewhat different from that which he had had to solve in the case of Cicero. He had now to deal with an author whose text, in the hands of recent editors, had suffered not from gross carelessness or inaccuracy in the reports of MS. readings, but from a superstitious adherence to the MS. tradition. The commonest instance of this was the insertion or omission of the letter *m* at the end of nouns—producing absurd confusions between the accusative and ablative cases. So far had this gone that Alschefsky, Weissenborn, and Hertz had edited *in medio sarcinas coniciunt* (10. 36. 1) for *in medium,* while Alschefsky did not scruple to print *in lapidem consedit.* Much was done by Madvig, not only in the way of clearing up the relations of the MSS. to each other, but by exploding these and similar ineptitudes : much more by his own brilliant emendations, the genius of which, as they succeed each other in long order, is astonishing, while many are absolutely certain. To have restored, or done much towards restoring, the text of Livy, is Madvig's unquestioned glory. It would be difficult to exaggerate either the importance of the work, or the learning, acuteness, and genius required for it.

The edition of Livy, in which Ussing was associated with Madvig, followed in the few years succeeding 1861. In 1871 Madvig brought out the first volume of his *Adversaria Critica*, or miscellaneous emendations in Greek and Latin texts.[1] This is a work of unequal merit. The introductory chapter, on the general causes of corruption in manuscripts, is, so far as I know, the only attempt at a comprehensive treatment of the subject. It would, indeed, gain by more actual demonstration from the admitted mistakes found in the manuscripts themselves. Madvig confines himself mainly to cases which in his strong opinion require emendation. There are really plenty of instances in which there can be no doubt in any one's mind. Such instances may be found by scores by any one who will take the trouble to examine the numerous *apparatus critici* now generally accessible, such as Ribbeck's to Vergil or Ritschl's to Plautus. In these one can trace the whole process of corruption, whether by confusion of letters, false division of words, abbreviations, repetitions, omissions, intrusion of glosses, or alteration of forms to suit the supposed exigencies of grammar. A good chapter might easily be written to supplement Madvig's essay. It would amply confirm what his sagacity has on the whole discerned without so minute a sifting of the materials.

The method of emendation pursued by Madvig in his Cicero, his Livy, and *Adversaria* (i. e. in the most valuable part of them) has beyond all question exercised a powerful influence on the progress of philological science. It is the proceeding of an original and master mind, not of an intelligent learner. He has taught scholars to demand a solid reason for an emendation ; he has pointed out, with perfect clearness and sobriety, the various kinds of errors to which manuscripts are liable ; and in his best work he has striven to correct texts, as far as possible, according to the indications given by the manuscripts

[1] The second volume appeared in 1873, the third—a much smaller book —in 1884.

themselves.   Much, in short, which has been done for Greek
by Cobet has been done for Latin by Madvig.   Not, of course,
that Lachmann and Ritschl and (more indirectly) Mommsen
have not, in their way, each made invaluable contributions to
the art and science of criticism ; but I doubt whether the
results of their labours have been put before the world in
a form so comprehensive, so simple and so accessible.   Lachmann's Lucretius is, in its way, as important a work as Madvig's
Livy: but Lachmann leaves his main conclusions as to the
text of Lucretius to be learned as the reader goes on with the
book.   So clearly does Madvig, on the other hand, expound
his method at the beginning of his Livy, that his preface can
easily be used, as I can gratefully testify, for a text-book in
a philological class.

To return, however, to the *Adversaria*.   There are faults in
the book which it would be wrong to ignore — Madvig did not
carry out, in the case of authors of whom his knowledge was
comparatively superficial, the principles which he lays down or
suggests in his *De Finibus* and *Livy*.   As Mr. Mayor[1] well says,
' It is plain at first sight that Madvig's knowledge of metre was
imperfect ; many of his guesses on minor authors are hasty,
and would have been abandoned by him on second thoughts ;
in some cases the common lexicons prove the correctness of
readings which he condemns.   His familiarity with ante- and
post-classical Latin was by no means on a par with his mastery
of Ciceronian and Livian style.   Nor does he display that nice
sense of usage which makes the study of I. F. Gronovius,
Ruhnken, Heindorf, Cobet, so instructive.   Robust common
sense, revolting against impossibilities in thought or expression,
a clear perception of what the context required, a close
adherence to the *ductus litterarum*, seem to me his great merits
as a critic.'

When Madvig[2] says of Plautus ' videri sibi Plauti Comoediis
ne plane nativum quidem sermonem Latinum et suopte
ingenio sese moventem contineri, sed non raro Graeca

[1] *Classical Review*, 1. 124.   [2] *Adv.* 2. 4.

vertendo, imitando, novam versus formam sequendo et ei
obediendo inflexum,' it is quite clear, in my judgement, that he
makes a great mistake. In the severe professorial lecture which
Ritschl reads him in the third volume of his *Opuscula Philologica*, Madvig is charged directly with the lack of historical
sense. Thus baldly stated, this charge cannot for a moment
be entertained; for in the wider application, no scholar shows
more historical sense than Madvig, nor was he ignorant of the
progress which the study of old Latin had made in the hands
of Ritschl and his school. But with the study itself it seems
to me that, for some reason or other, he was not in
intelligent sympathy. Whether national prejudice, or the
isolation of his position at Copenhagen, had any share in producing this result, so unlike the man and so unworthy of him,
is a question to be asked. However this may be, Ritschl has
the advantage of being in the right, and such further advantage
as may be derived from the adoption of a high scolding attitude,
and the liberal use of such words as Hybris, Authadeia,
Nemesis, and *Geistlosigkeit.*

I pass now to a brief mention of Madvig's writings on
Roman history and antiquities. The most important of these
are, first, the papers published in the *Opuscula* and *Kleine
Schriften*; *De iure et condicione coloniarum populi Romani*;
De tribunis aerariis disputatio: *Die römischen Officiere*; and
finally the two volumes entitled *Die Verfassung und Verwaltung
des römischen Reiches* (1881–2).

The results of the two first-named dissertations have been
long worked up into the treatises of other scholars. The
paper on the Roman officers is intended as a clear exposition
for the benefit of educated readers generally, and gives a
perfectly lucid explanation of the facts. The two volumes on
the Roman Constitution and Administration deserve special
notice for more reasons than one. Madvig's object in writing
the book, which has by the bye, a pathetic interest as the work
of a blind man, can best be expounded in his own language
(p. iv. foll.) :—

'The sketch here attempted is not the offspring of a definite intention to write such a book.   But a study of Latin literature, carried on almost without interruption for fifty years, has impressed upon me the necessity of giving a clear notion, both for my own sake and my hearers' sake, of the national life and the whole circumstances which gave that literature its general and special characteristics . . . My early studies fell into the period when the traditional accounts of early Roman history had received their death-blow at the hands of Niebuhr, who pointed out their many weaknesses, gaps, and discrepancies. My own aim was to gain a firm ground to start from.   I threw aside all prejudice; but I could not approve of the capricious and sometimes wild way of going to work which I seemed to observe in others, both in the handling of authorities and in the forming of groundless hypotheses . . . This position, first indicated in my paper on the Roman colonies in 1832, I have never abandoned . . . My aim has been to combine freedom from prejudice with sound sense, a natural and simple mode of theorizing, and a candid recognition of the peculiarities of the ancient world.   The only originality I care for is that of abandoning the claim to be original.   My chief object has been to grasp, explain, and combine the facts which stand out clearly in the period which we can safely regard as historical. Starting from these I have tried, in dealing with the Roman Constitution, to follow the connexion of its original principles with their late devolpment, and so to work back into the darkness of antiquity.   And, again, I have tried either to answer, or at any rate to place in a correct and simple light, such difficulties as arise with regard to the special development of these principles.   In all cases I have followed the indications before me, but have stopped short where all intelligible traces are obliterated . . .

. . . I am not altogether satisfied with Mommsen's proceeding in his *Staatsrecht.*   To begin with the *magistratus,* passing over the senate and people, is to build without sufficient foundation.   An impression of strain and of artificiality is produced by the work. An effort is made to explain the origin of existing forms and arrangements by reference to general conceptions and theories supposed to have existed in the minds of the Romans ; and the author shows an inclination to form combinations and hypotheses which cannot always be called natural or reasonable. In saying this, however, I wish to express my fullest recognition of Mommsen's extraordinary learning and acuteness, and of his absolutely unrivalled mastery over the materials which lie outside the region of Latin literature.'

Madvig, in fact, does not in this work aim at being either original or exhaustive. The compass of his book is too small to allow of so full a citation of references as is given by Marquardt and Mommsen. He does not write so much for the purpose of giving new theories, as to present in a form comprehensive and generally intelligible to the classically-educated public, the outlines of the Roman constitution and administration. This his book does, not only with clearness, but in such a way as to leave the impression of an individual personality working upon the materials. On the general point at issue between Mommsen and Madvig it would be presumptuous in me to offer an opinion ; nor will the question, perhaps, be decided in our generation. One thing however is to my mind highly probable ; and that is that the investigations into primitive usages now being carried on with such activity by anthropologists will in time throw fresh light upon the origins of Greek and Roman Institutions, if indeed they do not altogether revolutionize our historical methods.

For the general interest of the matter I quote Madvig's judgement [1] on the character of Julius Caesar :

' It has lately been the fashion, I know not whether in deference to Mommsen, or to the imperial author of the *Vie de César,* to take a high tone in glorification of Caesar's clear and magnificent ideas, and his plans for reforming the state and the empire of Rome. The suggestion is that, had he lived,

[1] i. 525.

a structure would have arisen very different from that reared by Augustus. I give the fullest recognition to Caesar's strategic genius, to his clear political vision and his energetic will. But the truth must be told, that we know absolutely nothing of these plans and ideas. In real history you will not find a Caesar who had a consistent notion of constructing a new and better state. What you do find is a man convinced of his own worth, ambitious, and intolerant of rivals. It is, finally, extremely doubtful whether Caesar would have hit upon a much better solution of the problems before him than Augustus did. These problems were colossal, and capable only of a very slow and imperfect solution. The one great reform which Caesar effected, the reformation of the calendar, was not a political reform. The fact that in his late years he was preparing for a war with Parthia does not prove that he was meditating organic changes. Even genius, we shall remember, has its limitations in the sphere of its time and circumstances.'

This verdict will no doubt be challenged; but I should imagine that the estimate of Livy and Dionysius, with which the book concludes, will meet with general acceptance. I offer a condensed paraphrase of it.

'Livy's history was accepted in his own and in the following generation, a period, it must be remembered, of great literary activity, as on the whole adequate and sufficient. No one attempted to do the work over again, and the later historians were generally content to abridge him. The ancients as a whole had too little general experience, too little capacity for appreciating the difference between one nation and another, between one period of civilization and another, between primitive and fully developed political institutions, between fable and assured fact, to write great histories in our sense of the word. Much of the confusion of thought which runs through Livy's account of the Roman constitution may be found in contemporary or nearly contemporary writers, such as Velleius and Asconius; nor does any one seem seriously to have cared to get to the root of the matter. To carry the

imagination back from the refined civilization of Augustan
Rome to the rude and limited world of Italian antiquity would
have been an effort quite beyond the capacities of that age.'

'Livy aims at no more, and no more was expected of him or
of any one else, than to give a tasteful and well-drawn picture
of the national history as it was accepted at his time; to adorn
it with life-like descriptions of characters and events, and to
make it reflect the inspiring idea of the greatness of the Roman
empire. His superficiality, carelessness, and critical incapacity
have been often noticed. But it should be remembered in his
favour that he lets us honestly see how scanty his authorities
often were; that he does not overlay his work with symmetrical
fictions, or spoil its Latin tone by an admixture of foreign
ideas ; and, finally, that his Latin terminology gives a firmness
and clearness to his outlines which is entirely wanting in the
Greek Dionysius. For Dionysius, in the antiquarian part of
his book, is a mere Greekling. He has no acquaintance with
Roman public life and its forms. While he praises the public
institutions of Rome, he is still vain enough to console himself
with the idea that Rome owed everything to the Greeks ;
a notion which leads him into the most shameless misrepre-
sentation, as when, for instance, he ascribes to the Romans of
remote antiquity a complete acquaintance with Greek cities and
Greek life.'

This clear, sound, and independent judgement, formed
always on first-hand study, is one of Madvig's greatest
characteristics. But I think that his interests were wider than
those of the mere philologist. He is no specialist, if by
specialist be meant a man whose moral and intellectual being
is genuinely satisfied with the investigation of particular points,
or the exclusive cultivation of a single unimportant branch of
study. And this I suppose is the real meaning of this vaguely
applied word. Madvig was forced by circumstances and by the
possession of an extraordinary genius for the restoration of
texts into spending the best part of his life, the years between
twenty and sixty, upon difficult problems of textual criticism.

But a perusal, however superficial, of the essays forming the *Kleine philologische Schriften* (1875), will convince the reader that Madvig's eye was constantly directed to the wider aspects of his studies. He never lost sight of the real position and value of classical philology. In his *Kleine Schriften* is printed a little paper on the retention of classical study in schools (p. 285 foll.). He shows that he is under no illusions on the subject. It is not in the literary enjoyment afforded by the Greek and Latin writers, nor in the gymnastic training given to the mind by mastering their grammar, that he places their educational value : but in the fact that they offer the necessary and the only means of obtaining a first-hand view of the Graeco-Roman world, and therefore of the fore-time of European civilization.

Again, the essays on Language in general, on *Gender in Language* (1835), *On the Nature and Development and Life of Language* (1842), *On the Origin and Character of the signs by which Language indicates grammatical distinctions* (1884–5), are in the way very instructive. Not being based on a really wide induction, or on any but a surface acquaintance with the results of comparative philology, they will not live as contributions to that science. But they have the great merit of clearness, insight, and a resolute antagonism to anything like the obscurity or vaporous writing into which, in dealing with these nearly impenetrable subjects, it is so easy to fall. These essays are then of value not only as being stimulating and suggestive, but as holding before the student the duty of lucid and patient thinking, of which, whatever the state of our knowledge, there is likely to be need for a long time.

Was it these general linguistic studies, or more extended historical work, to which Madvig had hoped to be able to devote himself as to *graviora studia* ? I suppose that, had his interests been narrower, he might have accomplished even more than he did in the reign of critical philology. One is irresistibly driven to compare him with his younger contemporary, Theodor Mommsen. He had not the strange power

of imagination, partly legal and political, partly poetical, nor
the astonishing impulse towards making new and ever new
discoveries, which characterize that great scholar. Since his
Livy was published he doubtless read much, but did little,
compared with Mommsen, to further the progress of original
investigation. Research has in the last quarter of a century
been growing more multitudinous and minute, and yet the
demand for general views of antiquity remains, and rightly
remains, the same. The contents of the seven-sealed book
are still an organic whole, and so is the knowledge of them :
to touch any part with success, one ought to be master of all.
The scholar is the servant of two masters—each, like two
Roman *collegae,* with plenary authority—width of view and
study of detail. Every day new facts, affecting languages, metre,
syntax, manuscript tradition, historical documents, are multi-
plying round him, so that no day in his life ought to be
so occupied *ut non lineam ducendo exerceat artem.* But when
will the picture appear ? or will it ever appear ?

The impression left on my mind by much in Madvig's
writing, and confirmed by his whole career, is that his ideal
was not so much to live for his studies as to render, through
his studies, solid service to his country. His services to
education, not only in the university of Copenhagen, but
throughout Denmark, seem to have been solid and valuable.
The disastrous cry which demands or approves the separation
of learning from education would not, I imagine, have awakened
much sympathy in his breast. One does not, unless I am
much mistaken, come upon any complaints in his books of
the tedium of giving lectures, or the interference of this
occupation with his studies ; although in a man of his genius
such complaints might have been natural and excusable.
Indeed his writings as a whole do not give the idea of having
exhausted all that his mind had to give. This impression is
confirmed by what I find Professor Gertz saying about him.
' He was always impressing upon the students that the
ultimate and highest aim of their studies was to gain a sure

insight into history, a clear and living idea of the life of the
Greek and Roman world.   Both in his lectures and in his
written works he made solid contributions towards this end.
His power of acute criticism, it is true, never deserted him
in his lectures any more than in his books.   He made a strong
point of defining clearly what, in his opinion, we know and
what we do not know. . . . His pictures of ancient life were
in consequence, at times fragmentary ; but one was always
comforted by the feeling that one was on sure ground with
him.   Where the materials allowed it, he could give sketches
as interesting, as full of life and soul, as any one.   And his
viva voce exposition lacked, almost entirely, the cumbrousness
which characterizes his written style. . . .

   ' His interests were by no means confined to his special
studies.   They embraced almost all sides of human knowledge
and practice.   He was not only at home, to a remarkable
degree, in many other departments of science (to say nothing
of general literature), but has been known to make suggestions of the greatest value to men whose studies lay outside
his own beat.   He was therefore the hero of the Danish
students, and up to the end of his life liked to mingle in
their society.   It was thus only natural that the University
of Copenhagen repeatedly elected him as its representative,
and the Academy of Sciences as its president . . . . It is to
him that Denmark owes the best organization of her higher
schools that she has ever enjoyed.   As inspector of schools
he impressed scholars and masters alike with his kindness.'

   Professor Mayor [1] gives an interesting account of his meeting
Madvig at Leyden in 1875.   'I saw,' he says, ' the first meeting
between him and Cobet, and remembered the description
given by the aged Gersdorf some ten years before, of the
meeting between Friedrich Jacobs and his old correspondent
Gottfried Hermann.   Madvig had a singular grace and ease
of manner . . . . Cobet, in proposing Madvig's health as the
acknowledged master of the critical art, added ; but we will

   [1] *Classical Review* i. 124.

not make a pope of you ; *pugnabimus tecum, contendemus tecum, eoque vehementius pugnabimus, quo te vehementius admiramur.* Madvig began his reply thus : *Post Cobetum latine loqui vereor ;* but soon passed from compliments to give some admirable advice to the students.'

On the second of December 1886 Madvig had intended to read a paper at the philological society on the political pamphlets of the later republican period. At noon however, on returning from his walk, he felt indisposed. All seemed to be going well till the forenoon of the twelfth, when his doctor declared himself well satisfied with his patient, to whom he had given leave to get up. Madvig was in the act of rising when he suddenly exclaimed ' It is all dark,' sank backwards and expired. The force and clearness of his intellect remained unimpaired to the last.

This was the peaceful end of an honourable life. His name will be remembered, as long as the historical sciences continue to exist. He cultivated to the utmost the virtue which it is the scholar's point of honour to possess, the love of truth. He fell into some mistakes from haste and carelessness, but never erred from want of sense, and insisted indeed in applying everywhere the rule of reason. In the study of minute points, he never lost his hold on the general bearing of philological questions or on the wider aspects of his science. He was, finally, one of the great reformers in the history of philology, who, by sweeping away bad work and false method, have made the way easier for those who came after him.

II.

THE ORIGINAL FORM OF
THE ROMAN SATURA[1].

(Originally published at the Clarendon Press in 1878.)

————••————

THE name *satura*, which has given so much trouble to scholars, should to all appearance be compared with feminines formed from adjectives, such as *noxia*, a fault, *dira*, a curse, and others of the same kind. The meaning seems to be a medley. Varro quoted by Diomedes (3. p. 486 Keil) says, 'Satura est uva passa et polenta et nuclei pini ex mulso consparsi:' and Festus p. 314, 'Satura et cibi genus ex variis rebus conditum est et lex multis aliis legibus confecta. Itaque in sanctione legum adscribitur "neve per saturam abrogato aut derogato."' How the word first came to be applied to a form of literature is not ascertainable. It may be that its use in this connection was metaphorical; it may be that *satura* (i. e. *satura fabula*) was from the first the term for a dramatic performance or a story which was a medley of scenes or incidents. When Juvenal speaks of 'nostri farrago libelli' he is doubtless alluding to the then accepted explanation of *satura* as an *olla podrida* or dish of various ingredients : but it must be remembered that all our Latin authorities on this matter speak at a time when the word has become fixed

[1 Mr. Nettleship contributed an article on this subject to the third edition of Smith's *Dictionary of Antiquities* (1891). I have noted below (pp. 33, 34) the two details about which he seems to have changed his opinion since 1878.]

in its literary sense of a medley of metres, or of prose and verse. It is probable, however, that the word *satura* was familiar to the Romans long before the existence of the literary composition so named, and before those who used it had many metres to mingle. The Roman scholars who treat of the name were partly too familiar with it, partly too careless in their etymological researches, to give its real origin a thorough examination.

An attempt will be made in the following pages to define somewhat more precisely than has hitherto been done what was the original form of the *satura*, and to trace the course of that development which, under the pressure of various circumstances, brought it to the shape which it assumed in the hands of Juvenal, and in which it is most familiar to us.

Livy 7. 2. 4, in describing the origin of dramatic performances at Rome says, 'Sine carmine ullo, sine imitandorum carminum actu ludiones ex Etruria acciti, ad tibicinis modos saltantes, haud indecoros motus more Tusco dabant. Imitari deinde eos iuventus simul inconditis inter se versibus coepere : nec absoni a voce motus erant. Accepta itaque res saepiusque usurpando excitata. Vernaculis artificibus, quia *ister* Tusco verbo ludio vocabatur, nomen histrionibus inditum, qui non, sicut ante, Fescennino versu similem incompositum temere ac rudem alternis iaciebant, sed inpletas modis saturas descripto iam ad tibicinem cantu motuque congruenti peragebant. Livius post aliquot annos, qui ab saturis ausus est primus argumento fabulam serere,' &c.

The passage is confused and difficult : but it seems fair to infer from it that Livy meant by the word *satura* a simple scene without a plot, acted at first without, but afterwards (under Etruscan influence) with, a regular musical accompaniment and corresponding gestures. He contrasts *saturae modis inpletae* or *saturae* regularly finished with a musical setting, to the irregular dialogue in verse, resembling the Fescennine, which existed before. Of the words *saturae modis inpletae*, the most important are apparently *modis inpletae*. There is nothing to prevent us from supposing that Livy would have applied the word *satura* to the previously existing irregular dialogue. A musical and rhythmical setting was first given to this dialogue on the introduction of the Etruscan art.

It follows with more certainty from the words of Livy that the performance to which he gives the name of *satura*, never developed into a play with a regular plot. Livius Andronicus, he says, was the first artist who gave up *saturae*, and under Greek influence introduced a regular play—*argumento fabulam serere ausus est.* In other words, the Greek play, with its various scenes united by the thread of a single story, drove the *satura* from the stage.

The fair inference from the whole passage seems to be twofold. First, that a *satura* differed from a play mainly in having no plot. Secondly, that the *satura* had in it an element of dialogue. This fact seems to follow by implication both from Livy's positive statements about the *satura* and from his omitting to mention the dialogue of Livius' plays as in any way a new factor in the development of the theatrical art. The new element is not the dialogue, but the plot.

To this view it may be objected that there is no proof of the rude performance which Livy calls *satura* standing in any real relation to the *satura* of literature, claimed by Horace[1] and Quintilian as an unquestionably Italian production. If however it can be shown, as I think it can, that the *satura* of literature bears features of strong resemblance to the *satura* mentioned by Livy, much will be done towards removing this objection. And, before going further, we may observe that Livy evidently uses the word *satura* as implying a form of art perfectly well known to his readers, and not in any way needing to be distinguished from the literary *satura* with which of course they were perfectly familiar.

Let us assume then that the *satura* existed in old times in Italy as a rude form of dramatic art similar to, though not

---

[1] *Graecis intacti carminis.* Quintil. 10. 1. 93 : *Satura quidem tota nostra est.*

identical with, the Fescennine verses. When we are enabled
to take up the thread of its continuous history we find it
driven from the stage and become a form of literature proper.
We have no record of the process by which the stage was
gradually occupied by the *Atellana*, the *mimus*, and the
exodium : but there seems to be no doubt that by the time
of Ennius [1] the *satura* had come to be cultivated exclusively
as a branch of literature, a literary luxury, it may almost be
said, capable of a tone somewhat more serious than would
have been suited for the stage and the general public. The
satura of Ennius was, in form, a mixture or medley of metrical
pieces in which the element of dialogue was in all probability
present. Little enough remains of Ennius' productions in
this line; but we may be sure that, like all his other works,
his *saturae* were strongly tinged by Greek influence. It is
difficult to suppose that the dialogue or contest between
Life and Death mentioned by Quintilian (9. 2. 36) in the
same breath with the fable of Prodicus about Virtue and
Vice was not a copy of some Greek model; perhaps we may
note here a touch of the popular Greek philosophy or
reflection which, as we shall see, is so obvious in the later
satura. Another interesting notice of the *satura* of Ennius
is preserved by Gellius (2. 29), who tells us that Ennius
worked the fable of the tufted lark and its young ones, with
great skill and grace, into a *satura*. This may remind us of
the way in which Horace uses the fable of the town and
country mouse, and again suggests a trace of connection with
Greek literature. For Ennius, in versifying a fable of Aesop,
may possibly have translated some Greek metrical version
of the story, such as Socrates is said to have amused himself
with making in the long hours of his imprisonment.

The writings of Pacuvius in this department being entirely
lost, it is necessary to pass on to the great change in the form

---

[1] Horace's words (*S.* I. 10. 66), '*quam rudis et Graecis intacti carminis
auctor,*' imply that in his opinion Ennius was the first writer who attempted
the literary *satura*.

and character of the *satura* introduced by Lucilius. In his
hands the *satura* did not lose its character as a brief narrative
or picture of life with an element of dialogue. So much is
clear if only from the remains of the third book, from which
Horace copied the Journey from Rome to Brundisium; from the
scene in the fourth book between Aeserninus and Pacideianus;
from the rustic supper in the fifth book, and the convivial
scenes of the fourteenth and twentieth. The dialogue of
Lucilius seems partly to have assumed the form of an address
to a friend or enemy (as in books 3, 5, 26, 30); partly to have
been carried on between the characters in the *satura* itself
(as in the twenty-eighth book); partly to have taken the more
formal shape (of which Juvenal is so fond) of an address by the
poet to his readers. Like the *satura* of Ennius, too, that of
Lucilius had its points of contact with Greek philosophy[1],
whether sceptical or reflective : witness the beginning of the
first book and the mention of Lucilius' contemporary Carneades.
These are points of resemblance between the *satura* of Lucilius
and that of Ennius ; but they are unimportant, and have been
to a great extent forgotten, in comparison with the points of
difference. Lucilius was the first writer who impressed on the
satura that character of invective which it to a great extent
preserved in the hands of Horace, Persius, Juvenal, and others

[1] Lactantius, 5. 14. 3 : *Lucilii, apud quem disserens Neptunus de re
difficillima ostendit non posse id explicari,* ' *nec si Carneaden ipsum Orcu*'
remittat' [book 1, fragm. 12, Müller]. Compare also 26. fragm. 59, *lutrarum*
(so Müller) *exactorem Albanum et fulguritorem arborum* (of Jupiter) :
27. 35. *nescis, ubi Graeci, ubi nunc Socratici charti?* and 28. 1 (as restored
by Munro),

> *Hoc cum feceris,*
> *Cum ceteris reus una tradetur Lupo.*
> (*A*) *Non aderit.* (*B*) ἀρχαῖς *hominem et* στοιχείοις *simul*
> *Privabit.* (*A*) *Igni cum et aqua interdixerit,*
> *Duo habet* στοιχεῖα; *adfuerit.* (*B*) *Posterioribus*
> στοιχείοις, *si id maluerit, privabit tamen.*

The line 26. 71, *sin autem hoc vident, bona semper petere sapientem putant,*
has the ring of the schools : so *Inc.* 101, *nondum etiam, qui haec omnia
habebit, Formosus, dives, liber, rex solus feretur?* (The references are to
Müller's edition).

(e. g. Albucius[1]), and which apparently in the view of a large section of the Roman literary public became essential to it. Personal the *satura* always is, it is always serious : but in the hands of Lucilius and those who imitated him it underwent a new Greek influence, that of the old Attic comedy, and became the instrument not only of personal reflection or advice or expostulation, but of personal attack. The movement is significant of a change in the spirit of the satirist and in that of his age. It was not only that the *satura* of Ennius may have seemed to Lucilius[2] cumbrous, grotesque, wanting in dignity ; it may also have appeared at once too general and too cold in its contents to suit the concluding years of the seventh century of the city. Ennius wrote at a time when the Romans, after their newly won triumph over Carthage, could content themselves with merely enjoying and reproducing the literature of Greece, and applying its forms to the decoration of their own achievements. Before the time of the Gracchi there is little trace in Roman literature of the deep feeling of corruption in the governing classes which meets us from the time of Lucilius to the end of the republic. But in the hands of Lucilius the *satura* becomes the scourge of incapacity in high places : he is the chronicler of the real Rome of his time, painting with all sincerity like a shipwrecked sailor on his votive board (as Horace says) the picture of his own life and that of his countrymen. The Rome[3] of Lucilius is a city in which the pleasures

---

[1] *Cuius Luciliano charactere sunt libelli* (Varro, *R. R.* 3. 2. 17) : see Teuffel, *Gesch. d. röm. Litt.* § 189, 1 [in the latest German edition of 1890 and in Warr's translation § 192. 1. Albucius seems to have been really named Abuccius.]

[2] Hor. S. 1. 10. 54. *Non ridet versus Enni gravitate minores ?*

[3] 1. 16 : *Infamem vitam turpemque odisse popinam.*

4. 3 :   *O Publi, O gurges, Galloni : es homo miser, inquit ;*
         Cenasti in vita nunquam bene, cum omnia in ista
         Consumis squilla atque acupensere cum in decumano.

Ib. 5 : *Occidunt, Lupe, saperdae te et iura siluri.*

6 :   *Quod sumptum atque epulas victu praeponis honesto.*

5. 29 : *Vivite lurcones, comedones, vivite ventres.*

Ib. 33 : *Nam si quod satis est homini id satis esse potesset,*

of money-getting and the banquet and the brothel are drawing away men's minds from honest living and public spirit and that manly virtue, which, teaching the due limits of desire and the real value of material prosperity, bids men put their country first, their parents second, and their friends last. All men have but one profession—to deceive, to flatter, to pretend, every man's hand against every man, and reputation depending upon wealth and love of display. Turning to political life , Lucilius sees the *nobiles* sinning unpunished and beating off all attacks by their mere nobility. In war [2] Roman armies are defeated

> *Hoc sat erat: nunc cum hoc non est, qui credimu' porro*
> *Divitias ullas animum mi explere potesse?*
>
> 6. 3 : *Nequitia occupat hos, petulantia prodigitasque.*
>
> 30. 24 : *Quem sumptum facis in lustris, circum oppida lustrans!*
>
> Inc. 4 : *Nunc vero a mane ad noctem, festo atque profesto,*
> *Toto itidem pariterque die populusque patresque*
> *Iactare indu foro se omnes, decedere nusquam :*
> *Uni se atque eidem studio omnes dedere et arti :*
> *Verba dare ut caute possint, pugnare dolose ;*
> *Blanditia certare, bonum simulare virum se ;*
> *Insidias facere, ut si hostes sint omnibus omnes.*
>
> Ib. 5 : *Aurum atque ambitio specimen virtutis virique est :*
> *Quantum habeas tantum ipse sies tantique habearis.*
>
> [1] 6. 2 :   *Peccare inpune rati sunt*
> *Posse ; et nobilitate facul propellere iniquos.*

Compare the series of personal attacks, 11. 10, 11, 12, 13.

> 11. 4 : *Praetor noster ad hoc quam spurcus sit ore, &c.*
>
> 14. 15 : *Publiu' Pavu' Tuditanus mihi quaestor Hibera*
> *In terra fuit : lucifugus, nebulo, id genus sane.*
>
> [2] 1. 30 : *Et mercede merent legiones* [see *Essays in Latin Literature* p. 344]
>
> 31 : *Munu' tamen fungi et muros servare potissint.*
>
> 2. 11 :   *Hostilius contra*
> *Pestem permitiemque catax quam et Maniu' nobis.*
>
> 13. 2 : *Aut forte omnino ac fortuna vincere bello.*
> *Si forte ac temere omnino, quid rursum ad honorem?*
>
> 15. 12 :   *dum miles Hibera*
> *Terra seice* (so Müller) *meret ter sex, aetate quasi, annis.*
>
> 26. 45 : *At Romanus populus victus vi superatus proeliis*
> *Saepest multis, bello vero nunquam, quo sunt omnia.*
>
> Ib. 46 : *Contra flagitium nescire, bello vinci a barbaro*
> *Viriato Hannibale* (so rightly Munro, following the MSS.).
>
> Ib. 47 : *Percrepa pugnam Popili, facta Corneli cane.*

through the sheer ignorance of their commanders—a Mancinus, a Manilius, a Popilius Laenas. Roman soldiers serve a whole life-time in Spain; Viriathus, a barbarian Hannibal, conquers them in war. In the dumb sense of a coming change the *satura* becomes more personal, and grapples more closely than before with life and public affairs. The practical and political stamp which almost all Roman writing bore from the time of the Gracchi to that of Augustus is now for the first time clearly manifest.

Estimating the literary value of what remains to us of the satire of Lucilius, Munro says[1], 'As for the author himself, I must confess that a continuous perusal of his remains has ended in much disappointment. True it is that most of the fragments are quite insignificant, single lines or pieces of lines, quoted to illustrate some unusual word. But my disappointment extends equally to the longer and more ambitious pieces, such for instance as that on Virtue preserved to us by Lactantius; the ideas are commonplace, the language often unpoetical, the rhythm loose and disjointed; there is not the slightest trace of the graceful touch of Horace or the powerful pathos of Juvenal. In style generally how infinitely does he fall below the consummate elegance and finish of Terence, who was before him too in time! Then what a disgusting fondness he displays for coarseness and obscenity, descending often to downright bestiality! How Quintilian can speak of him as he does, adding that some even then placed him at the head of all Latin poets, is to me incomprehensible; I should say even Horace's estimate of him was too high, raised designedly not to excite the ill-will of his contemporaries: for Lucilius, as Cicero will attest, unquestionably had a brilliant reputation.

This criticism can hardly be called too severe, considering the character of our remaining fragments: yet it is possible perhaps even from them to divine why Lucilius was so popular.

---

[1] *Journal of Philology*, 7. 294. With regard to the age of Lucilius, Lucian Müller argues with much plausibility that the date of his birth commonly accepted from Jerome, B.C. 147, is some thirty years too late.

Fastidious [1] and sensitive as to his own reputation (possibly the more so from bad health), Lucilius was clearly conscious of having something new and true to tell his countrymen.   He felt that he had the originality of nature which justified his following a path different from that of the general public.   He cannot [2], he says, be persuaded to change his ways for those of the common Romans of his day ; though a Roman *eques,* he will not become a *publicanus ;* the tithes do not suit him ; being, as he is, Lucilius, he will not be another.   The world he sees around him is a world of avarice and pleasure-seeking and ambition ; but he is a true man who loves his friend, a true poet who loves the Muses [3] ; his papers are his friends to whom he commits all his secrets [4] ; his verse, like himself, shall be sincere and simple [5], not full of the artificial bombast of the tragedians [6], but the poetry of real life, which though deserving the praise of the wise shall yet not speak exclusively to the learned, but go straight to the heart of the intelligent

----

[1] 1. 2 :   *Quis leget haec ?*

26 5 :   *Evadat saltem aliquid aliqua quod conatus sum.*

14. 5 :   *Non paucis malle a sapientibus esse probatum*
              ἢ πᾶσιν νεκύεσσι καταφθιμένοισιν ἀνάσσειν !

5. 2 :   *Si tam corpus loco validum ac regione mearet*
              Scriptoris quam vera meat sententia cordi.

[2] 26. 13 :   *Mihi quidem non persuadetur publicis mutem meos.*

Ib. 14 :   *Publicanus vero ut Asiae fiam scripturarius*
              Pro Lucilio, id ego nolo, et uno hoc non muto omnia.

Ib. 15 :   *Denique adeo male me accipiunt decumae et proveniunt male.*

Ib. 24 :   *Ego si qui sum et quo folliculo nunc sum indutus non queo.*

[3] 30. 2 :   *Quantum haurire animus Musarum ec fontibu' gestit.*

27. 10 :   *Animum quaerunt amici, rem parasiti ac ditias.*

[4] Hor. S. 2. 1. 30 :
              Ille velut fidis arcana sodalibus olim
              Credebat libris, neque si male cesserat umquam
              Decurrens alio, neque si bene.

[5] 26. 4 :   *Ego quem ec praecordiis ecfero versum.*

3 :   *Populum aucupamur istis cum scriptoribus.*
              Voluimus capere animum illorum.

[6] 4. 20 :   *Tityi e pulmonibus atque adipe unguen*
              Excoctum attulit Eumenidum sanctissima Erinys.

Compare 26. 31.

classes of Rome and Italy. It is the aspirations and discontents of these classes that Lucilius feels and expresses. He does not write up to the taste of the select few[1], or down to that of the rabble, but aims at hitting the mean of cultivated good sense. If in the hands of Ennius the *satura* had worn the first stiffness of the artificial drama, here at length was a poet who could clothe the dry bones with life, and make the national literature speak with a new voice. Lucilius is the child of his time, who yet calls on his countrymen to return to the traditions of a better age; in this sense as well as in his freedom of speech a sort of parallel to Aristophanes. There is something in his remains, despite their crudity and want of form, of the ring of Gaius Gracchus[2]. Thus it happened that in his lifetime he outstripped his predecessors in popularity[3], and remained for long after the favourite of readers who preferred free utterance and genuine republican feeling to ideality and classical form. Those who preferred Lucilius to Horace are mentioned by Tacitus[4] in the same breath with those who preferred Lucretius to Vergil.

The great reputation of Lucilius has made it necessary to examine his claims to it at greater length than the limits of the subject would strictly justify. Fortune has probably been unjust to him, nor is it easy to find in his fragments that refinement of form (if this be the meaning of *gracilitas*, Gellius

---

[1] 26. I : *Persium non curo legere, Iulium Congum volo.* See Cic. *Fin.* I, § 7: *Nec vero, ut noster Lucilius, recusabo quominus omnes mea legant. Utinam esset ille Persius! Scipio vero et Rutilius multo etiam magis; quorum ille iudicium reformidans, Tarentinis ait se et Consentinis et Siculis scribere. Facete is quidem, sicut alias; sed neque tam docti tunc erant, ad quorum iudicium elaboraret, et sunt illius scripta leviora, ut urbanitas summa appareat, doctrina mediocris.*

[2] [In the *Dictionary of Antiquities* Mr. Nettleship writes: The remains of Lucilius' *saturae* attest beyond doubt an extraordinary vigour which breathes in almost every surviving line.]

[3] 30. 3, 4 : *Et sua perciperet retro rellicta iacere*
    Et sola in multis nunc nostra poemata ferri.

[4] *Dialogus* 23 : *Versantur ante oculos isti qui Lucilium pro Horatio et Lucretium pro Vergilio legunt.*

7. 14) [1] which the ancients praised. But whatever may have been his real excellencies, it is clear that in altering the character and compass of the *satura* he also narrowed it. Not only did he confine his metre for the most part to the hexameter, thereby limiting the freedom of form which was a main characteristic of the old *satura*, but he did much to make invective an integral part of its contents. If we read between the lines of Horace's criticism of Lucilius [2] we shall see, I think, that Horace takes exception quite as strongly to his limitation of the field of the *satura* as to the slovenly character of his versification. Taking very much the tone of Aristotle [3], when, in his remarks on the origin of comedy, he says that in the Margites Homer indicated the lines on which comedy should be composed, οὐ ψόγον, ἀλλὰ τὸ γελοῖον δραματοποιήσας, Horace complains that Lucilius is entirely the child of the old comedy ; *hinc omnis pendet* : his inspiration is drawn from that of Eupolis and Cratinus and Aristophanes, the metre alone is changed. But if Hermogenes and the singers of Catullus had read these comedians, they would have seen that the strength of the old comedy lay in its mastery of wit and ridicule, not in vehemence, still less in slovenliness and uniformity. The satirist's true virtue is not to be monotonous or cumbrous, but versatile, now grave, now gay, now appearing as the orator or the poet, now as the man of the world, with all his strength in reserve. A true picture of the *satura* as it should have been; for Horace was too fastidious to think that any one (certainly not Lucilius) had attained to this ideal. It is as if Horace had said 'Lucilius depends entirely on the old comedy, and yet all of it that he has really seized is the force of its invective. He has not caught the ring of its laughter, its wit, its play of feature and emotion : only if the Roman *satura* can do this will it be worthy of being named by the side of its model.'

---

[1] [Compare Fronto quoted on p. 91.]

[2] *S.* 1. 4, 1. 10. [This point is omitted in the article contributed to the *Dictionary of Antiquities.*]

[3] *Poet.* 4. 9.

In what sense the attempts of Varro of Atax[1], and the
other writers whom Horace leaves unnamed, served to form
a transition from Lucilius to Horace we cannot say. It is
somewhat strange that, deeply as Horace evidently felt the
shortcomings of Lucilius, he never disputes with him on the
subject of metre, but apparently accepts the hexameter as the
normal measure of the *satura*. Perhaps from this prejudice,
perhaps from the absence in it of all pretensions to poetry, he
never mentions the Menippean satires of Terentius Varro;
which, had they survived, would probably (to judge by the
remaining fragments) have been a more precious relic than the
long invectives of Lucilius. It is unnecessary to enter here
into the details of Varro's charming pictures of contemporary
life in Rome, or of the various points of social, moral, religious,
philosophical, or literary interest[2] on which they touched; all
that need here be pointed out is the *satura* of Varro was, as
Quintilian remarks[3], the old and genuine *satura*. It was
a medley, not of different metres only, but of prose and verse.
Its spirit is also that of the true *satura*. The speaker does not
preach at or abuse, but describes and reflects upon, the life of
his contemporaries, and that with a mellow and genial wisdom.
Like the fool in the tragedy, he stands at the centre of things,
professing to see through imposture, to read things as they are,

---

[1] Hor. *S.* 1. 10. 46 foll.:
   Hoc erat, experto frustra Varrone Atacino
   Atque quibusdam aliis melius quod scribere possem,
   Inventore minor.

[2] *Aborigines* (περὶ ἀνθρώπων φύσεως), Αμμον μετρεῖς (περὶ φιλαργυρίας),
'Ανθρωπόπολις (περὶ γενεθλιακῆς), *Bimarcus* (a dialogue between Varro, his
second self, and Manius), *Caprinum Proelium* (περὶ ἡδονῆς), *Cycnus* (περὶ
ταφῆς), *Devicti* (περὶ φιλονεικίας), 'Εκατόμβη (περὶ θυσιῶν), *Endymiones* (on
dreaming), *Eumenides* (a philosophical dinner), 'Εχω σε (περὶ τύχης), *Gloria*
(περὶ φθόνου), &c.

[3] 10. 1. 95: *Alterum illud etiam prius saturae genus, sed non sola*
carminum varietate mixtum condidit Terentius Varro .... Plurimos hic
libros et doctissimos composuit. The text of this passage has been much discussed, but the general sense is pretty plain. It seems possible that *prius*
may be a mere gloss explaining *illud*.

to expose the vanity of human wishes and the weakness or
hypocrisy of human pretensions : above all things he is a plain
speaker who will tell the world the truth to its face.   In this
spirit the Roman satirist and the Cynic philosopher are very
much at one.   Varro is made by Cicero to say that he did not
translate but imitated Menippus; which probably means that
he adopted the form of the *satura* as the best embodiment of
the ideas of Menippus[1].

Varro's was essentially a quiet genius, and it is partly, perhaps,
due to this fact that in spite of the genuinely Roman flavour
which they shared with all that he wrote, the Menippean satires
never won their way into general popularity, or enabled the
old-fashioned medley of metres, or of prose and verse, to
reassert itself as the recognised form of the *satura*.   Again, if
we may trust Cicero[2] and the fragments of the Menippean
satires themselves, it is evident that Varro adopted a graver,
more cultured, more philosophical, and less personal tone than
Lucilius.   He cares more for the sketch than for his own signa-
ture at the foot of it, and appeals to a public that can read
between the lines.   Possibly also the cumbrousness which is
never absent from the graver works of Varro may have haunted
him here also, and prevented his satires from being read outside of a small circle of students.

The satire of Horace was evidently, both in matter and in
form, intended as a protest against that of Lucilius.   Horace
indeed retains the hexameter; but in spite of its apparent
freedom, his versification is always, within the limits which he
has laid down for himself, finished and perfect; it is not the
writing of a man who dashes off his two hundred verses in the
hour.   It is more important to observe that the satire of Horace
lacks, to a great extent, the element of invective.   It is true
that there is much talk about himself and his detractors, but

[1] Cic. *Acad. Post.* I, § 8 : *Menippum imitati, non interpretati.*   It is
interesting to compare the tone of the Roman *satura* with that of the echoes
of Menippus preserved by Lucian.

[2] Cic. l. c.: *Multa admixta ex intima philosophia, multa dicta dia-
lectice.*

this is always, professedly at least, in self-defence : *hic stilus haud petet ultro Quemquam animantem* [1]. He follows Lucilius, he says, but with this exception. And it appears on examination that, putting aside the uniformity of its metre, the *satura* or *sermo* of Horace is very much the old-fashioned medley. He addresses the public on its own life, sometimes directly, sometimes in the form of a scene or a dialogue. It may be observed that the form of dialogue is preserved chiefly in his second book, where we find it in the second, third, fourth, fifth, and seventh satires. In the first book the fifth, seventh, eighth, and ninth are true *saturae*; the first, second, and third are ethical discourses ; the fourth, sixth, and tenth pieces of self-justification, personal or literary. In the second book Horace appears to have worked himself more thoroughly than in the first into the form and manner of the *satura* ; there is nothing there which is not either a scene or a conversation ; there is no mere direct moral address to the people, but each piece, like a philosophical dialogue, has a setting of its own.

It seems at first sight strange that Horace, whose genius was so admirably adapted for the kind of writing which the *satura* best represented, should so soon have given up the form of the *satura* for that of the epistle. I would suggest, that having deliberately abandoned the old-fashioned medley of prose and verse as an anachronism, and having elected to follow Lucilius in uniformity of metre and in the choice of the hexameter, he found that the dialogue, an essential element in the true *satura*, could not be carried on with success in this measure. The form of the epistle, supposed to be addressed to one person, and not necessarily involving dialogue or dramatization, was better fitted for the kind of discourse which Horace loves to pour out than that of the *satura*, which was supposed to be addressed to the general public and involved more or less of dramatic form. That Horace was a true prophet is clearly shown by the failure of Persius, who in his devotion to Horace has chosen to imitate the dialogue of the second book of the

[1] S. 2. 1. 39.

satires, and succeeded in producing a form of writing which
for crudeness and obscurity can hardly be exceeded, and which
goes far to make the reader forget his real power.

The older form of *satura*, the mixture of metre with metre
and prose with verse, had a brilliant revival in the hands of
Petronius, the power, pathos, and wit of whose pictures have
not only rescued from discredit and oblivion a form of literature
of which we should otherwise have remained nearly ignorant,
but have given the world an unique idea of the capacity of the
ancient Italian genius.   Nothing is a greater proof of the genius
of Petronius than the entire freedom of his style from the
mannerisms of his age.   While literature in general was growing
more and more corrupted by the artificial tinge with which the
schools of the rhetoricians were colouring it, Petronius writes
with perfect purity and dramatic propriety; his characters
standing out and speaking to us with all the vividness of real
life, while the writer himself remains in the background and
lets the play tell its own story.   Who can forget Giton or
Trimalchio or Eumolpus ?   How different this from the stiff
personifications of Persius; how far removed from the
hexameter *satura* as it reached its full development in the
hands of Juvenal, under whose treatment versification and
contents alike are cramped and confined.   Even the hexameter
of Juvenal is not the free measure of Horace, but the formal
epic verse as stereotyped by Vergil, and handled without any
Vergil's various power.   The language of Juvenal, again, is an
artificial dialect which no one, outside of a lecture-room, could
ever have spoken ; his style is full of inversion, *innuendo*, and
unnatural periphrasis.   Powerful as he undoubtedly is, he
knows little of the spirit of poetry ; much of his passion is
forced and his invective unreal; his scenes are cumbrously
put together, his character-drawing lacks life and delicacy.
Petronius is indeed obscene beyond all possibility of excuse ;
but it may be questioned whether Juvenal, who has none of
the sweetness and versatility and reserve of Petronius, and
whose coarseness is the dull rhetorical coarseness of a serious

mind, can after all claim much superiority on this score[1]. All Juvenal's pictures are drawn with the same monotonous power and in the same lurid colours. In the hands of the professed rhetorician the *satura* has lost almost all its kindliness, and speaks the language of moral indignation in the tone of an angry literary clique. As far as his form is concerned, it may be observed that a shadow of the proper form of the *satura* is left in the third and ninth satires, which are cast in the form of a dialogue ; but most of Juvenal's pieces are addressed to one person, and might more properly be called epistles.

We have seen how, amid the surroundings of the empire, which contributed so powerfully to blight the freshness and sincerity of literature, the *satura* came in Juvenal's hands almost to lose its original character. We may now attempt to answer the question whether there is, after all, any characteristic common to all its forms which it preserves from the beginning to the end of our acquaintance with it. It may then be observed, first, that the *satura* always contains a strongly-marked personal element. The writer in his own person addresses the general public or an imaginary companion. Even the dull *satura* attributed to Sulpicia is supposed to be a dialogue between herself and the Muse. Or, again, the satirist describes a scene in which he himself takes a part. It follows that dialogue, either obvious or suggested, is an integral part of the true *satura ;* the satirist talking to his readers or to one of the characters in the scene which he is describing. Secondly, the *satura* as we know it is a description of isolated scenes, but never contains a regular plot. This is a characteristic which is not wholly lost even in the writing of Juvenal.

[1] A certain *quota* of obscenity was probably considered a proper and conventional attribute of the *satura*. It may have been taken over by the literary men, with other properties, from the primitive *satura*, which resembled the Fescennine verses, as Livy says, and that probably not in its form only. Certainly there is a strong element of coarseness in Lucilius, Varro, Horace, Juvenal, and Petronius: nor is Persius altogether spotless. I should be disposed to refer this fact not to the moral obliquity of these writers, but to the conventional traditions of their art.

Now these attributes, so clearly discernible in the literary *satura* as we possess it, tally entirely with those which we may infer from Livy to have belonged to the early *satura*. As we remarked at starting, Livy clearly distinguishes the *satura* from a play with a regular plot, and he gives to understand by implication that it was a dialogue. Quintilian, and after him Diomedes [1], distinguish two kinds of *satura*, the older sort represented by Ennius and Varro, the later by Lucilius and his followers. As far as the original and proper form of the *satura* is concerned, this division, if the foregoing remarks are just, would appear to be arbitrary. Another point deserves attention. Quintilian claims the *satura* as an entirely Roman or Italian production, and describes it as originally a medley of various metres, or even of prose and verse. Livy speaks of it as a form of art existing as far back as the time when the Etruscan *ludiones* were introduced. Suppose that the *satura* was originally a native Italian form of drama, consisting of a simple scene or narrative from common life represented by two actors or perhaps by one, reciting a mimic dialogue; suppose this humble representation gradually banished from the stage by more finished importations from abroad, and then transferred to paper by literary men (like plays which are not intended for acting) and perhaps recited by them, with a certain amount of action or dramatization, to small circles of friends; and it will not be difficult to account for all the forms which the *satura* assumed in the hands of its various masters at different periods of Roman history. Its disappearance from the stage on the introduction of the Greek play is very analogous to the disappearance of the Saturnian metre on the introduction of the hexameter; and as the introduction of the hexameter put an end to all hope of the development of

---

[1] 3, p. 485, Keil : *Satira dicitur carmen apud Romanos nunc quidem maledicum et ad carpenda hominum vitia archaeae comoediae charactere conpositum, quale scripserunt Lucilius et Horatius et Persius. Et olim carmen quod ex variis poematibus constabat satira vocabatur, quale scripserunt Pacuvius et Ennius.*

a native Italian poetry, so that of the Greek play may have destroyed the beginnings of a native Italian drama. As soon as the *satura* became literary, it could not but become, to a certain extent, artificial ; and though it never wholly lost its scenic character, it naturally became more personal in the sense of including a justification of the writer's point of view [1], and thus came indirectly to be used as a channel for various kinds of political, literary, and even critical and grammatical *causeries* [2]. But there is really nothing to show that the *satura* was in any sense derived from a Greek source ; when Horace says that Lucilius is dependent on the old comedy, this, as we have seen, implies on more than that Lucilius imported into satire the manner and spirit of moral and political invective.

If my hypothesis as to the original form of the *satura* be correct, its character and development must have corresponded very nearly with that of the Greek μῖμος. In his Prolegomena to Persius, Otto Jahn has examined the relations of the μῖμος and the *satura* at considerable length, and has laid some stress on the tradition preserved by Joannes Lydus, that Persius studied and imitated the μῖμοι of Sophron. But the statement of Joannes Lydus must stand or fall with another which he makes in the same sentence, and which is now generally given up, that the model of Lucilius was Rhinthon. It is very probable, of course, that the Roman satirists studied Sophron ; but this does not prove that the *satura* was not, in its origin, a native Italian production ; unless we prefer to conjecture that both the μῖμος and the *satura* represented a rude form of dramatic art existing before the separation of the Greek and Italian nations.

But that the *satura*, after it had become an artificial literary production, was largely tinged by Greek influences, is not to be

---

[1] As in the case, especially, of Lucilius and Horace.

[2] See the fragments of Lucilius' ninth book. Dziatzko, in the *Rheinisches Museum*, 33. 104, suggests an analogy between the grammatical precepts of Lucilius and those of the γραμματικὴ τραγῳδία of Callias (Athenaeus 10, p. 453 e). It may be that the γραμματικὴ τραγῳδία suggested to Lucilius the grammatical discussions of his ninth book.

denied for a moment.   Among these influences that of the old
Attic comedy has been much dwelt upon by critics from
Horace downwards.   It is probably an accident that in our
remaining fragments of Lucilius no allusion is made to Eupolis,
Cratinus, or Aristophanes.   And although Lucilius Graecized
the form of his *saturae* by writing them in Greek metres, there
is little in his remains the spirit of which is not quite genuinely
Italian.   Perhaps the influence of the old comedy, though
real, was general and intangible, acting in the way of inspiration and suggestion[1].   For, as we have seen, there was much
in the political circumstances of the time at which Lucilius
lived to tempt the writer of *satura* out of the old ways into the
line of personal attack.   However the matter may really have
stood, it yet seems certain that no Roman satirist who intended
to follow in the line of Lucilius would neglect the study of the
old comedy.   When Horace says, or makes his friend say[2],

> *Quorsum pertinuit stipare Platona Menandro,*
> *Eupolin, Archilochum, comites educere tantos ?*

he gives concisely a very clear notion of the sum of Greek
influences which were recognized as bearing on the composition
of the *satura.*

The mention of Plato by Horace (whether he means the
philosopher or the comedian is uncertain) reminds us of the
relation between the *satura* and the Greek popular philosophy.
As Greek philosophy never wholly dispensed with the form of
dialogue, philosophy and the drama were early brought into
a curious literary alliance, which is well illustrated by the
tradition that Plato used carefully to study the mimes of
Sophron[3].   It is clear that the *satura* of Varro contained a great
deal of popular dialectic[4]; there is much too of this in Horace,

---

[1] Pers. I. 123 : *Audaci quicunque adflate Cratino*
      Iratum Eupoliden praegrandi cum sene palles.
[2] S. 2. 3. 11.
[3] Zeller, *Philosophie der Griechen*, 2ter Theil, erste Abtheilung, p. 344,
note 3 (3rd edition).
[4] See Cicero quoted above, p. 36, note 1, and the titles of the *saturae*,
p. 35, note 1.

and the satire of Persius, in the main a popular exposition of Stoicism, often takes the form of short question and answer, which reminds the reader of Arrian's Epictetus; and the method probably pursued *viva voce* in the Stoical and Academical schools. One of Persius' satires, indeed, is a direct imitation, in Roman guise, of a Platonic dialogue.

The name of Menander suggests the associations of the New Comedy ; a world of literature of which echoes alone remain to us. It may be said generally that the kind of lessons inculcated by the Roman satirists when they preach truthfulness and simplicity and moderation of life, reflects to a great extent the tone of the better comic drama. We have here a popular impression of the gathered experience won by great thinkers and men of action. The satirist may be supposed to have spoken to his Roman hearers in somewhat the same tones as Euripides and Menander to the Greeks, interpreting higher thoughts to them in a language which they could understand, through examples which they could imitate, and in a form of writing native to their own soil. The Roman theatre remained too exclusively Greek in its forms and traditions to prevent the *satura* from continuing to form a delight and diversion of literary circles. The influence of the New Comedy is felt most strongly interpenetrating the satire of Horace and Persius, in which subject, character, situation, and reflection continually suggest the moralizings of the stage. It is not necessary to go into the details of a phenomenon which is amply illustrated in the commentaries ; but it may be noticed in particular that the attack on military life which is a prominent feature in the writing of Persius and Juvenal may possibly have originated in an echo from the stage, of which the *miles gloriosus* or ἀλαζών had long been a familiar property.

III.

LITERARY CRITICISM IN LATIN ANTIQUITY[1].

('JOURNAL OF PHILOLOGY,' VOL. XVIII (1890).)

I.

It may be said in general that two main lines of literary
criticism may be distinguished in ancient as in modern times.
The first is the criticism of philosophy, which investigates the
principles of beauty, regards art and literature alike as manifestations of the human spirit at the utmost height of its effort,
and judges of literary and artistic productions according as they
approach the realization of their intention.   The second is the
isolated and spontaneous judgement of artists and men of
letters, sometimes accidental, occasional, and fragmentary,
sometimes regularly formulated, but never rising beyond the
point attained by the personal impressions of the critic.

In the wealth of ancient and modern literature it is no
doubt easy to find instances of critics who may be said to unite
both points of view.   Much of Ruskin's criticism, for instance,
may be called philosophical, as based upon thought, not indeed
consistent and articulate, but still genuine ; while much again

[1] Since these essays were written I have read Usener's admirable edition
of the remains of Dionysius's περὶ μιμήσεως (Bonn, Cohen, 1889).   The conclusions which I had only drawn generally and in outline I now find confirmed by the close reasoning applied to the subject in the *Epistulae Criticae*
added by the editor to his text.

is the utterance of personal intuition. Still, on the whole, the distinction may be maintained. Every one feels the difference (say) between Landor, Carlyle, and Matthew Arnold on the one hand, and Mr. Frederic Harrison on the other. Mr. Harrison, in writing of literature, never loses sight of the Comtist tradition. Mr. Arnold writes with sure literary instinct, but without reference to any definite system, unless indeed he may be said to have built up, bit by bit, a literary system of his own. Lessing based both his criticism and his dramatic creations on what he took to be the right interpretation of Aristotle. But Goethe speaks always from the fulness of his personal impression at the moment.

It is the weakness of philosophical criticism that when it leaves the hand of the master it crystallizes into a tradition, and becomes exclusive, didactic, and conventional. It has, however, a twofold source of strength. It grasps fundamental principles, and even in the narrowness of scholastic tradition, holds firmly by them. The great philosopher seizes the truth that great art and great literature are the expression of the whole moral and intellectual being of man at the crises which call it into activity. His followers may lay a pedantic stress either on the purely ethical element in good literature, as e. g. the Stoics did with Homer; or, again, they may lay too much stress on form and general excellence, and make a canon of classical writers as the Alexandrians and the later ancient critics did. But in either case the disciple is set in the right track, nor is he prevented from looking back, from the narrower position in which his teachers have placed him, to the wider field trodden by their master.

The weak point in the occasional or unsystematized criticism of poets and artists is, it need hardly be said, its fitful and personal character. It has, however, a point of strength which more than counterbalances this defect. It is simple, as springing directly from the artistic intuition, from the appreciation of art and life by genius: and it knows no limits, but embraces in a generous welcome everything which bears the stamp of merit ; moreover, it is often conveyed in such beauty of expression as to be in itself an artistic creation.

Literary criticism in Latin literature, like everything else in Latin literature, had its borrowed and its original element. It is therefore necessary, in order to get at a correct appreciation of the whole matter, to begin with a few words on the Greek or borrowed element. Greek criticism had concerned itself mainly with poetry and oratory, and where it touched history, had treated it largely from the literary point of view. With regard to poetry and oratory, the judgements of Aristotle are the most comprehensive embodiment of pure Greek feeling. The aim of tragedy is μίμησις πράξεως σπουδαίας, the representation of serious action. This is not a judgement which ran counter to the best contemporary Greek feeling, or which anticipated the feeling of modern times ; rather it expresses what was generally expected of tragedy in Greek literary society. For throughout all classical antiquity it is the conduct of the action, not the psychological development of individual character, which attracts the attention of the reader or spectator. Development of character there may be in ancient poetry, but it is incidental, and subordinate to the course and demands of the action.   This is a commonplace truth, so commonplace indeed as to be often forgotten by critics who insist on applying modern canons to ancient literature.

Turning to oratory, we find that with Aristotle the art of rhetoric is based upon the knowledge of human character, passion, and life in its widest sense.   But Aristotle's successors did not, on the whole, maintain their criticism at this high level. It was the rules of arrangement and the principles of harmonious prose composition which mainly occupied their attention ; or, to put the same thing in a historical form, Isocrates and the practical rhetoricians ousted the philosophers.   It could hardly be otherwise in the case of an art which, unlike poetry, had a definite practical object, with the prospect of professional success and reward.   Next to the name of Aristotle, that of Theophrastus stands out in the history of Greek literary

criticism. It is to him probably that we owe the first continuous history of the origin of the different kinds of poetry
and their logical arrangement. Further, it is certain that he
criticized poetry in the interests of education, attempting to
show what poets it would be most useful for an orator to read
who was anxious to perfect his style. Only fragments of his
criticism have come down to us in express quotation, e. g. that
on Herodotus and Thucydides in the *Orator* of Cicero 39.
*Quo magis sunt Herodotus Thucydidesque mirabiles : quorum
aetas cum in eorum tempora quos nominavi incidisset, longissime
tamen ipsi a talibus deliciis vel potius ineptiis afuerunt. Alter
enim sine ullis salebris quasi sedatus amnis fluit, alter incitatior
fertur et de bellicis rebus canit etiam quodam modo bellicum,
primisque ab his, ut ait Theophrastus, historia commota est, ut
auderet uberius quam superiores et ornatius dicere.*

Besides the name of Theophrastus, those of Aristarchus and
his master Aristophanes of Byzantium must claim our attention. These great scholars, besides spending great labour on
the critical study of texts, directed their attention to forming
a canon or selection of the best poets (Quint. 10. 1. 54).
*Apollonius in ordinem a grammaticis datum non venit, quia
Aristarchus atque Aristophanes neminem sui temporis in ordinem
redegerunt*[1]. They selected five from among the epic poets,
three from the *iambographi* or writers of lampoon, and four
elegiac poets. The selection had considerable influence on
educational practice, but did not, of course, and could not,
dominate the literary world in general.

We must not, either, omit to mention the hostile criticism
of Homer of which Zoilus, the author of the ' Ομηρομάστιξ, is
the chief representative. It is no doubt of no value except to
amuse and to show that the spirit of Macaulay was alive in the
third century B.C. One instance will suffice. In *Il.* 23. 100
Homer says ψυχὴ δὲ κατὰ χθονός, ἠΰτε καπνός, Ὤχετο τετριγυῖα.

---

[1] See also 1. 4. 3 (*grammatici*) *auctores alios in ordinem redegerunt, alios
omnino exemerunt numero.* Horace's *fiet Aristarchus* (*A. P.* 450) must
refer to literary criticism.

On which Zoilus observed ἀλλ᾽ ὁ καπνὸς ἄνω φέρεται (Lehrs, Aristarchus, p. 206 : Townley Scholia *ad l.*). Nor must we pass over the ethical criticism on Homer passed in the Stoical schools, who extracted from the poet precepts of conduct, nay even rules of diet. *Rursus quid virtus et quid sapientia possit Utile proposuit nobis exemplar Ulixen. Seditione, dolis, scelere atque libidine et ira Iliacos extra muros peccatur et intra*[1].

The whole subject of poetical composition was treated by an Alexandrian writer, Neoptolemus of Parium, of uncertain date. This essay was used by Horace as the basis of his *De Arte Poetica*[2]. I am not aware that at present anything more is known of the rules or principles laid down by Neoptolemus than the translations or paraphrases of them which the ancient Horatian commentator Porphyrion points out. To judge from these the work must have been a collection of literary precepts, sensible enough but not profound, embracing (perhaps among others) the following topics : (1) An analogy between painting and poetry. (2) Self-knowledge. (3) Modesty. (4) Arrangement. (5) Words. (6) History of metre. (7) The style of Tragedy and Comedy. (8) Relations of Tragedy and Epic. (9) Comedy. (10) The general treatment of dramatic writing. (11) Acts, actors, and chorus. (12) The satyric drama. (13) The metres of drama. (14) The history of drama. (15) The moral aim of poetry.

There was also a great deal of criticism more properly to be called literary or aesthetic, which cannot now, apparently, be referred to any certain author. Of this criticism, much of which is probably older, at least, than the last century of the Roman republic, probably the best extant example is preserved in the works of Dionysius of Halicarnassus[3]. This is not the criticism of the great philosophy, but represents the tradition of the later schools, the narrow channels of which confined and distributed a part, but a part only, of the wealth of philosophic thought and suggestion.

Dionysius is in favour of raising taste and criticism from the

[1] Horace *Epist.* 1. 2. 17, 15.   [2 See p. 70.]   [3] *Floruit* 29 B.C.

mire into which the Greeks had allowed it to sink, and setting
it again upon the elevation which it had occupied in earlier
and purer days, and to which Roman feeling would naturally
restore it. No careful reader of Dionysius, who studies him
side by side with Cicero and Varro, can fail to carry away the
impression that, although he is an original writer of perfectly
independent judgement, the whole caste of his criticism is that
of an older time ; that he adopts much of his mode of thought
and expression from the better traditions of the schools. It is
therefore fair to take his writings, on the whole, as a good
specimen of the best criticism of this sort. What then, briefly
speaking, are its characteristics ? Let us speak first of its more
strictly scholastic element. In this we may notice three main
tendencies : (1) to classify style under three distinct heads [1] :
(2) to make or accept canons of the best or classical writers :
(3) to write careful, but somewhat cut and dried, criticisms
upon them, criticisms which seldom lack sanity, care, and
insight, but which are rather dangerously suited for learning
by heart and handing on to future generations of pupils.

The general, as distinguished from the scholastic, notes
of this writing are, that whether it touches poetry, oratory, or
history, it is mainly directed to the consideration of style ; that
it affects a somewhat pedantic parallelism between painting
and the plastic arts on the one side, and literature on the other;
and that it introduces a number of technical terms of criticism
unknown at least to Plato and Aristotle. All these points will
be dealt with more fully hereafter.

Meanwhile, to pass at length to Latin literature. I will first
take the scholastic criticism, and state generally what seems to
have been its fortune and character in the hands of Latin
writers, and then try to substantiate my remarks in detail.
The tendency from the second century B. C. onwards seems to

---

[1] This seems to have been applied even to Homer ; Gellius 6 (7). 14 *sed ea
ipsa genera dicendi iam antiquitus tradita ab Homero sunt tria in tribus ;
magnificum in Ulixe et ubertum, subtile in Menelao et cohibitum, mixtum
moderatumque in Nestore*

have been to formulate the different styles in Latin terms, and
to make a kind of canon of Latin writers, with neat character-
izations of each.

The earliest existing example of this kind is the so-called
canon of Volcatius Sedigitus, to be assigned, most probably, to
the early first century B. C. (Gellius 15. 24). *Multos incertos
certare hanc rem vidimus, Palmam poetae comico cui deferant.
Eum meo iudicio errorem dissolvam tibi, Ut contra si quis
sentiat, nil sentiat. Caecilio palmam Statio do comico (? comoediae* or *comoedicam*): *Plautus secundus facile exsuperat ceteros: Dein Naevius qui servet pretio in tertiost (? qui mereat
pretium tertiust). Si erit quod quarto detur, dabitur Licinio:
Post insequi Licinium facio Atilium; In sexto consequetur hos
Terentius: Turpilius septimum, Trabea octavum optinet; Nono
loco esse facile facio Luscium, Decimum addo causa antiquitatis
Ennium.*

The writer of this stupid production, it will be observed,
finds it necessary to make ten places for the Latin comedians,
perhaps because it had been found that there were ten and no
more classical orators among the Greeks. I will quote one
more instance of this kind of criticism, perhaps the only one
which may fairly be assigned to an age older than that of
Varro: Gellius 6 (7). 14. 8 tells us that Varro recognized the
threefold division of style into ἁδρὸν ἰσχνόν and μέσον, giving
Latin equivalents for each term. He goes on to say *animad-
versa eadem tripertita varietas est in tribus philosophis, quos
Athenienses Romam ad senatum legaverunt impetratum uti
multam remitteret quam fecerat is propter Oropi vastationem.
. . . . . Erant isti philosophi Carneades ex Academia, Diogenes
Stoicus, Critolaus Peripateticus. Et in senatum quidem intro-
ducti interprete usi sunt C. Acilio senatore; sed ante ipsi
seorsum quisque ostentandi gratia magno conventu hominum
dissertaverunt. Tum admirationi fuisse aiunt Rutilius et
Polybius philosophorum trium sui cuiusque generis facundiam.
Violenta, inquiunt, et rapida Carneades dicebat, scita et teretia
Critolaus, modesta Diogenes et sobria.*

The context of this last passage in Gellius, coupled with the mention of the same embassy in 17. 21. 48 taken from the *De Poetis* of Varro, suggests that the account may come from one of Varro's numerous works on the history and criticism of literature. In any case it may be taken as a fair type of the ruder and less intelligent form of the scholastic tradition. Varro was the author of several works in which literary criticism formed, either directly or indirectly, a main element. *De Poetis* [1], *De Poematis*, περὶ χαρακτήρων, *De Actionibus Scaenicis, Quaestiones Plautinae.* The *De Actionibus Scaenicis* must, we must suppose, have been a technical treatise on the drama: the *Quaestiones Plautinae* were intended to sift the genuine from the spurious works of Plautus. The *De Poetis*, to judge from the quotation in Gellius 17. 21. 43, was a historical or biographical work on the lives of the poets. The *De Poematis* must almost certainly have contained a classification of the different kinds of poetry. The περὶ χαρακτήρων, I am inclined to suppose (though Ritschl thinks differently) was a treatise on the different χαρακτῆρες or styles [2], especially the three technically described in Greek as ἁδρόν, μέσον and ἰσχνόν, and in Latin as *uber, mediocris, gracilis.* Gellius 6 (7). 14 says *uberi dignitas atque amplitudo est, gracili venustas et subtilitas, medius in confinio est, utriusque modi particeps ... Vera autem et propria huiuscemodi formarum exempla in Latina lingua M. Varro dicit esse ubertatis Pacuvium, gracilitatis Lucilium, mediocritatis Terentium.* Quintilian (10. 1. 99) quotes a saying of Varro that the Muses, in the judgement of Aelius Stilo, would have spoken in the language of Plautus had they wished to speak Latin.

In the case of a prolific writer like Varro, the enormous

---

[1] In 17. 21. 43 foll. Gellius preserves a fragment from the first book of the *De Poetis*, giving several dates affecting Naevius, Ennius, Caecilius, Terence, Pacuvius, Accius, and Lucilius.

[2] So Caecilius of Καλὴ 'Ακτή wrote περὶ χαρακτῆρος τῶν δέκα ῥητόρων· Diomedes 483 : *poematos* χαρακτῆρες *sunt quattuor*, μακρὸς βραχὺς μέσος ἀνθηρός. Dionys. *Comp.* 21 p. 146 R. τοὺς χαρακτῆρας (τῶν συνθέσεων) καὶ τὰς διαφορὰς ... τὴν μὲν αὐστηράν, τὴν δὲ γλαφυρὰν ἢ ἀνθηράν, τὴν δὲ τρίτην κοινήν.

E 2

mass of whose work necessarily implies great haste in the composition, and frequent repetition of the same idea, it is impossible, as Ritschl has seen, to feel assured to which of his treatises the surviving fragments of his criticism respectively belong. His *saturae* too, it must be remembered, contained matter of the same kind. Nonius p. 374 Mer. quotes from the *Parmeno* the following ; *in argumentis Caecilius poscit palmam, in ethesin Terentius, in sermonibus Plautus.* Charisius (2. p. 241 Keil) preserves a similar passage, taken not from the critical treatises proper, but from the *De Sermone Latino ;* ἤθη, *ut ait Varro De Sermone Latino, nullis aliis servare convenit, inquit, quam Titinio, Terentio, Attae : πάθη vero Trabea, Atilius, Caecilius facillime moverunt.* This passage brings me to the consideration of one much more familiar, the lines (*Epist.* 2 1. 55) in which Horace sums up the criticism of the ancient poets current in his day. *Ambigitur quotiens uter utro sit prior, aufert Pacuvius docti famam senis, Accius alti, Dicitur Afrani toga convenisse Menandro, Plautus ad exemplar Siculi properare Epicharmi, Vincere Caecilius gravitate, Terentius arte.* In these verses Horace is probably firing his parting shot at the criticisms he was made to swallow in his boyhood ; but whose mainly are the criticisms? The sentence about Caecilius, *vincere Caecilius gravitate,* seems to me to coincide exactly with Varro's words, πάθη *Caecilius facillime movit ;* and besides Varro's labours in literary criticism we know of no other important writings in the same line which Horace would be likely to refer to, or which would have affected contemporary opinion. And the words, *ut critici dicunt,* a few lines above (51), may show that he is thinking of some formal treatise on poetry. The verdict quoted on Accius and Pacuvius reminds the reader very much of what Quintilian says (10. 1. 97) *Accio virium plus tribuitur, Pacuvium videri doctiorem, qui esse docti adfectant, volunt.* It is difficult to avoid the conclusion that Quintilian is alluding at least to the same school of criticism as Horace ; nor does it much matter whether this was the criticism of Varro himself or the opinion prevalent among the scholars of Cicero's age.

We can at any rate lay our finger upon its general character. It is careful to assign his place to every important poet ; and there is another point to which attention must be called. As Latin literature since Naevius had adopted Greek models and Greek metres, every Latin writer of any pretensions took some Greek author as his ideal of excellence in the particular style which he was adopting. Criticism accordingly drifted into the vicious course of comparison ; of pitting every Latin writer against a Greek writer, as though borrowing from a man would constitute you his rival. Thus Ennius, we have seen, was a Homer, Afranius a Menander, Plautus an Epicharmus, before the days of Horace : in Horace's time there were three Homers, Varius, Valgius, and Vergil. Cicero and Demosthenes were compared by the Greek critics in the Augustan age, and, by the time of Quintilian, Sallust has become the Latin Thucydides, Livy the Latin Herodotus. This is the same trifling proceeding which meets us in Plutarch's parallel lives, and which, strange to say, has shown so much vitality as hardly yet to have disappeared altogether from the field of amateur criticism.

The work of Varro *De Poematis* was in all probability an enumeration of the different kinds of poetry, made on the basis of some post-Aristotelian work, perhaps that of Theophrastus. We are not altogether without the means of judging what were its character and contents. The grammarian Diomedes has in his third book (p. 482 foll.) a section *De Poematis* or *De Poematibus*, which in its present form is undoubtedly at least as late as Suetonius, to whom much of it may probably be referred. The basis of it is, however, plainly much older. As Varro is quoted in it four times, it is not to much to infer that it contains a fair amount of Varronian material. Poetry is divided generally into *activum vel imitativum* (dramatic), *enarrativum vel enuntiativum* (narrative), and *commune vel mixtum* (narrative and dramatic combined). The different species of each genus are then enumerated. Most space is given to the *commune* or *mixtum*, which embraces *epos*, *elegia*, *epodi*, *satira*, and *bucolica*. Then the writer goes back to the drama, and gives an account of tragedy, comedy, the satiric drama, and the *mimus*.

So much is known, and would that more were known, of Varro's contributions to the history and criticism of poetry. We may now leave the scholastic criticism of the last century of the republic, and come to the criticism of genius, represented almost entirely by Cicero. In Cicero again we must distinguish the conventional element, which he took from the Greeks, and the original element born of his own mind. Let us first endeavour briefly to characterize the late Greek aesthetic criticism, which, so far as he followed the Greeks at all, Cicero seems to have followed here.

I would notice, in the first place, the comparison between the arts of painting and sculpture on the one hand, and literature on the other. This, as a commonplace of criticism, is at least as old as Neoptolemus of Parium : *Humano capiti cervicem pictor equinam Iungere si velit*, &c.[1] We must not look to these ancient writers for any profound analysis, such as Lessing attempted, of the difference between the two forms of art. With the ancients it is all superficial ; *ut pictura poesis*. It may however be interesting to quote one or two passages from Dionysius, which I have no doubt are fair specimens of the style which had long been current with the best literary critics. (Περὶ Συνθέσεως 21 pp. 145–6 Reiske) οἶμαί τε ἴδιον ἡμῶν ἑκάστῳ χαρακτῆρα, ὥσπερ ὄψεως, οὕτω καὶ συνθέσεως ὀνομάτων παρακολουθεῖν, οὐ φαύλως παραδείγματι χρώμενος ζωγραφίᾳ. ὥσπερ γὰρ ἐν ἐκείνῃ τὰ αὐτὰ φάρμακα λαμβάνοντες, ἅπαντες οἱ τὰ ζῷα γράφοντες, οὐδὲν ἐοικότα ποιοῦσιν ἀλλήλοις τὰ μίγματα, τὸν αὐτὸν τρόπον ἐν ποιητικῇ τε διαλέκτῳ καὶ τῇ ἄλλῃ ἁπάσῃ τοῖς αὐτοῖς ὀνόμασι χρώμενοι πάντες οὐχ ὁμοίως αὐτὰ συντίθεμεν. *De Isocr.* 2 (p. 541 R.) δοκεῖ δή μοι μὴ ἀπὸ σκοποῦ τις ἂν εἰκάσαι τὴν μὲν Ἰσοκράτους ῥητορικὴν τῇ Πολυκλείτου τε καὶ Φειδίου τέχνῃ, κατὰ τὸ σεμνὸν καὶ μεγαλότεχνον καὶ ἀξιωματικόν· τὴν δὲ Λυσίου τῇ Καλάμιδος καὶ Καλλιμάχου, τῆς λεπτότητος ἕνεκα καὶ τῆς χάριτος. *De Isaeo* 4 (p. 591 R.) εἰσὶ δή τινες ἀρχαῖαι γραφαί, χρώμασι μὲν εἰργασμέναι ἁπλῶς, καὶ οὐδεμίαν ἐν

---

[1] Horace, *A. P.* 1.

τοῖς μίγμασιν ἔχουσαι ποικιλίαν, ἀκριβεῖς δὲ ταῖς γραμμαῖς, καὶ πολὺ τὸ
χαρίεν ἐν ταύταις ἔχουσαι· αἱ δὲ μετ᾽ ἐκείνας εὔγραμμοι μὲν ἧττον,
ἐξειργασμέναι δὲ μᾶλλον, σκιᾷ τε καὶ φωτὶ ποικιλλόμεναι, καὶ ἐν τῷ
πλήθει τῶν μιγμάτων τὴν ἰσχὺν ἔχουσαι. τούτων μὲν δὴ ταῖς ἀρχαιοτέραις
ἔοικεν ὁ Λυσίας, κατὰ τὴν ἁπλότητα καὶ τὴν χάριν· ταῖς δὲ ἐκπεπονημέναις
τε καὶ τεχνικωτέραις ὁ Ἴσαιος. To show how common, nay, how
commonplace, is this form of criticism among the ancients,
who are nothing if not imitative, let me quote the following
passages from Cicero and Quintilian. Cic. *Orator* 36 : *in
picturis alios horrida, inculta, abdita, et opaca, contra alios
nitida, laeta, conlustrata delectant.* *Brutus* 70 : *quis enim
eorum, qui haec minora animadvertunt, non intellegit Canachi
signa rigidiora esse quam ut imitentur veritatem ? Calamidis
dura illa quidem, sed tamen molliora quam Canachi ; nondum
Myronis satis ad veritatem adducta, iam tamen quae non dubites
pulchra dicere ; pulchriora etiam Polycliti et iam plane perfecta,
ut mihi quidem videri solent. Similis in pictura ratio est ; in
qua Zeuxin et Polygnotum et Timanthem et eorum qui non
sunt usi plus quam quattuor coloribus, formas et lineamenta
laudamus ; at in Echione, Nicomacho, Protogene, Apelle, iam
perfecta sunt omnia. . . . Odyssia Latina (Livii) est sic tamquam
opus aliquod Daedali. . . . § 75 (Naevii) bellum Punicum quasi
Myronis opus delectat.* Ib. 228 : *Q. Hortensi admodum
adulescentis ingenium, ut Phidiae signum, semel aspectum et
probatum est.* 261 (of Caesar) : *cum ad hanc elegantiam
verborum Latinorum, quae, etiam si orator non sis et sis
ingenuus civis Romanus, tamen necessaria est, adiungit illa
oratoria ornamenta dicendi, tum videtur tamquam tabulas bene
pictas collocare in bono lumine.* 298 : *volvendi enim sunt libri
aliorum, tum in primis Catonis. Intelleges nihil illius linea-
mentis nisi eorum pigmentorum, quae inventa nondum erant,
florem et colorem defuisse.* In Quintilian (12. 10. 3 foll.) we
have this kind of disquisition in its crudest form ; *primi,
quorum quidem opera non vetustatis modo gratia visenda sint,
clari pictores fuisse dicuntur Polygnotus atque Aglaophon,
quorum simplex color tam sui studiosos adhuc habet, ut illa*

prope rudia ac velut futurae mox artis primordia maximis qui, post eos extiterunt, auctoribus praeferant, proprio quodam intellegendi, ut mea opinio est, ambitu. Post Zeuxis atque Parrhasius non multum aetate discrepantes circa Peloponnesia ambo tempora. . . plurimum arti addiderunt. Quorum prior luminum umbrarumque invenisse rationem, secundus examinasse subtilius lineas traditur. Nam Zeuxis plus membris corporis dedit, id amplius atque augustius ratus, atque, ut existimant, Homerum secutus, &c. § 10 *In oratione vero si species intueri velis, totidem paene reperias ingeniorum quam corporum formas. Sed fuere quaedam genera dicendi condicione temporum horridiora, alioqui magnam ingenii vim prae se ferentia. Hinc sunt Laelii, Africani, Catones etiam Gracchique, quos tu licet Polygnotos vel Callonas appelles. Mediam illam formam teneant L. Crassus, Q. Hortensius, &c.*

Another point which may be noticed in this later criticism is the growth of a number of new aesthetic terms, such as τραχύς, αὐστηρός, αὐθαδής, αὐχμηρός, εὐπινής, στρυφνός, συνεσπασμένος, ἀντίτυπος, ἀρχαϊκός, πυκνός, δεινός, συστρέφειν, ἀξιωματικός, τραγικός, σεμνός, δαιμόνιος, πνεῦμα, χάρις, Ἀφροδίτη, γλαφυρός, ἀνθηρός, στρογγύλος, κτενίζω, βοστρυχίζω, ἡδονή, πειθώ, ῥώμη, ἰσχύς, ἀφελής, μεγαλοφυής, μεγαλοπρεπής, περιττός : several of which passed into the Latin of the Ciceronian and Augustan ages.

It is, however, where he leaves the beaten track that Cicero strikes into a vein more genial and more worthy of himself. Of criticism on poetry we have little from him but detached utterances : but it is plain that his liking is for the grander and freer style of the older poets, which to the new Alexandrian school was antiquated and distasteful. To Cicero[1] Ennius, Pacuvius, and Accius *non verba sed vim Graecorum expresserunt poetarum.* Of Ennius [2] he says *o poetam egregium, quamquam ab his cantoribus Euphorionis contemnitur ;* his verses on Cassandra are *poema tenerum et moratum atque molle* [3] : he is *summus poeta* [4], *ingeniosus poeta* [5], just as to

---

[1] *Acad. Post.* I. 10.   [2] *Tusc.* 3. 45.   [3] *Div.* 1. 66.
[4] *De Or.* I. 198.   [5] *Mur.* 30.

Lucretius he is *Ennius noster*, the writer of *aeterni versus*[1].
It is much to be wished that we had more of this kind from
the hand of a man of genius, who was a considerable metrist
himself, and only fell short of being a poet. But Cicero
threw his whole strength into the criticism of oratorical prose.
Here at length we get something which was new of its kind.
The comparative greatness of the Roman dominion, and the
large experience which was the inheritance of Roman life,
opened to the Latin writers the knowledge of a world wider
than that of the Greek schools and their books of history and
criticism. Dionysius was not insensible of this when in his
treatise περὶ τῶν ἀρχαίων ῥητόρων (2 p. 447 Reiske) he attributes
to the judgement of the great Romans the return to good
taste which he notices as a fact within his own experience.
After complaining that the Attic Muse had been banished,
as it were, from her own home (τῶν ἑαυτῆς ἐκπεσοῦσα ἀγαθῶν),
that the ignorant had driven out the inquiring, the insane, the
temperate (ἡ ἀμαθὴς τὴν φιλόσοφον, καὶ ἡ μαινομένη τὴν σώφρονα),
he goes on to say that the ancient and temperate style of
rhetoric had regained its credit. αἰτία δ', οἶμαι, καὶ ἀρχὴ τῆς
τοιαύτης μεταβολῆς ἡ πάντων κρατοῦσα Ῥώμη, πρὸς ἑαυτὴν ἀναγκάζουσα
τὰς ἄλλας πόλεις ἀποβλέπειν· καὶ ταύτης τ' αὐτῆς οἱ δυναστεύοντες, κατ'
ἀρετὴν καὶ ἀπὸ τοῦ κρατίστου τὰ κοινὰ διοικοῦντες, εὐπαίδευτοι πάνυ καὶ
γενναῖοι τὰς κρίσεις γενόμενοι (p. 448).

The rest of this essay will be devoted to Cicero as a critic.
I shall endeavour to state, (1) what are the broad principles on
which he bases his criticism of oratorical prose; (2) to point
out by a few instances what are the marks of his critical genius
in detail; (3) to indicate his weakness as a critic of historical
writing, and to ask how far this was due to his own position,
and how far to the circumstances of his age.

(1) Cicero might fairly be judged as a critic by his Brutus
alone, which is a history of Latin oratory from the earliest times
to his own. The work, written in the year 46, bears evident
marks of haste, and covers a large field of history. It has,

---

[1] Lucretius i. 117, 121.

consequently, obvious imperfections of form.   The character-
izations of the mumerous orators who are passed in review are
not executed with equal care.   Its main importance, like that
of the *Orator*, a treatise on the form of prose writing published
in the same year, lies in its controversial character ; or rather,
in the fact that Cicero now found himself obliged to vindicate
his own literary principles against a new school.   As, in the
field of poetry, the younger men were emphasizing the merits
of the Alexandrian school, with its elaborate study of form
and its love for small subjects and recondite mythology, so
in the field of oratory the supremacy of Cicero and Caesar
was threatened by the new Atticist represented by Calvus.
The ideals of the Atticists were Lysias, for his simplicity, and
Thucydides, for his condensation and intensity.   Forced to
defend his own position, Cicero lays down a principle which,
so far as I know, had never been so clearly propounded before,
and which is true for all time.   This principle is, that, given
fair time and opportunity, the recognition of the many is as
necessary a test of excellence in an artist as that of the few.
The merit which obtains the verdict of the connoisseurs only is
a true merit, but it is incomplete.   *Hic Atticus*[1], *Quo modo
istuc dicis, inquit, ' cum tuo iudicio, tum omnium' ?   Semperne in
oratore probando aut improbando volgi iudicium cum intellegen-
tium iudicio congruit ?   an alii probantur a multitudine, alii autem
ab iis qui intellegunt ?   Recte requiris, inquam, Attice ; sed audies
ex me fortasse quod non omnes probent . . . Etenim necesse est,
qui ita dicit ut a multitudine probetur, eundem doctis probari.
Nam quid in dicendo rectum sit aut pravum ego iudicabo, si modo
is sum qui id possim aut sciam iudicare ; qualis vero sit orator,
ex eo quod quis dicendo efficiet poterit intellegi.   Tria sunt enim,
ut quidem ego sentio, quae sint efficienda dicendo ; ut doceatur is
apud quem dicatur, ut delectetur, ut moveatur vehementius.
Quibus virtutibus oratoris horum quidque efficiatur, aut quibus
vitiis orator aut non adsequatur haec aut etiam in his labatur et
cadat, artifex aliquis iudicabit.   Efficiatur autem ab oratore*

[1] *Brutus* § 183.

necne, ut ei qui audiunt ita adficiantur ut orator velit, volgi adsensu et populari approbatione iudicari solet. Itaque nunquam de bono oratore aut non bono doctis hominibus cum populo dissensio fuit. An censes, dum illi viguerunt quos ante dixi, non eosdem gradus oratorum volgi iudicio et doctorum fuisse? De populo si quem ita rogavisses, ' Quis est in hac civitate eloquentissimus,' in Antonio et Crasso aut dubitaret, aut hunc alius? illum alius diceret. Nemone Philippum, tam suavem oratorem, tam gravem, tam facetum, his anteferret, quem nosmetipsi, qui haec arte aliqua volumus expendere, proximum illis fuisse diximus? Nemo profecto ; id enim ipsum est summi oratoris, summum oratorem populo videri. Quare tibicen Antigenidas dixerit discipulo sane frigenti ad populum ' Mihi cane et Musis' ; ego huic Bruto dicenti, ut solet, apud multitudinem, ' Mihi cane et populo, mi Brute,' dixerim ; ut qui audient quid efficiatur, ego etiam cur id efficiatur intellegam. Credit eis, quae dicuntur, qui audit oratorem, vera putat, adsentitur, probat, fidem facit oratio ; tu artifex quid quaeris amplius? delectatur audiens multitudo et quasi voluptate quadam perfunditur : quid habes quod disputes? gaudet, dolet, ridet, plorat, favet, odit, contemnit, invidet ; ad misericordiam inducitur, ad pudendum, ad pigendum ; irascitur, miratur, sperat, timet ; haec perinde accidunt ut eorum qui adsunt mentes verbis et sententiis et actione tractantur ; quid est quod expectetur docti alicuius sententia? True, this is said of the oratorical style only ; but, taken in its length and breadth, it is true of all art. When, with Handel, we see the kingdoms of the world, stroke upon stroke, broken in pieces, or when with Beethoven we share in the tears and despair of a nation which has lost its hero, it is the universality of the triumph and of the sorrow which moves us, as much as the power and sincerity of the master who represents it.

If, according to Cicero, oratory must appeal to the many as well as the few, and no distinction can be recognized in presence of a great work, it is also necessary that a great style should combine all the elements of excellence, if it is to appeal broadly to the universal sense of beauty and grandeur, not to the artificially pampered taste of the few.   *Ornatur*[1] *igitur oratio genere primum et quasi colore quodam et suco suo. Nam ut gravis, ut suavis, ut erudita sit, ut liberalis, ut admirabilis, ut polita, ut sensus, ut doloris habeat quantum opus sit, non est singulorum articulorum; in toto spectantur haec corpore. Ut porro conspersa sit quasi verborum sententiarumque floribus, id non debet esse fusum aequabiliter per omnem orationem, sed ita distinctum, ut sint quasi in ornatu disposita quaedam insignia et lumina. Genus igitur dicendi est eligendum, quod maxime teneat eos qui audiant, et quod non solum delectet, sed etiam sine satietate delectet; non enim a me iam expectari puto ut moneam ut caveatis, ne exilis, ne inculta sit vestra oratio, ne volgaris, ne obsoleta; aliud quiddam maius et ingenia me hortantur vestra et aetates.* Mere sweetness and prettiness cloy the senses: *difficile enim dictu est quaenam causa sit cur ea quae maxime sensus nostros impellunt voluptate, et specie prima acerrime commovent, ab iis celerrime fastidio quodam et satietate abalienemur. Quanto colorum pulchritudine et varietate floridiora sunt in picturis novis pleraque quam in veteribus! quae tamen, etiamsi primo aspectu nos ceperunt, diutius non delectant; cum iidem nos in antiquis tabulis illo ipso horrido obsoletoque teneamur. Quanto molliores sunt et delicatiores in cantione flexiones et falsae voculae quam certae et severae! quibus tamen non modo austeri, sed, si saepius fiunt, multitudo ipsa reclamat. Licet hoc videre in reliquis sensibus, unguentis minus diu nos delectari summa et acerrima suavitate conditis, quam his moderatis, et magis laudari quod terram quam quod crocum sapere videatur; in ipso tactu esse modum et mollitudinis et levitatis; quin etiam gustatus, qui est sensus ex omnibus maxime voluptarius, quique dulcitudine praeter ceteros sensus commovetur, quam cito id quod valde dulce est aspernatur ac respuit!* .. § 101 *Qua re 'bene et praeclare' quamvis saepe nobis dicatur; 'belle et festive' nimium saepe nolo; quamquam illa ipsa exclamatio 'non potest melius' sit velim crebra; sed habeat tamen illa in dicendo admiratio ac summa laus umbram*

[1] *De Oratore* 3. 96.

aliquam et recessum, quo magis id, quod erit illuminatum, extare atque eminere videatur.

Cicero is no philosopher, nor indeed could the Romans, to whom philosophy in the real sense was little known except as a lesson of doctrines learned from the Greeks, have based their criticism on its principles. But Cicero makes up to a certain extent for this deficiency by his wide grasp of facts. The instinct of genius, trained and strengthened by long experience, but never forgetting itself, gave him the sympathy which enabled him to perceive the connexion between the inarticulate feeling of the multitude and the reasoned judgement of educated men. His criticism is that of the trained scholar, whose technical knowledge is penetrated and transformed by living insight, and sense of reality.

(2) If this is the general character of Cicero's criticism, it will be interesting to quote instances in detail of the power which makes his utterances a new creation. If I am not mistaken, his real self appears with more genuine power and impressiveness in these criticisms than in anything which he has left us. This must be my excuse for quoting from them at some length. While they reveal the real genius of Cicero, they are also a monument of the expressive power of the Latin language.

Brutus § 93 (Galba). *Quem fortasse vis non ingeni solum sed etiam animi et naturalis quidam dolor dicentem incendebat, efficiebatque ut et incitata et gravis et vehemens esset oratio ; dein cum otiosus stilum prehenderat, motusque omnis animi, tamquam ventus, hominem defecerat, flaccescebat oratio. Quod eis qui limatius dicendi consectantur genus accidere non solet, propterea quod prudentia numquam deficit oratorem, qua ille utens eodem modo possit et dicere et scribere ; ardor animi non semper adest, isque cum consedit, omnis illa vis et quasi flamma oratoris extinguitur. Hanc igitur ob causam videtur Laeli mens spirare etiam in scriptis, Galbae autem vis occidisse.*

§ 125 (Gaius Gracchus). *Sed ecce in manibus vir et praestantissimo ingenio et flagranti studio et doctus a puero, Gaius Gracchus. Noli enim putare quemquam, Brute, pleniorem aut*

uberiorem ad dicendum fuisse. Et ille, ' Sic prorsus,' inquit,
' existimo, atque istum de superioribus paene solum lego.'   Immo
plane, inquam, Brute, legas censeo.   Damnum enim illius imma-
turo interitu res Romanae Latinaeque litterae fecerunt.   Utinam
non tam fratri pietatem quam patriae praestare voluisset!
Quam ille facile tali ingenio, diutius si vixisset, vel paternam
esset vel avitam gloriam consecutus!   Eloquentia quidem nescio
an habuisset parem neminem.   Grandis est verbis, sapiens sen-
tentiis, genere toto gravis; manus extrema non accessit operibus
eius; praeclare incohata multa, perfecta non plane.   Legendus,
inquam, est hic orator, Brute, si quisquam alius, iuventuti; non
enim solum acuere, sed etiam alere ingenium potest.

139 (Antonius).   *Omnia veniebant Antonio in mentem; eaque*
suo quaeque loco, ubi plurimum proficere et valere possent, ut ab
imperatore equites, pedites, levis armatura, sic ab illo in maxime
opportunis orationis partibus collocabantur.   Erat memoria
summa, nulla meditationis suspicio; imparatus semper aggredi
ad dicendum videbatur, sed ita erat paratus, ut iudices illo
dicente nonnumquam viderentur non satis parati ad cavendum
fuisse.   Verba ipsa non illa quidem elegantissimo sermone;
itaque diligenter loquendi laude caruit, neque tamen est admodum
inquinate locutus.   Nam ipsum Latine loqui est illud quidem, ut
paulo ante dixi, in magna laude ponendum, sed non tam sua
sponte, quam quod est a plerisque neglectum; non enim tam
praeclarum est scire Latine quam turpe nescire, neque tam
id mihi oratoris boni quam civis Romani proprium videtur.
Sed tamen Antonius in verbis et eligendis (neque id ipsum
tam leporis causa quam ponderis,) et collocandis et comprehen-
sione devinciendis nihil non ad rationem et tamquam ad artem
derigebat: verum multo magis hoc idem in sententiarum orna-
mentis et conformationibus.   Quo genere quia praestat omnibus
Demosthenes, idcirco a doctis oratorum est princeps iudicatus.
Σχήματα *enim quae vocant Graeci, ea maxime ornant oratorem,*
quae non tam in verbis pingendis habent pondus, quam in il-
luminandis sententiis.   Sed cum haec magna in Antonio, tum
actio singularis; quae si partienda est in gestum atque vocem,

gestus erat non verba exprimens, sed cum sententiis congruens, manus, umeri, latera, supplosio pedis, status, incessus, omnisque motus ; vox permanens, verum subrauca natura. Sed hoc vitium huic uni in bonum convertebat. Habebat enim flebile quiddam in questionibus aptumque cum ad fidem faciendam tum ad misericordiam commovendam ; ut verum videretur in hoc illud, quod Demosthenem ferunt ei, qui quaesivisset quid primum esset in dicendo, actionem, quid secundum, idem, et idem tertium respondisse. Nulla res magis penetrat in animos, eosque fingit, format, flectit, talesque oratores videri facit quales ipsi se videri volunt.

143 (Crassus). *Huic* (i.e. *Antonio) alii parem esse dicebant, alii anteponebant L. Crassum. Illud quidem certe omnes ita iudicabant, neminem esse qui horum altero uno patrono cuiusquam ingenium requireret. Equidem quamquam Antonio tantum tribuo quantum supra dixi, tamen Crasso nihil statuo fieri potuisse perfectius. Erat summa gravitas, erat cum gravitate iunctus facetiarum et urbanitatis oratorius, non scurrilis, lepos ; Latine loquendi accurata, et sine molestia diligens elegantia ; in disserendo mira explicatio ; cum de iure civili, cum de aequo et bono disputaretur, argumentorum et similitudinum copia. Nam ut Antonius coniectura movenda, aut sedanda suspicione aut excitanda incredibilem vim habebat, sic in interpretando, in definiendo, in explicanda aequitate nihil erat Crasso copiosius ; idque cum saepe alias tum apud centumviros in M'. Curi causa cognitum est.*

148 (Scaevola and Crassus). *Crassus erat elegantium parcissimus, Scaevola parcorum elegantissimus ; Crassus in summa comitate habebat etiam severitatis satis, Scaevolae multa in severitate non deerat tamen comitas. Licet omnia hoc modo ; sed vereor, ne fingi videantur haec ut dicantur a me quodam modo ; res tamen sic se habet. Cum omnis virtus sit, ut vestra, Brute, vetus Academia dixit, mediocritas, uterque horum medium quiddam volebat sequi ; sed ita cadebat, ut alter ex alterius laude partem, uterque autem suam totam haberet.*

201 (Cotta and Sulpicius). *Quoniam ergo oratorum bonorum —hos enim quaerimus—duo genera sunt, unum attenuate presse-*

que, alterum sublate ampleque dicentium ; etsi id melius est, quod splendidius et magnificentius, tamen in bonis omnia quae summa sunt iure laudantur. Sed cavenda est presso illi oratori inopia et ieiunitas, amplo autem inflatum et corruptum orationis genus. Inveniebat igitur acute Cotta, dicebat pure ac solute ; et ut ad infirmitatem laterum perscienter contentionem omnem remiserat, sic ad virium imbecillitatem dicendi accommodabat genus. Nihil erat in eius oratione nisi sincerum, nihil nisi siccum atque sanum ; illudque maximum, quod cum contentione orationis flectere animos iudicum vix posset nec omnino eo genere diceret, tractando tamen impellebat ut idem facerent a se commoti, quod a Sulpicio concitati. Fuit enim Sulpicius vel maxime omnium, quos quidem ego audiverim, grandis et ut ita dicam tragicus orator. Vox cum magna tum suavis et splendida ; gestus et motus corporis ita venustus, ut tamen ad forum, non ad scaenam institutus videretur ; incitata et volubilis, nec ea redundans tamen nec circumfluens oratio.

261 (Caesar). *Caesar autem rationem adhibens consuetudinem vitiosam et corruptam pura et incorrupta consuetudine emendat. Itaque cum ad hanc elegantiam verborum Latinorum (quae, etiamsi orator non sis et sis ingenuus civis Romanus, tamen necessaria est) adiungit illa oratoria ornamenta dicendi, tum videtur tamquam tabulas bene pictas collocare in bono lumine. Hanc cum habeat praecipuam laudem, in communibus non video cui debeat cedere. Splendidam quandam minimeque veteratoriam rationem dicendi tenet, voce motu forma etiam magnificam et generosam quodam modo. Tum Brutus : Orationes quidem eius mihi vehementer probantur ; complures autem legi, atque etiam commentarios quos scripsit rerum suarum. Valde quidem, inquam, probandos ; nudi enim sunt, recti et venusti, omni ornatu orationis tamquam veste detracta. Sed dum voluit alios habere parata unde sumerent qui vellent scribere historiam, ineptis gratum fortasse fecit, qui volent illa calamistris inurere ; sanos quidem homines a scribendo deterruit, nihil est enim in historia pura et illustri brevitate dulcius.*

274 (Calidius). *Sed de M. Calidio dicamus aliquid, qui non fuit orator unus e multis, potius inter multos prope singularis fuit :*

*ita reconditas exquisitasque sententias mollis et pellucens vestiebat
oratio. Nihil tam tenerum quam eius comprehensio verborum,
nihil tam flexibile, nihil quod magis ipsius arbitrio fingeretur, ut
nullius oratoris aeque in potestate fuerit; quae primum ita pura
erat ut nihil liquidius, ita libere fluebat, ut nusquam adhaeres-
ceret. Nullum nisi loco positum et tamquam in vermiculato
emblemate, ut ait Lucilius structum verbum videres; nec vero
ullum aut durum aut insolens aut humile aut longius ductum:
ac non propria verba rerum, sed pleraque translata, sic tamen ut
ea non irruisse in alienum locum, sed immigrasse in suum
diceres; nec vero haec soluta nec diffluentia, sed astricta numeris
non aperte nec eodem modo semper, sed varie dissimulanterque
conclusis. Erant autem et verborum et sententiarum illa lumina,
quae vocant Graeci σχήματα, quibus tamquam insignibus in
ornatu distinguebatur omnis oratio . . . Accedebat ordo rerum
plenus artis, actio liberalis, totumque dicendi placidum et sanum
genus. Quodsi est optimum suaviter dicere, nihil est quod melius
hoc quaerendum putes. Sed cum a nobis paulo ante dictum sit,
tria videri esse quae orator efficere debet, ut doceret, ut delectaret,
ut moveret: duo summe tenuit, ut et rem illustraret disserendo et
animos eorum, qui audirent, devinceret voluptate; aberat tertia
illa laus, qua permoveret atque incitaret animos, quam plurimum pollere diximus, neque erat ulla vis atque contentio: sive
consilio, quod eos, quorum altior oratio actioque esset ardentior,
furere et bacchari arbitraretur, sive quod natura non esset ita
factus, sive quod non consuesset, sive quod non posset. Hoc unum
illi, si nihil utilitatis habebat, abfuit; si opus erat, defuit.*

301 (Hortensius). *Primum memoria tanta (erat), quantam
in nullo cognovisse me arbitror, ut, quae secum commentatus esset,
ea sine scripto verbis eisdem redderet, quibus cogitavisset. Hoc
adiumento ille tanto sic utebatur, ut sua et commentata et scripta
et nullo referente omnia adversariorum dicta meminisset. Ar-
debat autem cupiditate sic, ut in nullo umquam flagrantius
studium viderim. Nullum enim patiebatur esse diem, quin aut
in foro diceret aut meditaretur extra forum; saepissime autem
eodem die utrumque faciebat. Attuleratque minime volgare*

genus dicendi ; duas quidem res, quas nemo alius ; partitiones, quibus de rebus dicturus esset, et collectiones eorum quae essent dicta contra quaeque ipse dixisset. Erat in verborum splendore elegans, compositione aptus, facultate copiosus ; eaque erat cum summo ingenio tum exercitationibus maximis consecutus. Rem complectebatur memoriter, dividebat acute, nec praetermittebat fere quicquam quod esset in causa aut ad confirmandum aut ad refellendum. Vox canora et suavis, motus et gestus etiam plus artis habebat quam erat oratori satis.

It will have been noticed that the method of Cicero's criticism is a very simple one. It is to summarize in terse expressions the literary qualities of the speakers whom he passes in review, with little preface, and no attempt, such as a modern writer would make, to set their productions in their historical framework, or to trace the growth of style in its historical development. But in this Cicero is only the child of his time. He follows in the same track as the Greek critics, in all probability, had done before him, as undoubtedly Dionysius and the author of the περὶ ὕψους did after him. What is Cicero's own, and what should make these criticisms immortal, is their genius, their fulness of light, the perfect mastery of the writer over his thoughts, his power of moulding the Latin language to his purpose, the self-control which forbids him to use a word too much. His usual prolixity is thrown aside, and he returns to obey the true laws of expression. As a critic, Cicero can write with all Tacitus's terseness, and without any of Tacitus's affectation.

(3) In the *De Legibus*[1] (1 § 5) Atticus says to Cicero *postulatur a te iam diu flagitatur vel potius historia. Sic enim putant, te illam tractante effici posse ut in hoc etiam genere Graeciae nihil cedamus. Atque ut audias quid ego ipse sentiam, non solum mihi videris eorum studiis qui litteris delectantur, set etiam patriae debere hoc munus, ut ea, quae salva per te est, per te eundem sit ornata. Abest enim historia litteris nostris, ut et ipse intellego et ex te persaepe audio. Potes autem tu profecto*

[1] See also *De Orat.* 2. 51 foll.

satis facere in ea, quippe cum sit opus, ut tibi quidem videri solet, unum hoc oratorium maxime. We must, after all, pause before we laugh at the weakness and shallowness of this passage, for in the remarkable words *opus (historici) est unum oratorium maxime* Cicero sums up, not his own view only, but one which was very widely prevalent in antiquity The rhetoricians, in fact, claimed history as part of their province, and their criticism was naturally directed only to the form of writing, ignoring the whole question of research and philosophical treatment. Hence it was observed as a remarkable fact about Theopompus and Ephorus, that they had been pupils of Isocrates. Transplant this notion to Rome, where not only was rhetoric an important branch of education, but every circumstance of public life favoured the development of the great style of oratory and it is easy to see how style came to be regarded as the main merit of the historian. To be a great statesman at Rome it was necessary, besides being a soldier, to be an orator ; a master not only of the cultivated style which would appeal to the forty or fifty educated senators and *equites* who might meet to try a case in a court of law, but of the broader effects which alone could make an impression upon the great *contiones*. Oratory (not rhetoric) bade fair in the hands of a comprehensive genius like Cicero to absorb the whole field of knowledge and education. To Cicero, if we may trust him in the *De Oratore*, knowledge is the necessary condition of eloquence, but knowledge must be subservient to eloquence. One can hardly complain of him for adopting a point of view which after all was the prevalent one with the mass of educated men in classical antiquity. For with them literature was surbordinate to life. The idea of investigation, of painful study, undertaken merely for the sake of ascertaining the truth in regions of fact such as history or natural science, was comparatively unfamiliar to the literary aristocracies who ruled the ancient Graeco-Roman world. One might perhaps have expected it to be developed either in the schools of the philosophers or among the *grammatici* or scholars. But the centre of gravity of philosophy shifted, since the time of Aristotle, more and more towards problems of speculative ethics; while scholarship satisfied itself with verbal and textual criticism. Nothing gives a better indication of the manner in which the ancient world as a whole conceived the duty of a historian, than the fact that Livy's history of Rome, the defects of which are now familiarly known to every in- dustrious sixth-form schoolboy, was generally accepted as satisfactory, and only superseded by abridgements of itself.

What therefore Cicero desired in the matter of history was not a profound critical work investigating the origin and de- velopment of the Roman constitution. Can it be said that any of his contemporaries could have had this idea? It would be as reasonable to expect that they would have proposed the abolition of slavery, or devised a system of representative government. Cicero wanted a history of Rome written in a luminous narrative style, with due regard to literary form and with striking rhetorical illustrations of Roman manners and character, subsidiary no doubt to the main idea of celebrating the growth of the Roman empire. This was all that lay within his power; nor is it too much to say that had he been granted the leisure to execute it, the task would not have been beyond his capacity, if we may judge by the specimens of historical narrative which he has left in the *De Re Publica* and *De Legibus.*

This short survey of the literary criticism of the Ciceronian age may be closed with the observation that its original genius, so far as the surviving books allow us to judge, was Cicero; and that Cicero, in his criticisms on oratorical prose, not merely left proofs of his power which are in themselves gems of their kind, but laid down principles and adopted an attitude which have a wide significance for artistic criticism in general, as well as for the special branch of literature with which he was con- cerned; finally, that his faulty judgement in regard to history was, when the circumstances of his age are considered, not only excusable but inevitable. In the following essay I shall en- deavour to sketch the history of literary criticism in Latin from Horace to Tacitus.

II.

The change of tone which strikes us at once on passing from the criticism of the Ciceronian to that of the Augustan age was, as we saw in the last essay, partly prepared by the Alexandrian and so-called Attic tendency, headed, to all appearance, by Calvus and his friends, which roused Cicero to a public assertion of his own principles in the *Brutus* and the *Orator*. The Alexandrian school liked obscure subjects, short poems, long preparation, elaborate workmanship : the so-called Atticists professed a passion for purity, simplicity, and condensation. Cicero cared more for breadth, grasp, and general inspiration, than for perfection in detail. Horace, and the school or society to which he belonged, that of Varius and Vergil, no doubt sympathized, so far as feeling for finish and preparation went, with the Alexandrians as against Varro and Cicero.

But it would be a great mistake to suppose that Horace, who sneers at Calvus and Catullus, was a thorough partisan, or even a partisan at all, of the Alexandrian set. His ideal is not Alexandria, but Greece ; Greece as in the spirit and form of art the true mistress of Rome. He is as patriotic a Roman as Cicero, as anxious to serve the literary interests of his country. He feels indeed that the lessons to be learned from Greece have not yet been exhausted, and that they must be exhausted before the Latin writer could show any masterpieces to equal their models ; but it is of Latin literature that he is thinking. The Alexandrian school, he may well have thought, was impotent to produce more than translation, imitation,and paraphrase ; of but little avail to Latin literature in the proper sense. This his unrivalled sense and literary tact would at once enable him to discover, supported as it was by his knowledge of life and its realities. For Horace was no mere student. He had seen much of the rough side of life in his youth, and had taken of mankind in general such measure as a man of more shrewdness and character than sympathetic power would take under the circumstances. His mind was versatile and many-sided, and so was his poetry. Lampoon, *satura*, epistles, and lyric in in its highest flights,—nothing came amiss to him. The centre of his taste, his point of judgement, is the firm and unalterable instinct of the cultured man of the world. Hence the ease and sureness with which he takes up his critical attitude, whether he is speaking of satire or lyric or epic or the drama.

The earliest critical utterances of Horace are to be found in his *Saturae*, the fourth and tenth of the first book. Here, under the form of polemic against Lucilius, he asserts his own sound, if too exclusive, principle. The *satura* of Lucilius was too hasty, too slovenly, to be taken as a model for this form of composition. And, again, the Old Attic Comedy is not the only type for the Latin writer of *saturae*, who should preserve the wider traditions of that form of writing. In general, indeed, says Horace, do not suppose poetry is a matter for the crowd. It is the gift and privilege of the few [1]; *neque enim concludere versum Dixeris esse satis, neque si quis scribat uti nos Sermoni propiora, putes hunc esse poetam. Ingenium cui sit, cui mens divinior atque os Magna sonaturum, des nominis huius honorem. . . . Nulla taberna meos habeat neque pila libellos. . . Nec recito cuiquam nisi amicis, idque coactus. . . Satis est equitem mihi plaudere.*

But some ten years later Horace took the opportunity of expressing his views in the form of a regular treatise, the *Epistula ad Pisones* [2]. The Greek framework of this piece was the treatise of Neoptolemus of Parium, of which I have already given some account (p. 48). If we try to penetrate Horace's motive in going back upon this formal essay and applying it to the circumstances of literary Rome as he knew it, we may discover a fresh interest in what at first sight seems a dry collection of commonplace. Leaving the Greek rules, let us take as worthy of special attention the Latin applications. These fall under some five heads.

[1] I. 4. 40 and 71.

[2] [The chronological order of Horace's works and the relation of the *Ars Poetica* to a Greek original are discussed in Mr. Nettleship's *Essays in Latin Literature* pp. 164, 173 foll.]

(1) 45–72. Horace claims for himself and his friends that they be allowed the same liberty in coining new words as has always been conceded to his predecessors: *Quid autem Caecilio Plautoque dabit Romanus, ademptum Vergilio Varioque? Ego cur, acquirere pauca Si possum, invideor, cum lingua Catonis et Enni Sermonem patrium ditaverit, et nova rerum Nomina protulerit? Licuit semperque licebit Signatum praesente nota procudere nomen.*

(2) 133–135. He cautions the Latin poet who translates or paraphrases from the Greek against an over-anxiety to be literal, or to bind himself strictly to the plan and character of his original. *Nec verbum verbo curabis reddere fidus Interpres, nec desilies imitator in artum, Unde pedem proferre pudor vetet aut operis lex.* In his general treatment let him look to Homer, not to the conventional later epic: *Nec sic incipies ut scriptor cyclicus olim, 'Fortunam Priami cantabo et nobile bellum.'*

(3) 234–250. Hints as to the handling of the satyric drama in the Roman stage. The language of the *Fauni* or *Satyri* should be of a colour between that of the tragic and the comic stage: Silenus should not talk in the manner of Davus.

(4) The treatment of the dramatic iambic. 250–274. The old metre of Ennius and Plautus is to be discarded, and far more care taken that the iambus should be treated as a foot consisting of a short and a long syllable.

(5) General warnings. 325–333. Poetry is not to be taken up lightly; nor again is it to be supposed that inspiration without sense will be sufficient. Beware of corrupting social influences and the love of money (382–390): nothing but the combination of industry and judgement with genius will effect anything (365–390: 419 to the end).

Putting aside the visible irritation of Horace against the formal critics of the older school and the smarts left by Orbilius's cane; putting aside also his well-justified contempt for the crowd of writers who were taking up poetry merely because it was fashionable to do so; what must we suppose were the motives which induced him to go back upon the treatise of

Neoptolemus, or whatever Greek work or works formed the basis of the *De Arte Poetica?* The answer probably is, that being dissatisfied both with the critical principles of the Ciceronian age as represented by Varro and Cicero, and with the petty industry and conceits of the Alexandrians, he wished to recall his countrymen to the critical canons on which the great works of Hellas seemed to be based. That he should not have gone back directly to Aristotle instead of to an author who probably only embodied Aristotelian precepts at second or third hand, may at first sight appear surprising. But it is, in fact, not more surprising than that Cicero should (as he does) have recourse, for the great mass of his philosophy, not directly to Plato or Aristotle, but to their degenerate successors. It may also be that the minute rules laid down by Horace's authority were better fitted to give an air of precision to his work than the broader principles of Aristotle. However this may be, I would suggest that Horace's chief aim in the *De Arte Poetica* is to recall his countrymen to the thoughts and mind of the great Greek masters in their length and breadth ; *Grais ingenium, Grais dedit ore rotundo Musa loqui. Vos exemplaria Graeca Nocturna versate manu, versate diurna.*

He takes up the same text, but treats it with riper judgement and in a less scholastic tone, in the two epistles of the second book. These are the best of Horace's critical utterances. The pedantic framework of Greek texts and Greek words has disappeared, and the genius of the poet speaks unfettered. The theme is, again, the rights of himself and his school ; mere antiquity is nothing ; nothing will excuse the lack of finish ; a fine line or fine word here and there will not compensate for general carelessness ; and more of the same kind which it is unnecessary to repeat here. For it is Horace's incomparable manner, his ease and the sureness of his tread, which really interests the reader of these two epistles. What can be more beautiful in its way than the following (*Ep.* 2. 2. 109–125)?

At qui legitimum cupiet fecisse poema Cum tabulis animum censoris sumet honesti ; Audebit, quaecumque parum splendoris

habebunt Et sine pondere erunt et honore indigna ferentur Verba,
movere loco, quamvis invita recedant, Et versentur adhuc inter
penetralia Vestae ; Obscurata diu populo bonus eruet, atque
Proferet in lucem speciosa vocabula rerum, Quae priscis me-
morata Catonibus atque Cethegis Nunc situs informis premit
et deserta vetustas ; Adsciscet nova, quae genitor produxerit usus ;
Vemens et liquidus puroque simillimus amni Fundet opes,
Latiumque beabit divite lingua : Luxuriantia compescet, nimis
aspera sano Levabit cultu, virtute carentia tollet, Ludentis
speciem dabit et torquebitur, ut qui Nunc Satyrum, nunc agrestem
Cyclopa movetur.

If the sane judgement of Horace sometimes lacks sympathy
and generosity, especially when he is speaking of the older
poets admired by Varro and Cicero and Orbilius, the defect is
amply supplied by Ovid. His luxuriant genius was naturally
combined with a comprehensive sympathy, which refused to
excommunicate the real poets of any age or style [1] ; *Ennius*
arte carens, animosique Accius oris, Casurum nullo tempore
nomen habent : Varronem primamque ratem quae nesciet aetas,
Aureaque Aesonio terga petita duci ? Carmina sublimis tunc
sunt peritura Lucreti, Exitio terras cum dabit una dies : Tityrus
et fruges Aeneiaque arma legentur, Roma triumphati dum caput
orbis erit. Or again [2], *Utque suo Martem cecinit gravis Ennius*
ore, Ennius ingenio maximus, arte rudis, Explicat et causas
rapidi Lucretius ignis Casurumque triplex vaticinatur opus.
One cannot but admire, as in the case of Cicero, the generous
desire to recognize merit, the perfect mastery of critical
language, the rapid flowing manner, half concealing the delicate
care with which each weighty expression is wrought out.

As Homer was attacked by Zoilus, so Vergil was criticized
by Carvilius Pictor in his *Aeneidomastix,* and in the same
spirit of petty cavil. None the less did Vergil and Horace
become classics soon after their death. The result was that
they drove out the taste for the older poets, and even for the
writers of the Ciceronian age. Not that there were not many

[1] *Am.* I. 15. 19.   [2] *Trist.* 2. 423.

antiquarians or lovers of the ancients among the Roman *litterati* as long as Latin literature existed. But the new school carried with it, during the first century, many of the most genial minds. To Persius, for instance, the love of Pacuvius and Accius is a mere morbid survival[1]: *Est nunc Brisaei quem venosus liber Acci, Sunt quos Pacuviusque et verrucosa moretur Antiopa, aerumnis cor luctificabile fulta.* If Persius only once says in terms that Horace in his ideal, his constant imitation of him—for it must always be remembered that in the ancient world to imitate a poet was to show one's admiration of him—is a living witness to the fact. Lucan's *Pharsalia* teems with imitations of Vergil; may not then Lucan and Persius be taken respectively as representatives of the Vergilian and Horatian schools?

It is worth while to ask in this place whether Eumolpus, the poet in Petronius, may not be taken as a representative of the serious school whose champions, during the age of Nero, were Persius in satire, Lucan in epic, and Seneca in tragedy. No Latin satirist, so far as we can judge from the remains, approaches Petronius in delicacy of *innuendo*; and it requires some careful reading to discern what I believe is now hardly disputed, that the hexameters of Eumolpus on the civil war are a parody of Lucan's *Pharsalia.* His iambics on the *Troiae Halosis* seem to me to be no less clearly a parody of Seneca. Now Eumolpus is a declared admirer of the Vergilian and Horatian school[2]; *Multos (inquit Eumolpus) carmen decepit. Nam ut quisque versum pedibus instruxit sensumque teneriorem verborum ambitu intexuit, putavit se continuo in Heliconem venisse. Sic forensibus ministeriis exercitati frequenter ad carminis tranquillitatem tamquam ad portum feliciorem refugerunt, credentes facilius poema extrui posse quam controversiam sententiolis vibrantibus pictam. Ceterum neque generosior spiritus vanitatem amat, neque concipere aut edere partum mens potest nisi ingenti flumine litterarum inundata. Refugiendum est ab omni verborum, ut ita dicam, vilitate, et sumendae*

[1] I. 76.   [2] Petronius 118.

voces a plebe semotae, ut fiat ' Odi profanum vulgus et arceo.'
Praeterea curandum est ne sententiae emineant extra corpus
orationis expressae, sed intexto vestibus colore niteant. *Homerus*
testis et lyrici Romanusque Vergilius et Horatii curiosa fe-
licitas. Observe the direct contradiction in these words to
Cicero's deliverance [1]; *ut porro conspersa sit quasi verborum*
sententiarumque floribus, id non debet esse fusum aequabiliter
per omnem orationem, sed ita distinctum, ut sint quasi in
ornatu disposita quaedam insignia et lumina. The true poet,
according to Eumolpus, must be a deep student of literature ;
every sentence must be thought out, and the tissue of the
composition consciously interwoven with the fibres of older
writing ; there must be nothing careless, no brave neglect, but
all must be a delicate web of rich and carefully wrought colours.
Now in his first satire Persius takes up somewhat the same
parable. Poetry, he complains, is thought an easy matter [2] :
Ecce modo heroas sensus adferre videmus Nugari solitos Graece,
nec ponere lucum Artifices, nec rus saturum laudare ; . . . In
udo est Maenas et Attis, Nec pluteum caedit, nec demorsos sapit
ungues. All that is wanted is to write verses, anyhow, so that
they are written, and to give good dinners and ask your friends
to come and applaud. This serious, perhaps over-serious, tone
is probably what Petronius is personifying in the character
of Eumolpus, as he certainly seems to be in another passage,
which reminds the reader strangely of Persius. This is the
eighty-eighth chapter, where Eumolpus delivers a sermon on
the current lack of true philosophy and religion. *Ubi est*
dialectica, ubi astronomia, ubi sapientiae cultissima via ? Quis
unquam venit in templum, et votum fecit 'si ad eloquentiam per-
venisset' ? Quis ' si philosophiae fontem attigisset' ? Ac ne bonam
quidem mentem aut bonam valetudinem petunt, sed statim an-
tequam limen Capitolii tangant, alius donum promittit si
propinquum divitem extulerit, alius si thesaurum effoderit, alius si
ad trecentiens sestertium salvus pervenerit. Ipse senatus, recti
bonique praeceptor, mille pondo auri Capitolio promittere solet,

[1] *De Oratore* 3. 96. [See p. 60.]   [2] 1. 69, 105.

et ne quis dubitet pecuniam concupiscere, Iovem quoque peculio exornat. This may almost be described as a prose version of Persius 2. 8—14, 55—63, 70. *'Mens bona, fama, fides,' haec clare et ut audiat hospes: Illa sibi introrsum et sub lingua murmurat, ' O si Ebulliat patruus, praeclarum funus' et ' O si Sub rastro crepet argenti mihi seria dextro Hercule ! pupillumve utinam, quem proximus heres Impello, expungam'.— Hinc illud subiit, auro sacras quod ovato Perducis facies ... Aurum vasa Numae Saturniaque impulit aera, Vestalisque urnas et Tuscum fictile mutat. O curvae in terras animae et caelestium inanes ! Quid iuvat hoc, templis nostros immittere mores Et bona dis ex hac scelerata ducere pulpa ?. . . At vos Dicite, pontifices, in sancto quid facit aurum.*

In corroboration of this view it may be added that Petronius in his *satura* adopts the form of the Varronian *satura Menippea*, the genuine medley of prose and verse, the genuine literary drama with its various characters. He does not write in hexameters, as Horace and his imitator Persius. In fact, he does not like the Vergilian and Horatian school as represented by the serious Stoical poets, Lucan, Persius, and Seneca. Would that more of his *satura* had survived, and that he could have told us definitely whether his heart was, as I suspect, and as he seems to hint in his first chapter, with Varro and Cicero.

The sharp conflict between the Ciceronians and anti-Ciceronians, the enemies of the new educational method based on *declamatio*, and its champions, are clearly enough described in the first two chapters of Petronius. They are to a certain extent toned down in Quintilian, who, however, on the whole throws the weight of his authority against the modern tendency. Before proceeding to examine his literary criticism in detail, it is necessary to say a few words on his position at Rome, which, to a certain extent, seems to have influenced his attitude as a critic.

M. Fabius Quintilianus was born at Calagurris in Spain about 35 A.D. But he passed his youth and most of the remaining part of his life in Rome, where his father was by profession a teacher of rhetoric. He himself was an active pleader in the courts, and a professor (probably the most celebrated in Rome) of declamation and eloquence. In the year 88 (*aet.* 53) he was placed at the head of the first state-supported (*publica*) school in Rome, with a salary from the public treasury. His great work, the *Institutio Oratoria,* was begun probably in his fifty-sixth year, having been preceded by a smaller book *De Causis Corruptae Eloquentiae,* or the reasons of the decline in prose writing.

The *Institutio Oratoria* is thus the work of a man qualified by every external circumstance for his task. Quintilian had full experience both of life and education ; he was thoroughly familiar, not only with every detail of the ordinary educational *curriculum,* and the technicalities of declamation, but also with the practice of the courts. The most talented youths in Rome, such men as Tacitus and the younger Pliny, were his pupils.

John Stuart Mill called the *Institutio Oratoria* a great work ; and a modern reader must undoubtedly admire not only its good sense and manly tone, but its breadth of conception, and the depth and variety of educational principles brought to bear upon the one point, the education of a speaker. Quintilian writes with a full mind and a complete devotion to his profession. But what I tried to point out with regard to Cicero is still truer of Quintilian. In his view oratory includes the whole of literary education. It is the Ciceronian ideal, worked out with more system, and in fuller and more practical detail, than was possible to Cicero. Oratory is the great liberal profession, the profession of the lawyer, senator, and statesman ; let it then be made to cover the whole field of literature. This is Quintilian's idea, not an ignoble one ; and from it proceeds whatever is strong and weak in his literary criticism.

Quintilian is by no means indifferent to the ethical element in literary or oratorical performance. A great orator, to him as to Cato, is *vir bonus dicendi peritus.* After reading the gross flattery which he administers to Domitian not only as an able administrator and general but as a literary man [1], one is somewhat surprised at the boldness of his moral pronouncements [2] *ne futurum quidem oratorem nisi virum bonum : ne studiis quidem operis pulcherrimi vacare mens nisi omnibus vitiis libera potest.*   But it is fair to remember that in the narrower sense of the word there seems to be no doubt that the morality of Quintilian was unimpeachable; and this is something when we recall what is said of Remmius Palaemon and Hamillus.   Again, Quintilian expressly says [3] that he is speaking rather of his ideal than of any probable reality; *cum proprie et ad legem ipsam veritatis loquendum erit, eum quaero oratorem quem et ille (Cicero) quaerebat.*   Practically, he says, one must judge of a great orator by his motive and general intention.   Even if Demosthenes and Cicero are chargeable with the faults alleged against them by their enemies, it must be said that the public career of Demosthenes compensated for his shortcomings, and that Cicero was never lacking in the *voluntas boni civis.*   Granting this, an indulgent casuistry will allow some freedom to a great orator [4]; *da nunc ut crimine manifesto prematur dux bonus, et sine quo vincere hostem civitas non possit: nonne ei communis utilitas oratorem advocabit ?*

All this, perhaps, would hardly be worth quoting were it not that Quintilian's somewhat pretentious moral overture leads us to expect something more than a mere recurrence to the ordinary canons of human judgement.   One would be glad to know whether he would have thought it a necessary virtue in a *bonus grammaticus* to read and conscientiously study the Greek authors on whom he passes formal critical judgements. For it is, alas! too plain that, whether Quintilian had or had not read them, he contents himself in many cases with merely repeating the traditional criticisms of the Greek schools upon some of the principal Greek authors.

[1] Preface to the fourth book, and 10. 1. 91.   [2] 12. 1. 3, 4.
[3] 12. 1. 19.   [4] 12. 1. 43.

In the first chapter of his tenth book Quintilian proposes a course of reading calculated to form the taste of a young man aspiring to success as a speaker. The list of books falls into two parts, the first of which comprises the Greek, the second the Latin classics. The order observed in both parts is the same, viz. poetry, the drama, history, oratory, and philosophy. And in both Quintilian represents himself as ranking his authors in order of merit (*ordinem ducere*).

In the case of the first list, or list of Greek authors, he gives his readers fair warning that he is only repeating other people's criticisms, not pronouncing his own. In § 27 he mentions Theophrastus by name ; in § 52, speaking of Hesiod, he says *datur ei palma* &c.: in § 53, the second place is given to Antimachus by the consent of the *grammatici* : Panyasis is thought (*putant*) *in eloquendo neutrius aequare virtutes.* Callimachus (58) *princeps habetur* (*elegiae*), *secundas confessione plurimorum Philetas occupavit.* In 59 only three *iambographi* are referred to, those, namely, who were allowed by Aristarchus. The *novem lyrici* (61) were probably also a selection of Aristarchus : in any case they are the *Pindarus novemque lyrici* (for this need not be taken to mean strictly ten) of Petronius's first chapter.

It will be worth while to go as far as possible towards ascertaining from what source or sources Quintilian took his borrowed criticisms. The first step is to compare them in detail with those contained in the second book of the περὶ μιμήσεως, or, as it used to be called, *De Veterum Censura,* of Dionysius. The remains of this work only survive in a fragmentary epitome ; but it is quite clear from the coincidences between what survives and the criticisms of Quintilian either that Quintilian has borrowed from a fuller version of Dionysius, or that both authors are using an older authority. From the fact that Dionysius, though mentioned elsewhere by Quintilian, is never alluded to in this context, I am disposed to conclude that the last is the truth. Let us compare Dionysius and Quintilian in detail.

80 *LITERARY CRITICISM IN LATIN ANTIQUITY.*

(Homer.) Dionysius περὶ μιμήσεως 2 p. 19 Usener [1]: τῆς μὲν Ὁμηρικῆς ποιήσεως οὐ μίαν τινὰ τοῦ σώματος μοῖραν, ἀλλ' ἐκτύπωσαι τὸ σύμπαν, καὶ λάβε ζῆλον ἠθῶν τε τῶν ἐκεῖ καὶ παθῶν, καὶ μεγέθους, καὶ τῆς οἰκονομίας, καὶ τῶν ἄλλων ἀρετῶν ἀπασῶν, εἰς ἀληθῆ τὴν παρά σοι μίμησιν ἠλλαγμένων. Quintilian 10. 1. 46 *hic enim, quemadmodum ex Oceano dicit ipse omnium amnium fontiumque cursus initium capere, omnibus eloquentiae partibus exemplum et ortum dedit. . . Adfectus quidem vel illos mites vel hos concitatos nemo erit tam indoctus qui non in sua potestate hunc auctorem habuisse fateatur. . . . . . (Auditorem) intentum proposita rerum magnitudine . . . facit . . In . . dispositione totius operis nonne humani ingenii modum excedit ? . . . ut magnum sit virtutes eius non aemulatione, quod fieri non potest, sed intellectu sequi.* The points common to both writers here are (a) that Homer is admirable in every respect, not in one only: (b) that he is a master in particular of the ἤθη and πάθη, of μέγεθος, and of οἰκονομία. Compare Ovid's *Aspice Maeoniden, a quo, ceu fonte perenni, Pieridum vates ora rigantur aqua.*

(Hesiod). Dionysius p. 19. Ἡσίοδος μὲν γὰρ ἐφρόντισεν ἡδονῆς καὶ ὀνομάτων λειότητος καὶ συνθέσεως ἐμμελοῦς. Quintilian 52 *raro adsurgit Hesiodus, magnaque pars eius in nominibus est occupata ; tamen utiles circa praecepta sententiae levitasque verborum et compositionis probabilis, daturque ei palma in illo medio genere dicendi.*

(Antimachus). Dionysius l. c. Ἀντίμαχος δ' εὐτονίας καὶ ἀγωνιστικῆς τραχύτητος καὶ τοῦ συνήθους τῆς ἐξαλλαγῆς. Quintilian 53 *contra in Antimacho vis et gravitas et minime vulgare eloquendi genus habet laudem. Sed quamvis ei secundas fere grammaticorum consensus deferat, et affectibus et iucunditate et dispositione et omnino arte deficitur, ut plane manifesto appareat, quanto sit aliud proximum esse, aliud secundum.*

(Panyasis). Dionysius l. c. Πανύασις δὲ τάς τ' ἀμφοῖν ἀρετὰς ἠνέγκατο καὶ αὐτῶν πραγματείᾳ καὶ τῇ κατ' αὐτὸν οἰκονομίᾳ διήνεγκεν.

---

[1] [*Dionysii Halicarnassensis librorum de imitatione reliquiae*, edidit H. Usener, Bonnae 1889. Mr. Nettleship does not follow Usener's text absolutely.]

Quintilian 54 *Panyasin ex utroque mixtum putant in eloquendo neutriusque aequare virtutes, alterum tamen ab eo materia, alterum disponendi ratione superari.* So far it seems clear that both Quintilian and Dionysius are following the *grammatici*, i. e. probably Aristarchus and Aristophanes. The passage about Panyasis is very important as bearing on this point : Quintilian, while saying evidently much the same as Dionysius, says not *putat Dionysius* but *putant*. After this Quintilian has some criticisms which are not in Dionysius, viz. on Archilochus, Apollonius Rhodius, Aratus, Theocritus, Pisander, Nicander, Euphorion, Tyrtaeus, Callimachus, and Philetas.

(Pindar). Dionysius l. c. Ζηλωτὸς δὲ καὶ Πίνδαρος ὀνομάτων καὶ νοημάτων ἕνεκα καὶ μεγαλοπρεπείας καὶ τόνου καὶ περιουσίας καὶ κατασκευῆς καὶ δυνάμεως καὶ πικρίας μετὰ ἡδονῆς, καὶ πυκνότητος καὶ σεμνότητος καὶ γνωμολογίας καὶ ἐνεργείας καὶ σχηματισμῶν καὶ ἠθοποιΐας καὶ αὐξήσεως καὶ δεινώσεως· μάλιστα δὲ τῶν εἰς σωφροσύνην καὶ εὐσέβειαν καὶ μεγαλοπρέπειαν ἠθῶν. Quintilian 61. *novem lyricorum longe Pindarus princeps spiritus magnificentia, sententiis, figuris, beatissima rerum verborumque copia, et velut quodam eloquentiae flumine.*

(Simonides). Dionysius, p. 20. Σιμωνίδου δὲ παρατήρει τὴν ἐκλογὴν τῶν ὀνομάτων, τῆς συνθέσεως τὴν ἀκρίβειαν· πρὸς τούτοις, καθ' ὃ βελτίων εὑρίσκεται καὶ Πινδάρου, τὸ οἰκτίζεσθαι μὴ μεγαλοπρεπῶς, ἀλλὰ παθητικῶς. Quintilian 64. *Simonides tenuis alioqui sermone proprio et iucunditate quadam commendari potest : praecipua tamen eius in commovenda miseratione virtus, ut quidam in hac eum parte omnibus eius operis auctoribus praeferant.*

(Stesichorus). Dionysius l. c. ὅρα δὲ καὶ Στησίχορον ἔν τε τοῖς ἑκατέρου τῶν προειρημένων (Pindar and Simonides) πλεονεκτήμασι κατορθοῦντα, οὐ μὴν ἀλλὰ καὶ ὧν ἐκεῖνοι λείπονται κρατοῦντα· λέγω δὲ τῇ μεγαλοπρεπείᾳ τῶν κατὰ τὰς ὑποθέσεις πραγμάτων, ἐν οἷς τὰ ἤθη καὶ τὰ ἀξιώματα τῶν προσώπων τετήρηκε. Quintilian 62. *Stesichorus quam sit ingenio validus materiae quoque ostendunt, maxima bella et clarissimos canentem duces, et epici carminis onera lyra sustinentem. Reddit enim personis in agendo simul loquendoque debitam dignitatem, ac si tenuisset modum, videtur*

*aemulari Homerum potuisse; sed redundat atque effunditur,
quod ut est reprehendendum, ita copiae vitium est.*

(Alcaeus). Dionysius l. c. Ἀλκαίου δὲ σκόπει τὸ μεγαλοφυὲς
καὶ βραχύ, καὶ ἡδὺ μετὰ δεινότητος, ἔτι δὲ καὶ τοὺς σχηματισμούς, καὶ
τὴν σαφήνειαν, ὅσον αὐτῆς μὴ τῇ διαλέκτῳ τι κεκάκωται· καὶ πρὸ
ἁπάντων τὸ τῶν πολιτικῶν πραγμάτων ἦθος. Πολλαχοῦ γοῦν τὸ μέτρον
τις εἰ περιέλοι, ῥητορικὴν ἂν εὕροι πολιτείαν. Quintilian 63. *Alcaeus
in parte operis ‘aureo plectro’ merito donatur, quia tyrannos
insectatus multum etiam moribus confert; in eloquendo quoque
brevis et magnificus et diligens et plerumque oratori similis:
sed et lusit et in amores descendit, maioribus tamen aptior.*

In § 65 Quintilian proceeds to the old Comedy, about
which there is nothing in Dionysius as we now have him.
In the section on Aeschylus, Sophocles, and Euripides Dionysius (p. 21) and Quintilian (66–68) have nothing in common.
But it is curious that both should proceed from the Attic
tragedy to Menander (Quintilian 69–72).

Passing to the historians, Quintilian (73) merely condenses
what is said much better and more fully by Dionysius (p. 22).
Τὸ σύντομόν ἐστι παρὰ Θουκυδίδῃ ... Ἐν μέντοι τοῖς ἠθικοῖς κρατεῖ
Ἡρόδοτος, ἐν δὲ τοῖς παθητικοῖς ὁ Θουκυδίδης ... Ῥώμῃ δὲ καὶ ἰσχύϊ καὶ
τόνῳ καὶ τῷ περιττῷ καὶ πολυσχηματίστῳ παρηυδοκίμησε Θουκυδίδης·
ἡδονῇ δὲ καὶ πειθοῖ καὶ χάριτι ... μακρῷ διενεγκόντα τὸν Ἡρόδοτον
εὑρίσκομεν. *Densus et brevis et semper instans sibi Thucydides,
dulcis et candidus et fusus Herodotus: ille concitatis, hic remissis
affectibus melior, ille contionibus, hic sermonibus, ille vi, hic
voluptate.*

On Theopompus Quintilian (74) is very scanty, but what he
says is not in Dionysius.   On Philistus Quintilian gives a very
little of what Dionysius says (p. 24).   Ephorus, Clitarchus, and
Timagenes (Quintilian 74, 75) are omitted by Dionysius. Xenophon is counted among the historians by Dionysius (p. 23),
among the philosophers by Quintilian (82)[1].   There is a general

---

[1] Usener shows (p. 113) that this view was an old one.   Xenophon is
spoken of as a philosopher by Cicero (*De Orat.* 2 § 58), Diogenes Laertius
ii. 48, and Dio Chrysostom, all probably from an ancient authority.

agreement in the criticism, Dionysius being much the fuller :
Dionysius's words καθαρὸς τοῖς ὀνόμασι καὶ σαφὴς καὶ ἐναργής, καὶ
κατὰ τὴν σύνθεσιν ἡδὺς καὶ εὔχαρις are faintly represented by
Quintilian's *iucunditatem inadfectatam, sed quam consequi nulla
adfectatio possit.*

In speaking of the philosophers it is to be noticed that both
Dionysius (p. 26) and Quintilian (81) put Plato and Xenophon
before Aristotle.   About Aristotle Dionysius says παραληπτέον
δὲ καὶ 'Αριστοτέλη εἰς μίμησιν τῆς τε περὶ τὴν ἑρμηνείαν δεινότητος καὶ
τῆς σαφηνείας, καὶ τοῦ ἡδέος καὶ πολυμαθοῦς· τοῦτο γάρ ἐστι μάλιστα
παρὰ τοῦ ἀνδρὸς λαβεῖν.   So Quintilian (83) *quid Aristotelem ? quem
dubito scientia rerum an scriptorum copia an eloquendi suavitate
an inventionum acumine an varietate operum clariorem putem.*

The following sections in Quintilian (83–84), on Theophrastus and the Stoics, have nothing corresponding to them
in Dionysius.   Nor can it be said that in their remarks upon
the orators Demosthenes, Aeschines, and Hyperides (Quintilian 76–7) there is much notable coincidence between the two
critics.

The general conclusion seems to be that for much of his
criticism on the Greek poets, historians, and philosophers
(if not for that on the orators), Quintilian is indebted to
Theophrastus and later writers, as Aristophanes and Aristarchus [1].   It is not, therefore, much to the point to inquire
how far he had studied or even read the authors upon whom
he passes judgement.   Doubtless he was familiar with his
Homer, his tragedians, his Menander ; he had probably
read Thucydides, Herodotus, and Xenophon ; but it would

---

[1] Usener, on a comparison of the criticisms in Cicero (especially the
Hortensius), Dionysius, Quintilian, and Dio Cassius, sums up his conclusion
thus : *Iudicia de poetis scriptoribusque Graecis non a Dionysio Quintilianus
mutuatus est. Igitur ne Dionysius quidem sua profert, sed diversum uterque
exemplum iudiciorum ut plerumque consonantium expressit. Fontis utrique
communis antiquitatem Hortensius Tullianus cum Dione comparatus
demonstravit. Posteriore tempore cum eruditionis copia in angustae memoriae
paupertatem sensim contraheretur, iudiciis neglectis sola electorum auctorum
nomina relicta sunt, et laterculi formam induerunt.* (p. 132.)

be rash to credit him with a wide knowledge of Greek literature. When speaking of the less known authors he sometimes
avowedly quotes the judgements of others ; sometimes he lets
the reader clearly perceive that he is talking at second-hand.
This carelessness and indolent repetition of scholastic conventionalities is a great blot upon his work.

We must, however, do him the justice of supposing that
his criticisms of the masters of Latin literature (§§ 85 *foll.*)
are, on the whole, independent. Let me endeavour briefly to
sum up the chief points in them which seem to require attention.

(1) They are vitiated throughout by the idea of making
canons of classical Latin authors to correspond as closely
as possible with the Greek canons. Vergil leads the van
among the poets as the Latin Homer ; Macer and Lucretius
follow as representing Hesiod and the didactic poets. The
elegiac poets, Propertius and Tibullus, follow next, answering
to Tyrtaeus ; then the satirists, who of course have no
Greek counterparts ; then the writers of lampoon, Catullus,
Bibaculus, and Horace, to match Archilochus ; the lyric poets,
Horace corresponding to Pindar ; the dramatist, comic and
tragic, among whom Varius is singled out as equal to any
of the Greeks : the historians, Sallust being matched with
Thucydides and Livy with Herodotus ; the orators, Cicero
being of course compared in detail with Demosthenes ; and
the philosophers, among whom we are told that Cicero is
aemulus Platonis. It is needless to point out the weakness
of this criticism, nor, after what has been already said, is
there any difficulty in explaining its *genesis.* It is much more
important to ask what is its positive value, what idea it gives
us of Quintilian's literary insight.

(2) It will be observed, first, that Quintilian is a Ciceronian, and that he is so both as against the younger school of his
own day and as against the pre-Ciceronian literature. Ennius
he sets aside with a few respectful words (88) : Pacuvius and
Accius, one must almost suppose, he had never read : *virium
tamen Accio plus tribuitur, Pacuvium videri doctiorem, qui esse*

docti adfectant, volunt (97). If he had read them, then, he did
not think it worth his while to pass an independent judgement
upon them. The comedians, Plautus, Caecilius, and Terence,
he will hardly notice ; so far, he thinks, do they fall below their
Greek originals. Lucretius he totally misconceives, even
granting his point of view, for can it be said that there are no
fine passages of rhetoric in the *De Rerum Natura*? The
criticisms on the post-Ciceronian writers are for the most part
(remembering always that Quintilian is thinking of the needs of
an orator) sound and well expressed, notably that upon Ovid.
*nimium amator ingenii sui : si imperare ingenio suo quam in-
dulgere maluisset* (98). But they are mostly too short, and leave
the impression that the writer is anxious to get to the end of
them. In speaking of Cicero, however, Quintilian rises to the
height of real enthusiasm, and has left a passage (105–112)
which deserves to be quoted entire, as perhaps the most
typical instance of what his thoughtfulness and insight can
attain to :

*Oratores vero vel praecipue Latinam eloquentiam parem facere
Graecae possunt. Nam Ciceronem cuicunque eorum fortiter
opposuerim. Nec ignoro quantam mihi concitem pugnam, cum
praesertim non id sit propositi, ut eum Demostheni comparem
hoc tempore ; neque enim attinet, cum Demosthenem in primis
legendum vel ediscendum potius putem. Quorum ego virtutes
plerasque arbitror similes, consilium, ordinem, dividendi, prae-
parandi, probandi rationem, omnia denique quae sunt inventionis.
In eloquendo est aliqua diversitas ; densior ille, hic copiosior, ille
concludit astrictius, hic latius, pugnat ille acumine semper, hic
frequenter et pondere, illi nihil detrahi potest, huic nihil adici,
curae plus in illo, in hoc naturae. Salibus certe et commisera-
tione, quae duo plurimum in adfectibus valent, vincimus. Et
fortasse epilogos illi mos civitatis abstulerit ; sed et nobis illa,
quae Attici mirantur, diversa Latini sermonis ratio minus per-
miserit. . . . Cedendum vero in hoc, quod et prior fuit, et ex magna
parte Ciceronem, quantus est, fecit. Nam mihi videtur M.
Tullius, cum se totum ad imitationem Graecorum contulisset,*

effinxisse vim Demosthenis, copiam Platonis, iucunditatem Iso-
cratis.   Nec vero quod in quoque optimum fuit studio consecutus
est tantum, sed plurimas vel potius omnes ex se virtutes extulit
immortalis ingenii beatissima ubertas.   Non enim 'pluvias,' ut
ait Pindarus, 'aquas colligit, sed vivo gurgite exundat,' dono quo-
dam providentiae genitus in quo totas vires suas eloquentia
experiretur.   Nam quis docere diligentius, movere vehementius
potest ?   Cui tanta umquam iucunditas affuit ? ut ipsa illa quae
extorquet impetrare eum credas, et cum transversum vi sua iudi-
cem ferat, tamen ille non rapi videatur sed sequi.   Iam in omnibus
quae dicit tanta auctoritas inest ut dissentire pudeat, nec advocati
studium, sed testis aut iudicis adferat fidem ; cum interim haec
omnia, quae vix singula quisquam intentissima cura consequi
posset, fluunt inlaborata, et illa, qua nihil pulchrius auditum est,
oratio prae se fert tamen felicissimam facilitatem.   Quare non
immerito ab omnibus aetatis suae regnare in iudiciis dictus est,
apud posteros vero id consecutus, ut Cicero iam non hominis
nomen sed eloquentiae habeatur.   Hunc igitur spectemus, hoc
propositum nobis sit exemplum, ille profecisse se sciat cui Cicero
valde placebit.

This refined and carefully written criticism, in which hardly
a word could be missed, may (granting the writer's point of
view) be regarded as a classical monument of what educated
insight, with manly and sober sense to support it, can effect.
But genius is absent from the passage, as indeed from every
word that Quintilian wrote.   For that we must go to a far
greater than Quintilian, one who was probably his pupil, and
whose critical *dicta*, in form much resembling those of Quintilian,
breathe a very different spirit, the author of the *Dialogus de
Oratoribus.*

Quintilian, writing for his pupils, takes the line natural for
a man who stood in his day at the head of the educational
profession.   His main question, put into modern language, is
' What is the best reading on which to form a good oratorical
style ? '   Tacitus is not so directly concerned with the literary
and professional aspects of the question.   He penetrates to the

heart of his subject, and asks under what social conditions do great writing and great speaking arise? seeing clearly (and this is the important point which characterizes the treatise) that literature must be taken and judged as the expression of national life, not as a matter of form and of scholastic teaching.

The first fifteen chapters of the *Dialogus* contain a discussion on the comparative advantages offered respectively by the life of the active lawyer and that of the poet. We are here concerned not with these, but with the remainder of the dialogue, in which Aper and Messalla defend respectively the modern and the older style of Latin eloquence.

Aper takes very much the same line as is suggested by Eumolpus in Petronius. He limits the field to a comparison between the orators of the Ciceronian age and those of his own, excluding the consideration of Cato and the Gracchi. In a vivid and lucid statement he lays down the principle that literary style changes with the times; that this has always been the case; that Cato improved upon Appius Claudius, Gracchus on Cato, Crassus on Gracchus, Cicero on Crassus. *Non esse unum eloquentiae vultum, sed in illis quoque quos vocatis antiquos plures species deprehendi, nec statim deterius esse quod diversum est*[1]. The orator who gave the impulse in the modern direction was Cassius Severus, and he did so deliberately; *non infirmitate ingenii nec inscitia litterarum transtulisse se ad aliud dicendi genus contendo, sed iudicio et intellectu. Vidit namque, ut paulo ante dicebam, cum condicione temporum et diversitate aurium formam quoque ac speciem orationis esse mutandam.* The present age cannot put up with the lengthiness and tediousness of the Ciceronians. It requires rapid and brilliant embodiment of thought; the orator must aim at the beauty of poetry, must form himself on Horace, Vergil, and Lucan. One great merit of Cicero was that his sense and taste were far in advance of contemporary opinion (*nec ulla re magis oratores aetatis eiusdem praecurrit quam iudicio*)[2]. He was the first orator who developed style in its perfection.

[1] C. 18.   [2] C. 22.

You may find memorable sayings in Cicero, at least in the later speeches composed in his old age ; his earlier orations give you nothing to carry away (*nihil excerpere, nihil referre possis*).   To sum up in Aper's own words : *Ego autem oratorem, sicut locupletem et lautum patrem familiae, non eo tantum volo tecto tegi quod imbrem ac ventum arceat, sed etiam quod visum et oculos delectet ; non ea solum instrui supellectile quae necessariis usibus sufficiat, sed sit in apparatu eius et aurum et gemmae, ut sumere in manus et aspicere saepius libeat.   Quaedam vero procul arceantur ut iam oblitterata et* [*olentia*] ; *nullum sit verbum velut rubigine infectum, nulli sensus tarda et inerti structura in morem annalium componantur, fugitet foedam et insulsam scurrilitatem, variet compositionem, nec omnes clausulas uno et eodem modo determinet.*

The reply of Messalla on behalf of the Ciceronian orators is opened by the statement that, different as they are, Cicero, Calvus, Asinius Pollio, Caelius, the sane complexion of their style is the same ; *omnes eandem sanitatem prae se ferunt.* Their intention, their spirit, is akin.   The modern manner, with its prettiness and wanton tricks, is the manner of the decadence.   The cause of the decline is a moral one.   The education of children has passed from the hands of the parents into those of Greek nurses and slaves, none of whom pauses to think what should or should not be said in the presence of a child.   Again, while the youths of the Ciceronian age (to take the instance of Cicero himself) were brought into personal contact with the great masters of philosophy, oratory, and law, as Philo, Antonius, and Mucius Scaevola, boys are now sent to the professional rhetoricians to be taught to declaim, i. e. to practise speaking on fictitious themes—*fictis nec ullo modo ad veritatem accedentibus controversiis*[1].   *Apud maiores nostros iuvenis ille qui foro et eloquentiae parabatur, imbutus iam domestica disciplina, refertus honestis studiis, deducebatur a patre vel a propinquis ad eum oratorem qui principem in civitate locum*

---

[1]   C. 31.   The same complaint, as to the unreality of these *declamationes,* is to be found in Petronius, c. 1.

obtinebat. Hunc sectari, hunc prosequi, huius omnibus dictioni-
bus interesse sive in iudiciis sive in contionibus assuescebat, ita ut
altercationes quoque exciperet et iurgiis interesset, utque sic
dixerim, pugnare in proelio disceret[1]. But what is the result of
the modern training ? Forgetting that great speaking is rooted
in wide knowledge and many accomplishments, the young
speakers of to-day make bad blunders even in common expressions, know nothing of *leges* or *senatus consulta*, laugh at the
civil law, and are terrified at the notion of studying philosophy.
In paucissimos sensus et angustas sententias detrudunt elo-
quentiam velut expulsam regno suo, ut quae olim omnium artium
domina pulcherrimo comitatu pectora implebat, nunc circumcisa
et amputata, sine apparatu, sine honore, paene dixerim sine
ingenuitate, quasi una ex sordidissimis artificiis discatur. Ego
hanc primam et praecipuam causam arbitror esse cur in tantum
ab eloquentia antiquorum oratorum recesserimus[2].

In the rhetorical schools[3] it is difficult to say whether more
harm is done by the place or the companionship or the style of
teaching. *Nam in loco nihil reverentiae, scilicet in quem nemo*
nisi aeque imperitus intret ; in condiscipulis nihil profectus, cum
pueri inter pueros et adulescentuli inter adulescentulos pari
securitate et dicant et audiantur ; ipsae vero exercitationes magna
ex parte contrariae. The *suasoriae* are given to boys, the *con-*
troversiae to youths : *quales per fidem et quam incredibiliter*
compositae ! Sequitur autem ut materiae abhorrenti a veritate
declamatio quoque adhibeatur. Sic fit ut tyrannicidarum prae-
mia aut vitiatorum electiones aut pestilentiae remedia aut incesta
matrum, aut quicquid in schola quotidie agitur, in foro raro vel
nunquam, ingentibus verbis persequantur. But a great style,
like a fire, requires fuel to sustain it, motion to arouse it, activity
to strengthen it (*magna eloquentia, sicut flamma, materia alitur et*
motibus excitatur et urendo calescit). The force of genius, the
brilliancy of style, depends upon the adequacy of the subject
dealt with ; *crescit enim amplitudine rerum vis ingenii, nec quis-*
quam claram et illustrem orationem efficere potest nisi qui causam

[1] C. 34.   [2] C. 32.   [3] C. 35.

parem invenit. No doubt, he goes on to say, the Roman republic paid its price for its great eloquence. *Est magna illa et notabilis eloquentia,* he says in a vein worthy of Carlyle, *alumna licentiae, quam stulti libertatem vocant, comes seditionum, effrenati populi incitamentum . . . contumax, temeraria, arrogans, quae in bene constitutis civitatibus non oritur. . . Nec tanti rei publicae Gracchorum eloquentia fuit ut pateretur et leges, nec bene famam eloquentiae Cicero tali exitu pensavit* [1].

Striking and beautiful as this criticism is, it must be observed (1) that no answer is given to the objections brought by Aper to the style of the republican oratory as unsuited to the new conditions of things ; and (2) that the speaker falls into a singular inconsistency when he first lays down the principle that a great style is born of great events and great surroundings, and then proceeds to condemn those very events and surroundings as leading to the ruin of republics. This inconsistency is not removed by the fact that he makes a moral and healthy education the first element in the production of a great speaker. For it is an essential condition of this training, as he himself emphatically states, that the young man should be constantly hearing eminent orators and witnessing the real conflicts of the forum ; and the eminent orators cannot exist without these conflicts, which on his own showing are destructive of healthy public life. Tacitus (for we can hardly doubt that Messalla represents the views of Tacitus) is looking one way and rowing the other. He speaks or appears to speak with bitter regret of a time which he nevertheless describes as disastrous. He ought surely to have gone on to condemn eloquence altogether, or at any rate to limit it strictly to the field of forensic business.

But these observations need not preclude us from awarding to the *Dialogus de Oratoribus* the palm among the pieces of literary criticism which have come down to us from Latin antiquity. The only work which can be compared with it is the *Brutus* of Cicero. But this falls behind Tacitus's book, not merely because Cicero wrote it in a hurry and with some

---

[1] C. 40.

consequent loss to completeness and literary form, but also
because a century of eventful history has given Tacitus a wide
experience and a deeper knowledge of the relation between
literature and life. Cicero had witnessed no organic change
in the constitution of Rome. The progress which he records
is gradual, merely an advance from comparative rudeness to
comparative polish; and the change is only a literary change,
not determined by any great alteration in the complexion of
society or politics. But in Tacitus's time the substitution of
monarchy for republic had divided literature into republican
and imperial, Ciceronian and non-Ciceronian. Some at least
of the factors which go to produce social and literary mutation
have not escaped his notice. The most important of these is
the degeneracy of theme. The writer or speaker whose surroundings suggest great subjects, subjects likely to draw out
the full moral and intellectual powers of the man, will speak in
the grand manner; but an ignoble national life will produce
ignoble art.

Fronto, the tutor of Marcus Aurelius, is little more, so far as
literary criticism goes, than an unimpeachable and intelligent
professor. He is an antiquarian; in other words, he goes back
to the literature of the third and second centuries B.C., and does
not care to bring his reading down later than Cicero. His
utterances do not go beyond neatly formulated criticisms of the
old scholastic type. One or two instances will suffice. *Ad
Verum* I. I. (p. 113 Naber); *Quid si quis postularet ut Phidias
ludicra aut Canachus deum simulacra fingeret? aut Calamis
Turrena aut Polycletus Etrusca? Quid si Parrhasium ver-
sicolora pingere iuberet, aut Apellen unicolora, aut Nealcen
magnifica, aut Nician obscura, aut Dionysium inlustria, aut
lasciva Euphranorem, aut Pausiam proelia? In poetis autem
quis ignorat ut gracilis sit Lucilius, Albucius aridus, mediocris
Pacuvius, inaequalis Accius, Ennius multiformis? Historiam
quoque scripsere Sallustius structe, Pictor incondite, Claudius
lepide, Antias invenuste, Sisenna longinque, verbis Cato mul-
tiiugis, Coelius singulis. Contionatur autem Cato infeste,*

Gracchus turbulente, Tullius copiose.   Iam in iudiciis saevit idem Cato, triumphat Cicero, tumultuatur Gracchus, Calvus rixatur   Or again (*De Feriis Alsiensibus*, 3. p. 224 N.) *mox, ut te studium legendi incessisset, aut te Plauto expolires, aut Accio expleres, aut Lucretio delenires, aut Ennio incenderes.*

Thus in the person of Fronto does Roman literature look back, wistfully but ineffectually, to the original sources of its inspiration.   The story is now ended ; the creative force which had successively produced the styles of Cicero, Sallust, Livy, and Tacitus is exhausted ; and with the death of style comes the death of criticism.   The short survey which I have attempted in these two essays will have shown, I hope, that, for bad or good, the literary criticism of the Romans has had its say in the history of European literature.   For bad, in that their scholastic tradition set on foot the habit of mechanical comparison between the classical writers of different ages and countries ; for good, in that principles of criticism, new and true, and full of suggestion for the future, were struck out in the course of a great history, finding worthy spokesmen in Rome's two greatest men of letters, Cicero and Tacitus.

IV.

THE HISTORICAL DEVELOPMENT OF
CLASSICAL LATIN PROSE.

('JOURNAL OF PHILOLOGY,' VOL. XV (1886 .)

WERE any one asked who in his opinion were the main
representatives of Latin Prose style, there can I suppose be
little doubt that he would mention Cicero, Livy, and Tacitus.
These three names, in fact, mark three definite stages in the
development of classical Latin Prose. To speak more accu-
rately, there are two stages, each of which marks the extreme
point of a line of tendency. These stages are represented
respectively by the styles of Cicero and of Tacitus, between
whom Livy, who has a manner peculiar to himself, occupies
the middle place.

The elements of a good style are two, luminousness and
beauty. By luminousness I mean its power of representing
thought and passion. To express thought it must be lucid, to
represent thought and passion it must be simple and strong.
By beauty I mean such a choice of words, and such an arrangement of them, as satisfies the requirements of the ear.

In a masterly style these two elements are combined in
a manner which is felt to defy dissection, and to require none.
The impression produced is one and indivisible, and we do
not care to analyze it. Such a passage as the conclusion of
Cicero's second Philippic speaks home to us with a living

impression of unity and directness which we acknowledge without question. We admire and ask for nothing more[1].

But Rome was not built, nor the Latin prose of Cicero formed, in a day. It is possible to trace with tolerable clearness the course of literary development of which it is the climax, and to observe the laborious process by which, from writer to writer, the combination of luminousness with beauty was gradually perfected.

Isidore 1. 38. 2 preserves a tradition, which probably comes from Varro, that the first Latin prose was written by Appius Claudius Caecus. *Tam apud Graecos quam apud Latinos longe antiquiorem curam fuisse carminum* (supply probably *Varro ait) quam prosae. Omnia enim prius versibus condebantur, prosae autem studium sero viguit. Primus apud Graecos Pherecydes Syrus soluta oratione scripsit. Apud Romanos autem Appius Caecus adversus Pyrrhum solutam orationem primus exercuit. Iam ex hinc et ceteri pro se eloquentiam condiderunt.*

This notice probably represents the accepted literary tradition of Rome; and whatever truth there may be in it, it is quite clear that for the purposes of oratory Latin prose composition must have been in existence before the Punic wars. We have Cicero's express testimony to the existence of *mortuorum laudationes* in rude prose[2]. In an ancient city community like that of Rome—a community in which the people

---

[1] § 118. *Resipisce, quaeso, aliquando rem publicam, M. Antoni; quibus ortus sis, non quibuscum vivas, considera. Mecum, ut voles; redi cum re publica in gratiam. Sed de te tu ipso videris; ego de me ipse profitebor. Defendi rem publicam adulescens, non deseram senex; contempsi Catilinae gladios, non pertimescam tuos. Quin etiam corpus libenter obtulerim, si repraesentari morte mea libertas civitatis potest, ut aliquando dolor populi Romani pariat quod iam diu parturit. Etenim si abhinc annos prope viginti hoc ipso in templo negavi posse mortem immaturam esse consulari, quanto verius nunc negabo seni? Mihi vero, patres conscripti, etiam optanda mors est, perfuncto rebus iis quas adeptus sum quasque gessi. Duo modo haec opto, unum ut moriens populum Romanum liberum relinquam, alterum ut ita cuique eveniat, ut de re publica quisque mereatur.*

[2] Brutus, § 61: *Nec vero habeo quemquam antiquiorem (Catone) cuius quidem scripta proferenda putem, nisi quem Appii Caeci oratio haec ipsa de Pyrrho et nonnullae mortuorum laudationes forte delectant.*

had to be persuaded—some kind of oratory must have arisen at a very early period.   We may however almost say of Latin prose as we may of Latin poetry, that in order to study it we must begin at the end.   The earliest specimens of Latin prose style which now survive are the fragments of the speeches and histories of the elder Cato (for the *Res Rustica* as we have it is written in no style at all), and Cato, whose life extended from 234–149 B.C., or eighty-five years, comes at the end of what we may call the Italian period proper, and at the moment when the study of Greek literature was beginning to change the form of Latin composition.   Anti-Hellenist as he was, it is difficult to suppose that Cato altogether escaped the influence of the new fashion, and in his old age it is known that he took to the study of Demosthenes and (to a certain extent) to that of Thucydides.   Let us take some specimens of Cato's oratory from the few fragments which survive.

Meyer, Fragmenta Oratorum Romanorum, p. 41[1]. *Tuum nefarium facinus peiore facinore operiri postulas, succidias humanas facis, tantas trucidationes facis, decem capita libera interficis, decem hominibus vitam eripis, indicta causa, iniudicatis, incondemnatis.*

Ib. p. 43. *Dixit a decemviris parum sibi bene cibaria curata esse.   Iussit vestimenta detrahi, atque flagro caedi.   Decemviros Bruttiani verberavere: videre multi mortales.   Quis hanc contumeliam, quis hoc imperium, quis hanc servitutem ferre potest?   Nemo hoc rex ausus est facere: eane fieri bonis, bono genere gnatis, boni consulitis?   Ubi societas, ubi fides maiorum?   Insignitas iniurias, plagas, verbera, vibices, eos dolores atque carnificinas per dedecus atque maximam contumeliam, inspectantibus popularibus suis atque multis mortalibus, te facere ausum esse?   Sed quantum luctum quantumque gemitum, quid lacrimarum quantumque fletum factum audivi!   Servi iniurias nimis aegre ferunt.   Quid illos, bono genere gnatos, magna virtute praeditos, opinamini animi habuisse atque habituros, dum vivent?*

---

[1] [Editio auctior, Turici 1842: Mr. Nettleship does not follow Meyer's text absolutely.]

The following fragment is from the *Oratio pro Rhodiensibus* (Meyer, p. 104).

Scio solere plerisque hominibus rebus secundis atque prolixis atque prosperis animum excellere, superbiam atque ferociam augescere atque crescere. Quod mihi nunc magnae curae est, quod haec res tam secunde processit, ne quid in consulendo adversi eveniat, quod nostras secundas res confutet, neve haec laetitia nimis luxuriose eveniat. Adversae res edomant, et docent quid opus sit facto. Secundae res laetitia transversum trudere solent a recte consulendo atque intellegendo. Quo maiore opere dico suadeoque, uti haec res aliquot dies proferatur, dum ex tanto gaudio in potestatem nostram redeamus.

Atque ego quidem arbitror, Rhodienses noluisse nos ita depugnare, uti depugnatum est, neque regem Persen vicisse. Non Rhodienses modo id noluere, sed multos populos atque multas nationes idem noluisse arbitror. Atque haud scio an partim eorum fuerint, qui non nostrae contumeliae causa id noluerint evenire: sed enim id metuere, si nemo esset homo, quem vereremur, quodque luberet faceremus, ne sub solo imperio nostro in servitute nostra essent: libertatis suae causa in ea sententia fuisse arbitror. Atque Rhodienses tamen Persen publice numquam adiuvere. Cogitate, quanto nos inter nos privatim cautius facimus. Nam unus quisque nostrum, si quis advorsus rem suam quid fieri arbitratur, summa vi contra nititur ne advorsus eam fiat: quod illi tamen perpessi.

Ea nunc derepente tanta nos beneficia ultro citroque tantamque amicitiam relinquemus? Quod illos dicimus voluisse facere, id nos priores facere occupabimus?

Qui acerrime advorsus eos dicit, ita dicit, hostes voluisse fieri. Ecquis est tandem vostrum qui, quod ad sese attineat, aequom censeat poenas dare ob eam rem quod arguatur male facere voluisse? Nemo, opinor: nam ego, quod ad me attinet, nolim.

The next is from the *Origines*, book 4 p. 19, Jordan):

Di immortales tribuno militum fortunam ex virtute eius dedere. Nam ita evenit, cum saucius multifariam ibi factus esset, tamen vulnus capiti nullum evenit, eumque inter mortuos

defatigatum vulneribus atque quod sanguen eis defluxerat cogno-
vere, eum sustulere, isque convaluit, saepeque postilla operam
rei publicae fortem atque strenuam praehibuit, illoque facto, quod
illos milites subduxit, exercitum servavit. Sed idem benefactum
quo in loco ponas nimium interest. Leonides Laco, qui simile
apud Thermopylas fecit, propter eius virtutes omnis Graecia
gloriam atque gratiam praecipuam claritudinis inclutissumae
decoravere monumentis, signis statuis elogiis historiis aliisque
rebus: gratissimum id eius factum habuere. At tribuno militum
parva laus pro factis relicta, qui idem fecerat atque rem serva-
verat.

Ea omnia, as Gellius [1] says of the speech *pro Rhodiensibus,*
distinctius numerosiusque fortassean dici potuerunt, fortius atque
vividius potuisse dici non videntur. The style is clear and
forcible, it is therefore luminous : but harmony, and therefore
beauty, it has none. The sentences follow the thoughts,
without any idea of rhythm to modify them ; *succidias humanas*
facis, tantas trucidationes facis, decem funera facis, decem capita
libera interficis. There are but few connecting particles, those
employed being of the simplest kind, such as relatives, condi-
tionals, or adversatives. Verbs are constantly placed in the
same position at the end of the sentence, without any attempt
to vary the sound : *excellere, augescere, crescere : processerit,—*
eveniat,—confutet,—eveniat: proferatur,—redeamus. The order
of the words is sometimes entirely without art ; *secundae res*
trudere solent a recte consulendo atque intellegendo. The same
idea is reiterated by the use of words almost synonymous ;
rebus secundis atque prosperis atque prolixis: superbiam atque
ferociam: multos populos atque multas nationes. Words are
repeated for emphasis and distinctness, to the destruction of
true rhetorical effect ; *adversae res, secundae res : depugnare uti*
depugnatum est: adversus rem suam,—adversus eam: dicit,—
ita dicit. In the same careless spirit Cato (in the *pro Rhodien-*
sibus) begins three consecutive sentences with *atque.*

Very much the same characteristics meet us in the fragments

[1] 6 (7). 3. 52.

of the historian Cassius Hemina, whose *floruit* is assigned to
B.C. 146 or thereabouts.

Fragm. ap. Peter H. R. Rell. p. 98 *Pastorum volgus sine
contentione consentiendo praefecerunt aequaliter imperio Remum
et Romulum, ita ut de regno pararent inter se. Monstrum fit:
sus parit porcos triginta: cuius rei fanum fecerunt Laribus Grun-
dulibus.* Ib. p. 107 *Mirabantur alii, quomodo illi libri durare
possent. Ille ita rationem reddebat: lapidem fuisse, quadratum
circiter in media arca evinctum candelis quoquo versus. In eo
lapide insuper libros insitos fuisse: propterea arbitrarier, non com-
putuisse. Et libros citratos fuisse: propterea arbitrarier, tineas non
tetigisse. In iis libris scripta erant philosophiae Pythagoricae.*

Of the speeches of Metellus Macedonicus, who was praetor
148 and consul 143 B.C. we have the following fragments (*de
ducendis uxoribus*, Meyer p. 161); the first of which reflects what
was evidently the current style of the time :

*Di immortales plurimum possunt, sed non plus velle debent
nobis quam parentes. At parentes, si pergunt liberi errare, bonis
exheredant. Quid ergo nos a dis immortalibus diutius expectemus,
nisi malis rationibus finem faciamus? His demum deos propitios
esse aequum est, qui sibi adversarii non sunt. Di immortales
virtutem approbare, non adhibere debent.*

There is more structure in the following :

*Si sine uxore esse possemus, Quirites, omnes ea molestia care-
remus: sed quoniam natura ita tradidit, ut nec cum illis satis
commode, nec sine illis omnino vivi possit, saluti perpetuae potius
quam brevi voluptati consulendum.*

After the death of Cato the stream of Greek influence flowed
stronger and ever stronger into the channel of Italian thought
until the end of the Ciceronian age.   In the few fragments of
the speeches of Scipio Aemilianus (184–129 B.C.) and C. Laelius
(consul 140) it is, I think, possible to trace an attempt to realise
a more artistic manner of expression. Take the following from
Scipio (Meyer p. 184) :

*Omnia mala, probra, flagitia, quae homines faciunt, in duabus
rebus sunt, malitia atque nequitia.   Utrum defendis malitiam,*

an nequitiam, an utrumque simul? Si nequitiam defendere vis,
licet. Sed tu in uno scorto maiorem pecuniam absumpsisti quam
quanti omne instrumentum fundi Sabini in censum dedicavisti.
Si hoc ita est, quis spondet mille nummum? Sed tu plus tertia
parte pecuniae paternae perdidisti atqui absumpsisti in flagitiis.
Si hoc ita est, quis spondet mille nummum? Non vis nequitiam.
Age, malitiam saltem defendas. Sed tu verbis conceptis coniuravisti
sciens sciente animo tuo. Si hoc ita est, quis spondet mille nummum?

Meyer p. 192. *Docentur praestigias inhonestas : cum cinae-*
dulis et sambucis psalterioque eunt in ludum histrionum. Discunt
cantare quae maiores nostri ingenuis probro ducier voluerunt.
Eunt, inquam, in ludum saltatorium inter cinaedos virgines
puerique ingenui. Haec mihi cum quispiam narrabat, non
poteram animum inducere ea liberos suos homines nobiles docere.
Sed cum ductus sum in ludum saltatorium, plus medius fidius in
eo ludo vidi pueris virginibusque quingentis : in his unum, quod
me rei publicae maxime miseritum est, puerum bullatum, petitoris
filium, non[1] *minorem annis duodecim, cum crotalis saltare, quam*
saltationem impudicus servulus honeste saltare non posset.

In the first of these fragments, and to a certain extent in the
second, we may observe the same simplicity of order, the same
tendency to repetition, as in Cato : but there is in the second
a great advance towards appreciation of rhythmical effect.

Isidore (2. 21. 3–5) has preserved the following examples of
climax from Scipio Aemilianus :

Ex innocentia nascitur dignitas, ex dignitate honor, ex honore
imperium, ex imperio libertas.

Vi atque ingratiis coactus cum illo sponsionem feci, facta spon-
sione ad iudicem adduxi, adductum primo coetu damnavi, dam-
natum ex voluntate dimisi.

The fragments of the orations of Gaius Gracchus (B.C. 154—
121), besides the genius and intensity which raised him, in the
opinion of Cicero, to the very highest position among Roman
orators, show also an advancing sensibility to the requirements
of harmonious composition.

---

[1] Surely *non* should be omitted.

Meyer p. 231. *Versatus sum in provincia, quomodo ex usu vestro existimabam esse, non quomodo ambitioni meae conducere arbitrabar. Nulla apud me fuit popina, neque pueri eximia facie stabant et in convivio liberi vestri modestius erant quam apud principia. . . Ita versatus sum in provincia, ut nemo posset vere dicere assem aut eo plus in muneribus me accepisse, aut mea opera quemquam sumptum fecisse. Biennium fui in provincia. Si ulla meretrix domum meam introivit, aut cuiusquam servulus propter me sollicitatus est, omnium† nationum †[2] postremissimum nequissimumque existimatote. Cum a servis eorum tam caste me habuerim, inde poteritis considerare, quomodo me putetis cum liberis vestris vixisse. . . Itaque, Quirites, cum Romam profectus sum, zonas, quas plenas argenti extuli, eas ex provincia inanes rettuli. Alii vini amphoras, quas plenas tulerunt, eas argento repletas domum reportaverunt.*

Meyer p. 234. In the following fragment there is considerable elaboration of structure, and an almost musical cadence:

Si vellem apud vos verba facere et a vobis postulare, cum genere summo ortus essem, et cum fratrem propter vos amisissem, nec quisquam de P. Africani et Ti. Gracchi familia nisi ego et puer restaremus, ut pateremini hoc tempore me quiescere, ne a stirpe genus nostrum interiret, et uti aliqua propago generis nostri reliqua esset; haud scio an lubentibus a vobis impetrassem.

In narrative Gracchus had a rapid but somewhat rude and unconnected manner:

Meyer p. 236. *Nuper Teanum Sidicinum consul venit: uxor eius dixit se in balneis virilibus lavari velle. Quaestori Sidicino a M. Mario datum est negotium, uti balneis exigerentur qui lavabantur. Uxor renuntiat viro, parum cito balneas traditas esse et parum lautas fuisse. Idcirco palus destitutus est in foro, eoque adductus suae civitatis nobilissimus homo M. Marius. Vestimenta detracta sunt; virgis caesus est. Caleni ubi id audierunt, edixerunt nequis in balneis lavisse vellet, cum magistratus Romanus ibi esset. Ferentini ob eandem causam praetor noster*

---

[1] For *nationum, hominum natorum* and *latronum* have been proposed. I have conjectured *raponum* (*Essays in Latin literature,* p. 345).

quaestores arripi iussit: alter se de muro deiecit, alter virgis caesus est. . .

Quanta libido quantique intemperantia sit hominum adulescentium, unum exemplum [1] *vobis ostendam. His annis paucis ex Asia missus est, qui per id tempus magistratum non ceperat, homo adulescens pro legato. Is in lectica ferebatur. Ei obviam bubulcus de plebe Venusina venit, et per iocum, cum ignoraret qui ferretur, rogavit num mortuum ferrent. Ubi id audivit, lecticam iussit deponi, struppis, quibus lectica deligata erat, usque adeo verberari iussit, dum animam efflavit.*

Rude as these passages are as a whole, they have clauses in them of true rhythmical beauty. *Idcirco palus destitutus est in foro, eoque adductus civitatis suae nobilissimus homo M. Marius. His annis paucis ex Asia missus est, qui per id tempus magistratum non ceperat, homo adulescens pro legato. Is in lectica ferebatur. Ei obviam bubulcus de plebe Venusina venit, et per iocum, cum ignoraret qui ferretur, rogavit num mortuum ferrent.*

From this time the style of Latin prose becomes manifestly more formed and artistic. We may note the progress in the following fragments of Quintus Metellus Numidicus (consul 109 B.C.).

Meyer p. 274. *Nunc quod ad illum pertinet, Quirites, quoniam se ampliorem putat esse si se mihi inimicum dictitaverit, quem ego mihi neque amicum recipio neque inimicum respicio, in eum ego non sum plura dicturus. Nam cum indignissimum arbitror cui a viris bonis bene dicatur, tum ne idoneum quidem, cui a probis male dicatur. Nam si in eo tempore huiuscemodi homunculum nomines, in quo punire non possis, maiore honore quam contumelia adficias.*

Meyer p. 275. *Qua in re quanto universi me antestatis, tanto vobis quam mihi maiorem iniuriam atque contumeliam facit, Quirites, et quanto probi iniuriam facilius accipiunt quam alteri tradunt, tanto ille vobis quam mihi peiorem honorem habuit. Nam me iniuriam ferre, vos facere volt, Quirites, ut hic conquestio, istic vituperatio relinquatur.*

[1] *Uno exemplo?*

In the fragments of Lucius Licinius Crassus (140–91 B.C.), though a few archaisms still linger, a transition to the style of Cicero may be observed.

Meyer p. 310. '*Forte evenit ut in Privernati essemus.' Brute, testificatur pater, se tibi Privernatem fundum reliquisse. Deinde ex libro secundo ' In Albano eramus ego et Marcus filius.' Sapiens videlicet homo cum primis nostrae civitatis norat hunc gurgitem ; metuebat ne, cum is nihil haberet, nihil esse ei relictum putaretur.   Tum ex libro tertio ' In Tiburti forte adsedimus ego et Marcus filius.'   Ubi sunt ii fundi, Brute, quos tibi pater publicis commentariis consignatos reliquit ?   Quod nisi puberem te iam haberet, quartum librum composuisset, et se etiam in balneis locutum cum filio scriptum reliquisset. . .*

Brute, quid sedes ?   Quid illam anum patri nuntiare vis tuo ? quid illis omnibus, quorum imagines duci vides, quid maioribus tuis ?   Quid L. Bruto, qui hunc populum dominatu regio liberavit ?   quid te facere, cui rei, cui gloriae, cui virtuti studere ? Patrimonione augendo ?   At id non est nobilitatis.   Sed fac esse, nihil superest : libidines totum dissipaverunt.   An iuri civili ? Est paternum.   Sed dicet te, cum aedes venderes, ne in rutis quidem et caesis solium tibi paternum recepisse.   An rei militari ? qui nunquam castra videris ?   An eloquentiae, quae nulla est in te, et quicquid est vocis ac linguae, omne in istum turpissimum calumniae quaestum contulisti ?   Tu lucem aspicere audes, tu hos intueri ? tu in foro, tu in urbe, tu in civium esse conspectu ? tu illam mortuam, tu imagines ipsas non perhorrescis ? quibus non modo imitandis, sed ne conlocandis quidem tibi ullum locum reliquisti.

P. 313. *An tu, cum omnem auctoritatem universi ordinis pro pignore putaris, eamque in conspectu P.R. concideris, me his existimas pignoribus terreri ?   Non tibi sunt illa caedenda, si L. Crassum vis coercere : haec tibi est excidenda lingua, qua vel evulsa spiritu ipso libidinem tuam libertas mea refutabit.*

L. Licinius Crassus died in 91 B.C., and we are now, not only in the natural sequence of events, but in the progress from cause to effect, brought to consider the style of Cicero.   For, as we have seen, Crassus seems to have cultivated and brought to a considerable height of excellence the periodic manner of writing which the genius of Cicero perfected. Cicero says in the *Orator* (§ 223) that the clause which he most likes should consist of two κόμματα or short sentences, a κῶλον or longer sentence, and a *comprehensio* or concluding period. *Crassus*, he says, *sic plerumque dicebat, idque ipse genus dicendi maxime probo.* He adds an instance from Crassus ; *Domus tibi deerat? At habebas. Pecunia superabat? At egebas. . . Incurristi amens in columnas: in alienos insanus insanisti : depressam, caecam, iacentem domum pluris quam te et fortunas tuas aestimasti.* And below he adds (§ 226) *ego illa Crassi et nostra posui, ut qui vellet auribus ipsis quid numerosum etiam in minimis particulis orati nis esset iudicaret.*

Crassus was a great student of Greek, and according to Cicero could speak it with as much ease as his mother tongue [1]. So it was also with Antonius ; and it was by these two great orators that Cicero was educated in his youth. The attempt to write a periodic style was the result of the study of Greek prose, and in particular that of Isocrates and Theopompus, the mechanical structure of whose writing Cicero thinks the most serviceable as a model for study (*Orator*, § 207). From the first Cicero's style is characterised by the wide compass and elaborate balance of his paragraphs. Take, for instance, the first sentences of his earliest work (*Inv.* I. 1). *Saepe et multum hoc mecum cogitavi, bonine an mali plus attulerit hominibus et civitatibus copia dicendi ac summum eloquentiae studium. Nam cum et nostrae rei publicae detrimenta considero et maximarum civitatum veteres animo calamitates colligo, non minimam video per disertissimos homines invectam partem incommodorum : cum autem res ab nostra memoria propter vetustatem remotas ex litterarum monumentis repetere instituo, multas urbes constitutas, plurima bella restincta, firmissimas societates, sanctissimas amicitias intellego cum animi ratione, tum facilius eloquentia comparatas.* This is his most redundant and diffuse manner,

[1] *De Oratore,* 2. § 2.

which continues with him, so far as we can see, until about his thirty-fifth year.   In the Verrine Orations he has, however, nearly mastered the art of expression.   His prose rises and falls, expands and contracts, strikes hard or gently, as he chooses. *In Verrem* Act. 1. 1.   *Inveteravit enim iam opinio perniciosa rei publicae vobisque periculosa, quae non modo [Romae, sed etiam] apud exteras nationes omnium sermone percrebruit, his iudiciis, quae nunc sunt, pecuniosum hominem, quamvis sit nocens, neminem posse damnari.   Nunc in ipso discrimine ordinis iudiciorumque vestrorum cum sint parati, qui contionibus et legibus hanc invidiam senatus inflammare conentur, reus in iudicium adductus est C. Verres, homo vita atque factis omnium iam opinione damnatus, pecuniae magnitudine, sua spe et praedicatione absolutus.   Huic ego causae, iudices, cum summa voluntate et expectatione populi Romani actor accessi, non ut augerem invidiam ordinis, sed ut infamiae communi succurrerem. Adduxi enim hominem in quo reconciliare existimationem iudiciorum amissam, redire in gratiam cum populo Romano, satis facere exteris nationibus possetis, depeculatorem aerarii, vexatorem Asiae atque Pamphyliae, praedonem iuris urbani, labem atque perniciem provinciae Siciliae.*   He has not, however, at this period, nor indeed for some years afterwards, entirely emancipated himself from the artificiality of the former generation. The peroration of the Verrines is a great effort, but one feels that it is an effort ; there is still a certain air of constraint about it.   How different is the following from the Laelius, written twenty-five years afterwards (B.C. 45).

    (§ 10)   *Ego si Scipionis desiderio me moveri negem, quam id recte faciam viderint sapientes, sed certe mentiar.   Moveor enim tali amico orbatus, qualis, ut arbitror, nemo umquam erit, ut confirmare possum, nemo certe fuit.   Sed non egeo medicina : me ipse consolor et maxime illo solacio, quod eo errore careo quo amicorum decessu plerique angi solent.   Nihil mali accidisse Scipioni puto : mihi accidit, si quid accidit : suis autem incommodis graviter angi non amicum, sed se ipsum amantis est.   Cum illo vero quis neget actum esse praeclare ?   Nisi enim, quod ille minime putabat, immortalitatem optare vellet, quid non adeptus est quod homini fas esset optare, qui summam spem civium, quam de eo iam puero habuerant, continuo adulescens incredibili virtute superavit: qui consulatum petivit numquam, factus est bis, primum ante tempus, iterum sibi suo tempore, rei publicae paene sero: qui duabus urbibus eversis inimicissimis huic imperio non modo praesentia, verum etiam futura bella delevit?*

As far as can be ascertained, Cicero is the first writer who attempted to form a systematic theory of what the rhythm of Latin prose should be. The rules which he lays down in the *Orator* are all based upon the idea of accommodating the rhythmical laws of Greek prose to the requirements of the Italian ear.

Cicero has been universally accepted as the great master of classical Latin prose, that is, of the prose which best represents the genius of ancient Italy when in the fullness of its life and activity. He won that position because his conception of oratory was the widest possible, because in his hands eloquence was made to include all accessible culture: again, because he set himself to study and interpret to his countrymen the great masterpieces of Greek literature; and again because, having these masterpieces before him, he determined that his style should be thoroughly Latin, that Greek culture should be used as an instrument towards developing the capacities of Italian thought and diction. The general character of his writing is determined by two facts: first, that the prose style of his age was, and that he knew it to be, formed by the exigencies of public life. It is the prose of the speaker more than of the writer. Secondly, it is the style of the Graecizing school, the school which felt the need of beauty and harmony as well as of perspicuity in expression. Every clause must be rhythmical: every clause must, as a general rule, be connected by some mark of expression with the preceding clause.

Now as far as the mere mechanism of this style is concerned, Caesar is as much a master of it as Cicero. He has the clearness of Cicero, and his cohesion. We must of course remember that while much of Cicero's writing has come down to us in its most finished shape, nothing of Caesar remains but his most carelessly written work; and thus we have no means of judging what was the main secret of his success as an orator, whether it lay in his style, or in the genius and power of the man, or, as is most probable, in both together. The general resemblance between Cicero and Caesar was undoubtedly felt in the first century A.D.[1] Where then lies the main difference between Cicero's style and Caesar's?

It must be pointed out that Cicero's success was not merely due to his having mastered the laws of prose rhythm, nor merely to his general power as a stylist. His mind was of the poetical and imaginative order, while Caesar's, manly, sound, and robust, was without a touch of poetry. Strength of passion Caesar has, but no imagination. Cicero, nearly a poet and a considerable master of metre and poetic diction, really writes a poetical prose. Poetical, not like that of Livy and Tacitus, because it is filled with mechanical reminiscences of passages from the poets, but because of the spontaneous bent of Cicero's own genius. His prose is not only harmonious and pleasant to the ear, but is charged with metaphorical expression to an extent altogether without parallel in any prose writer of his age. It rises far beyond the average writing of the gifted and cultivated Romans of that time. While it represents the highest stage then attained by the healthiest literary culture, it is also penetrated and illuminated by the individuality of Cicero's own imaginative temperament.

The tendency of Italian literary culture seems then to have set towards the formation of a broad, clear, and periodic style, the chief representatives of which, though in very different ways, are Caesar and Cicero. But we have now to note the existence of a very different tradition, of which the earliest existing representative may perhaps be said to be Cornificius, though by far its most remarkable champion in the last century of the republic is Sallust.

The remarkable treatise on rhetoric which bears the bastard

---

[1] See Tacitus, *Dialogus* 20-24.

Latin title *Auctor ad Herennium* is now generally attributed to Cornificius. It belongs to the first sixteen years, or there abouts, of the last century of the republic[1], and is in tone somewhat anti-Hellenic. The style is on the whole the style of the newer school, but many of the instances of various kinds of writing which the author has invented in his fourth book have the tinge of the archaic, unperiodic manner. Cornificius, however, was not powerful enough to create a typical style. It was reserved for Sallust to head a reaction against the Ciceronian manner. The peculiarities of Sallust's writing, which have been analysed carefully by Mr. A. M. Cook in his recent edition of the *Bellum Catilinae* (London, 1884), are, I suppose, in the main traceable to two causes: his admiration for Cato, and his admiration for Thucydides. These authors were to Sallust what Crassus and Isocrates were to Cicero. That Sallust borrowed many archaic words from Cato was a commonplace of criticism[2]; and I suspect also that he imitated Cato in the abrupt, unconnected character of his sentences. Cicero and Caesar like to extend their clauses and to connect them, so that one easily flows from another. In Sallust the clauses are comparatively independent, and the effect is produced by crowding one short sentence upon another. *Qui labores, pericula, dubias atque asperas res facile toleraverant, eis otium divitiae, optanda alias, oneri miseriaeque fuere. Igitur primo pecuniae, deinde imperii cupido crevit ; ea quasi materies omnium malorum fuere. Namque avaritia fidem probitatem ceterasque artes bonas subvertit: pro his superbiam crudelitatem, deos neglegere, omnia venalia habere edocuit. Ambitio multos mortales falsos fieri subegit, aliud clausum in pectore, aliud in lingua promptum habere, amicitias inimicitiasque non ex re sed ex commodo aestimare, magisque voltum quam ingenium bonum habere*[3].

In all this I think it highly probable that Sallust is following in the steps of Cato, of course under the conditions imposed by

[1] Mr. W. Warde Fowler has shown (*Journal of Philology*, 10. 197) that 84 B.C. is the latest date to which there is any positive allusion in the book.
[2] Quintilian, 8. 3. 29. [3] Sallust, *Cat.* 10.

a different age and state of culture. In pregnancy of thought and expression he would fain have figured as the Roman Thucydides; and indeed, if Quintilian's opinion could have exalted him to this position, he would have held it in the eyes of the world [1].

Cicero, writing towards the end of his life, complains in his *Orator* (§ 30) of a school of stylists who called themselves Thucydideans. His remarks are directed ostensibly to oratory, but I think it not unlikely he is aiming a side-thrust at Sallust. His protest in favour of a rhythmical as against an unrhythmical prose is in any case worth quoting here (§ 233): *Age sume de Gracchi apud censores illud, ' Abesse non potest quin eiusdem hominis sit probos improbare qui improbos probet' : quanto aptius si dixisset, ' quin eiusdem hominis sit, qui improbos probet, probos improbare?' Hoc modo dicere nemo umquam noluit, nemoque potuit quin dixerit: qui autem aliter dixerunt, hoc adsequi non potuerunt: ita facti sunt repente Attici. Quasi vero Trallianus fuerit Demosthenes!.... Res autem sic se habet, ut brevissime dicam quod sentio ; composite et apte sine sententiis dicere insania est, sententiose autem sine verborum et ordine et modo infantia : eius modi tamen infantia, ut ea qui utantur non stulti homines haberi possint, etiam plerumque prudentes : quo qui est contentus utatur.*

The consideration of the style of Sallust brings us to the commencement of the great change, which, beginning in the Augustan age, ended by forming the style of Tacitus. Livy stands at the meeting point of the older and the later periods. Among all the Latin writers he is perhaps the best representative of the periodic style; witness, among a thousand instances which I might quote, his character of Cicero. *Ingenium et operibus et praemiis operum felix, ipse fortunae diu prosperae et in longo tenore felicitatis magnis interim ictus vulneribus, exilio, ruina partium pro quibus steterat, filiae exitu tam tristi atque acerbo, omnium adversorum nihil ut viro dignum erat tulit praeter mortem ; quae vere aestimanti minus indigna videri potuit, quod*

[1] IO. I. IOI. *Nec opponere Thucydidi Sallustium verear.*

*a victore inimico nil crudelius passurus erat quam quod eiusdem
fortunae compos in eo fecisset.* (Fragm. 49.)

No doubt Livy must have agreed with Cicero that the style
best suited for a continuous history was that of Isocrates and
Theopompus, not that of Thucydides; not the abrupt and
broken manner, but the periodic. But there is a marked
difference between the period as constructed by Livy and as
constructed by Cicero. Cicero aims simply at such a balance
of clauses as will raise the expectation and satisfy the demands
of the ear: Livy wishes to do this and a great deal more.
Cicero's grammatical construction is perfectly simple, and not
modified by the exigencies of his theory of composition.
Livy, on the contrary, in order to build a harmonius clause,
tempers and varies his grammatical constructions so as to produce a welded mass of writing over which the reader must
pause before he can grasp it as what it is, a carefully articulated
whole. *Ipse fortunae diu prosperae et in longo tenore felicitatis
magnis interim ictus vulneribus :* this triply constructed sentence
would in Cicero or Caesar have been broken up into three.
Cicero aims always at being understood at first hearing or first
reading; his manner is that of an orator. Livy's style is the
style of a scholar, not of a statesman. He speaks not to be
heard but to be read, and aims mainly at satisfying the taste of
literary men and winning admiration for his art. His method
consists in ingenious condensation of thoughts and combination
of clauses. In the first he probably wishes to rival Sallust, in
the last to comply with the precepts of Cicero. It is also important to observe that when (as in the first decade) the subject
seems to require it, he adopts a poetical tone and colouring,
which suggests that he is writing with the ancient poets (if not
indeed with Vergil) open before him.

Quintilian twice tells us that Asinius Pollio found in Livy
something of a provincial tone (*Patavinitatem quandam*). The
information is given us in such a way as to leave us uncertain
of the real point of the criticism : 1. 5. 56. *taceo de Tuscis et
Sabinis et Praenestinis quoque : nam ut eorum sermone utentem*

Vettium Lucilius insectatur, quemadmodum Pollio reprehendit in Livio Patavinitatem. 8. 1. 2. *multos enim, quibus loquendi ratio non desit, invenias, quos curiose potius loqui dixeris quam Latine, quomodo et illa Attica anus Theophrastum, hominem alioqui disertissimum, adnotata unius adfectatione verbi hospitem dixit, nec alio se id deprendisse interrogata respondit, quam quod nimium Attice loqueretur. Et in Tito Livio, mirae facundiae viro, putat inesse Pollio Asinius quandam Patavinitatem.* Putting these two passages together, one may reasonably infer Pollio's meaning to have been that Livy showed his provincialism in an overstrained literary purism : that, like a student, he would sometimes take words from provincial Italians : that he was more anxious to form a *recherché* and scholarly style than a man would have been who had taken an active part in the public life of Rome.

It was not, however, the style of Livy nor even that of Cicero that was destined to prevail. Livy, indeed, is like no one before or after him. Like Horace, he brought to perfection a peculiar manner which no one was able to imitate And for the style of Cicero it soon appeared that there was no public. The extinction of the republican life of Rome destroyed the demand for the broad and massive oratory of the forum. The aristocracy and the *equites* found themselves more and more driven into forming a literary clique. For good or for evil they had now to shape their course in the presence of a power greater than their own. Oratory was driven from the forum into the law-courts, where it was of necessity confined to technical points, or it was shut up in the senate, where in many cases the expression of opinion was no longer free. And as the sphere of oratory became narrower, the cultivation of style became nicer and more minute. The character of Roman education was changing. Ennius and Accius and Pacuvius were driven from the field, and Vergil and Horace became the classical poets on whom the taste and thought of the rising generation were moulded. Their writings were learned by heart as a regular part of the school *curriculum*, and prose writing, in the hands of the more gifted authors, naturally took a poetical (I should rather have said a Vergilian) tinge. As before, indeed, the Roman youth were trained to be speakers. Well and good : but what if the conditions were absent under which alone a manly oratory could be developed? In the atmosphere that was now rising, nothing could in the long run thrive but the desire of pleasing a picked audience by finely-chosen words, pithy sentences, and artificial points[1]. In fine, men began to study, not things, but words and phrases. Before the first century had run its course, the change was complete, and Quintilian spends much of his force in a vain attempt to revivify the style and spirit of the republican literature.

The new tendency was greatly encouraged by an important change which now took place in the method of education. Rhetorical education in the time of Cicero and Caesar was planned upon broad outlines. The Greek classics were carefully studied, and youths were exercised thoroughly in Greek and Latin composition. The understanding was strengthened and the range of knowledge extended by the writing and reading out of essays on general topics, *proposita* as Cicero calls them, as the Greeks called them θέσεις, and by the treatment of *communes loci*, or the topics which were sure to come up in the course of any serious discussion on a matter of practice[2]. The written treatment of θέσεις and *communes*

---

[1] The name with which the change is associated is that of Cassius Severus: Tacitus, *Dialogus* 19 : *Nam quatenus antiquorum admiratores hunc velut terminum antiquitatis constituere solent, Cassium Severum, quem primum adfirmant flexisse ab illa vetere atque derecta dicendi via non infirmitate ingenii nec inscitia litterarum transtulisse se ad aliud dicendi genus contendo, sed iudicio et intellectu. Vidit namque, ut paulo ante dicebam, cum condicione temporum et diversitate aurium formam quoque et speciem orationis esse mutandam. Facile perferebat prior ille populus, ut imperitus et rudis, impeditissimarum orationum spatia. . . . . At hercule pervulgatis iam omnibus, cum vix in cortina quisquam adsistat quin elementis studiorum, etsi non instructus, at certe imbutus sit, novis et exquisitis eloquentiae itineribus opus est, per quae orator fastidium aurium effugiat.*

[2] The following evidence on this subject seems worth quoting : Cicerc

loci was the main if not the only exercise of originality known
to the educationists of Cicero's day.   But towards the end
of Cicero's life the habit of *declamatio*, or speaking in private
on fictitious themes, began to prevail.   It is probable that
young men aspiring to become orators also exercised their

Top. §§ 79–81. *Quaestionum duo genera, alterum definitum, alterum infinitum.   Definitum est quod* ὑπόθεσιν *Graeci, nos causam : infinitum, quod*
θέσιν *illi appellant, nos propositum possumus nominare.   Causa certis
personis, locis, temporibus, actionibus, negotiis cernitur aut in omnibus aut
in plerisque eorum : propositum autem in aliquo eorum aut in pluribus nec
tamen in maximis.   Part. Or.* § 61. *Duo sunt, ut initio dixi, quaestionum
genera, quorum alterum finitum temporibus et personis causam appello,
alterum infinitum nullis neque personis neque temporibus notatum propositum voco.   Sed est propositum latior quasi pars causae quaedam.* He
proceeds to distinguish the different kinds of *proposita*, speculative and
practical.

   Seneca *Contr.* i. praef. 12 (p. 50, Bursian).   *Declamabat autem Cicero non
quales nunc controversias dicimus, ne tales quidem quales ante Ciceronem
dicebantur, quas thesis vocabant.   Hoc enim genus materiae quo nos
exercemur adeo novum est, ut nomen quoque eius novum sit.   Controversias
nos dicimus ; Cicero causas vocabat.   Hoc vero alterum nomen Graecum
quidem sed in Latinum ita translatum, ut pro Latino sit, scholastica
controversia multo recentius est, sicut ipsa declamatio apud nullum antiquum
auctorem ante Ciceronem et Calvum inveniri potest, qui declamationem
distinguit ; ait enim ' declamare est domi non mediocriter dicere.'   Bene
alterum putat domesticae exercitationis esse, alterum verae actionis.   Modo
nomen hoc prodiit ; nam et studium ipsum nuper celebrari coepit ; ideo
facile est mihi ab incunabulis nosse rem post me natam.*

   Quintilian 12. 2. 25.   *Peripatetici studio quoque se quodam oratorio
iactant, nam thesis dicere exercitationis gratia fere est ab iis institutum.*
2. 1. 9. *An ignoramus antiquis hoc fuisse ad augendam eloquentiam genus
exercitationis, ut thesis dicerent et communes locos et cetera citra complexum
rerum personarumque quibus verae fictaeque controversiae continentur?
Ex quo palam est quam turpiter deserat eam partem rhetorices institutio
quam et primam habuit et diu solam. . . . Non communes loci, sive qui sunt
in vitia derecti, quales legimus a Cicerone compositos, seu quibus quaestiones
generaliter tractantur, quales sunt editi a Q. quoque Hortensio, ut ' sitne
parvis argumentis credendum' et pro testibus et in testes in mediis litium
medullis versantur?   Arma sunt haec quodammodo praeparanda semper,
ut iis, cum res poscet, utare. 2. 4. 24. Theses autem, quae sumuntur ex
rerum comparatione, ut ' rusticane vita an urbana potior,' ' iuris periti an
militaris viri laus maior,' mire sunt ad exercitationem dicendi speciosae
atque uberes.*

powers on *causae,* or fictitious cases of a definite character, corresponding generally to what was afterwards called *controversia.* It is however important to observe that the *declamatio,* with its two branches the *controversia* and *suasoria,* tended more and more to drive out the θέσις and *communis locus* in the schools. This we must infer from the words of the elder Seneca quoted in the note, *studium ipsum nuper celebrari coepit.* I understand Seneca to mean, not that *declamatio* was in his youth an absolutely new thing, but that it was new as an almost exclusive instrument of education.

In treating a θέσις or *communis locus* the student had to find and arrange his own facts : in a *declamatio,* whether it were a *controversia* or fictitious controversy on a point of law or politics, or a *suasoria,* in which advice was given to a fictitious person, the facts were found for him. In driving the θέσις from the schools, therefore, the masters were depriving rhetorical education of its most valuable element, of the element most likely to develop originality and encourage thoroughness.

The *declamatio,* as was natural, soon degenerated into a barren exercise which produced little save artificial antithesis and false points. Cornificius (4 § 25) says of a manly style, *sententias interponi raro convenit, ut rei actores, non vivendi praeceptores videamur esse.* But a *declamatio* could not exist without a number of pointed *sententiae.* As the elder Seneca, who witnessed the birth and growth of *declamatio,* well says (*Contr.* 9 praef. p. 241 Bursian) *qui declamationem parat, scribit non ut vincat sed ut placeat. Omnia itaque lenocinia conquirit : argumentationes quia molestae sunt et minimum habent floris, relinquit : sententiis, explicationibus audientis deliniri contentus est. Cupit enim se approbare, non causam. Sequitur autem hoc usque in forum declamatores vitium, ut necessaria deserant dum speciosa sectantur.*

Looking at the results of the system in his own time Quintilian says (7. 1. 41) *famam adfectantes contenti sunt locis speciosis :* and a little further on (44) he speaks of the *sententiae praecipites vel obscurae* (*nam ea nunc virtus est*) which had come to be the fashion.

Who, when he hears of obscurity, does not think of the memorable story quoted from Livy by Quintilian (8. 2. 18) *fuisse praeceptorem aliquem qui discipulos obscurare quae dicerent iuberet, Graeco verbo utens* σκότισον *: unde illa scilicet egregia laudatio, 'tanto melior ; ne ego quidem intellexi.'* Who has not struggled with the obscurity of Persius, the direct result of this training? *Et quod recte dici potest* (says Quintilian 8 prooem. 24 foll.) *circumimus amore verborum, et quod satis dictum est repetimus, et quod uno verbo patet, pluribus oneramus, et pleraque significare melius putamus quam dicere. Quid, quod nihil iam proprium placet, dum parum creditur disertum, quod et alius dixisset? A corruptissimo quoque poetarum figuras seu translationes mutuamur, tum demum ingeniosi scilicet, si ad intellegendos nos opus sit ingenio. Atqui satis aperte Cicero praeceperat 'in dicendo vitium vel maximum esse a vulgari genere orationis atque a consuetudine communis sensus abhorrere.' Sed ille est durus atque ineruditus : nos melius, quibus sordet omne quod natura dictavit,* &c.

These causes combined from several sides to popularize the abrupt and sententious style of Latin. The passion for *sententiae* or pithy sayings well expressed became dominant: Seneca the younger is full of them, and even Quintilian lays it down as a rule for a master's guidance that he should every day say something for his hearers to carry away (2. 2. 8 *ipse aliquid, immo multa, cottidie dicat, quae secum oratores referant*). An attempt was indeed made by Tacitus in his *Dialogus*, and by Quintilian in his *Institutio*, to galvanize the republican style into life[1] ; but the spirit of the age was too strong for them,

[1] The letters of the younger Pliny are also written in a style intended to recall that of Cicero. Pliny, it must be remembered, was a pupil of Quintilian, and it is surely very probable that Tacitus was also. This hypothesis would account for the style of the *Dialogus*, as well as for the striking similarity of its spirit and criticisms to those of Quintilian. I am glad to find that this view is also adopted by Dr. Eugen Gruenwald, in his tract

and Tacitus, with a true sense of the fact, abandoned the attempt. Few now understood the virtues of the ancient manner. To make an impression it was necessary to strike a series of sudden blows, to arrest the ear by a succession of smart points. The idea of forming harmonious clauses, of exhibiting thought and passion in perfect clearness, was thrown to the winds. The language was strained beyond its power. Becoming an end itself, it ceased to be the natural instrument for expression of thought and feeling. The reign of the artist is over and that of the *virtuoso* has begun, who writes, not to move the heart, but to display the capacity of his instrument. Men were now called upon to admire, not the adaptation of language to thought, but the language itself. It must be *recherché*, it must recall Vergil, it must say more than it ought to say. The process ended not merely in destroying the framework of Latin style, but in corrupting the clearness of the Latin language. Not only does the stately structure of the Ciceronian period crumble into dust in the Latin of the silver age, but the meaning of words is perverted. In Sallust, though the style has a false ring, the language, as a vehicle of thought, preserves its integrity. The younger Seneca, though always striving to make points, writes with perfect clearness ; but in Tacitus the language itself is touched with decay.

Let me not be misunderstood, or be supposed to wish for a moment to depreciate the genius of Tacitus. It would be unpardonable to represent him as other than what he is, a man of profound feeling, of splendid imagination and dramatic power. I am only concerned to show that the course of events had destroyed the literary structure of the language in which he had to write ; that he was a great artist working with bad tools. The very force of his genius makes him employ to excess the only means he has of making himself heard. His style is the natural result of the situation. Astonishing

entitled *Quae ratio intercedere videatur inter Quintiliani Institutionem Oratoriam et Taciti Dialogum.* (Berlin, 1883.)

in its condensation and in its pathos it is in composition structureless, in language strained and obscure[1].

There is no great Latin prose after Tacitus. Suetonius is an able writer, but no stylist; aiming much lower than Tacitus, he has none of his excellences, and succeeds in avoiding his faults. Suetonius is succeeded by writers of the stamp of Gellius and Fronto, and creative genius is extinct.

---

[1] I content myself with quoting the following specimens from the second book of the Histories: 48. *Pecunias distribuit parce nec ut periturus... Non enim ultima desperatione, sed poscente proelium exercitu remisisse rei publicae novissimum casum.*

49. *Othoni sepulchrum exstructum est modicum et mansurum.*

76. *Nec speciem adulantis expaveris.*

Ib. Abiit iam et transvectum est tempus, quo posses videri concupisse; confugiendum est ad imperium. An excidit trucidatus Corbulo?

V.

LIFE AND POEMS OF JUVENAL.

('JOURNAL OF PHILOLOGY,' XVI. (1888).)

———••———

IT is sometimes necessary to distinguish between the position which an author holds in the world of letters at large, and that which a nearer consideration of the circumstances of his life and times would dispose the student of history to assign him. The literary reputation of Juvenal is a case in point. The scourge of a corrupt age, the master of moral indignation, the great representative of the most original production of the Latin genius ; such is the idea of Juvenal which may be said to have prevailed, and still to prevail, in the modern literary world[1]. I am far from saying that such an estimate is false, but I think it partial and inadequate. Take Juvenal at his own estimate, assume that the pictures which he draws of contemporary life are in the main correct, study him alone and leave the younger Pliny and Quintilian and Suetonius and the inscriptions unread, and the ordinary

[1] This view seems in the main to be that of Professor Mayor, if I may judge by the preface to his new edition (1886). I wish it clearly to be understood that, while I venture to differ from Mr Mayor's general estimate of Juvenal's moral position, I cannot adequately express my admiration for his edition and indeed for his many unique contributions to Latin scholarship and the history of Latin literature. I suppose that in wealth of learning and freshness of interest combined, Mr. Mayor holds a position occupied by no scholar since Casaubon.

view of Juvenal becomes the natural one. But literary criticism
must in the present day be based upon history; and studied
historically the position of the famous satirist will, if I am not
mistaken, appear to be a peculiar and personal one, and his
satires, though containing a large element of truth, to represent
the partial and exaggerated views natural in such circumstances.

It is strange that so little should be known about the life of
so celebrated a writer. The biographies prefixed to his satires
in the manuscripts are as numerous as they are unsatisfactory.
Of these lives there are nine, seven of which are printed by
Otto Jahn in his edition of 1851. An eighth was published
from a Harleian MS. by Rühl in the *Neue Jahrbücher* of 1874
(p. 868); a ninth, which I am sorry to say adds nothing to the
information conveyed by the others, I have myself found in a
Bodleian manuscript of the thirteenth century[1]. In point of
Latin style, and presumably therefore of antiquity, the best of
these memoirs is that printed by Jahn as No. 1. The author
imitates the style of Suetonius, but not his clearness or accu-
racy. Of this memoir Borghesi[2] rightly observes that Suetonius
could never have written in so unsatisfactory a way of so
distinguished a contemporary.

The biographies all agree that Juvenal was the son or ward
of a freedman, that he was born at Aquinum, that he practised
declamation till middle life (*ad mediam aetatem*[3]) and that he
was banished in consequence of an attack made upon an actor.
The date of his birth is variously given in the three memoirs
which mention the fact. Two (2 and Bodl.) put it in the
reign of Claudius Nero (Claudius), another (3) in that of Nero
Claudius (Nero). The accounts of his exile present equally
serious discrepancies. For while one tradition (Lives 1, 2, 4, 7
and Schol. Iuv. 4. 38) represents him as banished to Egypt,

---

[1] See p. 144.   [2] *Œuvres* 5. 513.

[3] For *media aetas* Mr. Mayor quotes Plautus Aulularia 159, and Phaedrus
2. 2. 3: we may add Celsus 1. 3 *inediam facillime sustinent mediae aetates,
minus iuvenes, minime pueri et senectute confecti*: Martial 10. 32. 3 *talis
erat Marcus mediis Antonius annis Primus.*

another (5, 6) relegates him to Scotland, or the Scottish border. Again, in the accounts of the time and circumstances of his exile there are irreconcilable differences. According to Life (1) he was banished in his eightieth year, and died soon afterwards ; according to (4) he was banished by Domitian[1], and remained in exile, altering and enlarging his satires, till he died in the reign of Antoninus Pius : according to (6) he was banished by Trajan to Scotland and died there soon afterwards.

The tradition however is uniform that the pretext for his exile was furnished by some verses which he had written against the *pantomimus* Paris, a favourite of Domitian. The verses were, it is stated, inserted into the seventh satire (v. 90 foll.) *Quod non dant proceres, dabit histrio : tu Camerinos et Baream, tu nobilium magna atria curas ? Praefectos Pelopea facit, Philomela tribunos.* This story is confirmed to a certain extent by some lines of Sidonius Apollinaris (Carm. 9. 270–275) *Non qui tempore Caesaris secundi Aeterno incoluit Tomos reatu, Nec qui consimili deinde casu Ad vulgi tenuem strepentis auram Irati fuit histrionis exul.*

If any reliance can be placed on these words of Sidonius, if indeed we can be sure that they refer to Juvenal at all, and not to some other poet, then Juvenal must have been banished for having said or written something not only offensive to an actor but unpopular with the pit and gallery. If the actor was Paris the favourite of Domitian, the date of the poet's exile must be placed in or before A.D. 83, for Paris was put to death in that year[2].

It is in truth impossible to make anything out on this point from the biographies and the *scholia*. The compilers of these notes may have got hold of the fact that Juvenal was banished,

---

[1] So Schol. Iuv. 4. 38 : Schol. 7. 92 makes him banished by Claudius Nero : Schol. 15. 27 only says he served in Egypt, not that he was banished thither.

[2] Friedländer has pointed out that actors often took the names of celebrated predecessors, as shops in modern times sometimes continue to bear the old names. There was a Paris in the reign of Nero, as well as in that of Domitian, and three more afterwards. (*Sittengeschichte* ii. 3. Appendix 16.)

but have confused their tradition with the import of the lines
(7. 88 foll.) *Ille et militiae multis largitus honorem Semenstri
vatum digitos circumligat auro : Quod non dant proceres,* &c.
This passage, however, really contains no reflection whatever on
any actor : the indictment, if any, lies against the aristocracy.
The mention of Paris and of an actor here may have led to
these verses being connected with the story of the histrio who
caused Juvenal's banishment.   The words *satyra non absurde
composita in Paridem pantomimum poetamque semenstribus
militiolis emitantem* in Life (1), to which (2) adds *poetamque
Statium,* are clearly a mere plagiarism from the text.

But another circumstance may have contributed to form this
tradition. An inscription found at Aquinum contains a dedica-
tion to Ceres made by a D. Iunius Iuvenalis, flamen of Vespasian,
and holding some appointment (perhaps that of *tribunus* in
a *cohors Delmatarum*[1]).   Now, as in A.D. 103 the *cohors quarta
Delmatarum* was in Britain, while an unnumbered *cohors
Delmatarum* was there in 105, and the *prima cohors Delmatarum* in 124, scholars have been inclined to suppose that
Juvenal was actually, as some of the memoirs say, at one time
in Britain in a military capacity.   It should however be added
that other Dalmatian cohorts are known elsewhere—thus the
fifth *cohors Delmatarum* was in Germany in the year 116—and
that as the number of the cohort to which the inscription
attaches its D. Iunius Iuvenalis cannot be recovered, there is
really no evidence on which we are justified in connecting
Juvenal with Britain.

The inscription of Aquinum, then, throws no real light on
the question of Juvenal's banishment. And it should be added
that if Juvenal was sent to Britain in 103 or 124 *contra Scotos,*
as the memoirs say, *sub honore militiae,* this must have taken
place either under Trajan or under Hadrian.   But it is
inconceivable that either Trajan or Hadrian should have

[1] [Mommsen *C. I. L.* x. 5382, Dessau 2926 : the stone is now lost.
Some numeral must have followed *coh (ors)* : Mommsen conjectures *coh.* [*i*]
Delmatarum, ' cum facillime excideret I.']

committed to an aged literary man (for aged Juvenal must have been in 124) the command of a cohort on a dangerous frontier.

If useless with regard to the question of the banishment, the inscription may, perhaps, be turned to account in another way. The *Iuvenalis* whose name it bears was a *flamen* of Vespasian. So far as this fact goes, it affords a presumption that the inscription was put up in the reign of one of Vespasian's immediate successors, i. e. either of Titus or Domitian. If the *Iuvenalis* of the inscription is the poet, he must then, in the reigns of Titus or Domitian (79–96), have attained the age qualifying him for the post of *tribunus cohortis.*

Let us consider whether any light can be obtained by interrogating the memoirs with the help of such internal evidence as is afforded by the satires themselves. Were we dealing in this way with Vergil, Horace, or Ovid, we should meet, in all probability, with no difficulty. But Juvenal's manner is at times so unreal that it is impossible for the reader to be sure whether the poet is referring to contemporary events or only professing to do so. In the first satire, for instance, he speaks of Tigellinus as a formidable person (155, *pone Tigellinum: taeda lucebis in illa,* &c.) and suggests therefore that he is writing in the reign of Nero. Yet it is clear that the piece cannot have assumed its present form until after 100 A.D. in which Marius was condemned for his misgovernment in Africa. (49, *exul ab octava Marius bibit et fruitur dis Iratis.*)

There are however some undoubted marks of time in the satires which I will at once mention, taking the latest first and working backwards.

The latest is 15. 27 (assuming the satire to be really Juvenal's) *nuper consule Iunco.* Iuncus was consul in the year 127.

There is some doubt about 13. 16, *stupet haec, qui iam post terga reliquit Sexaginta annos, Fonteio consule natus*[1]. A Fonteius

---

[1] Friedländer (*Sittengeschichte* iii.3. Appendix 5) refers *stupet* to Juvenal, and therefore puts the poet's birth in 67 A. D. But surely *stupet* refers to Juvenal's friend.

Capito (the *praenomen* is lost) was consul with C. Julius Rufus
A.D. 67, and this would bring the thirteenth satire down to 127 :
but C. Fonteius Capito was consul in 59 with C. Vipstanus
Apronianus.   As Fonteius was the first consul in 67 and would
therefore give his name to the year, recent commentators refer
the verse of Juvenal to 67 : but this is not a necessary interpretation.   The reference may be to C. Fonteius Capito,
consul 59 : for though the *Fasti Consulares* make him second
consul after Apronianus, Pliny (*H. N.* 7. 84) and *C. I. L.* 6. 2002
quote his name first.   The alternative dates for this satire are
then 127 and 119.

A line of the sixth satire (407, *instantem regi Armenio
Parthisque cometen*) is rightly referred by all commentators to
the comet of 115 A.D.   The earthquakes mentioned in the same
passage may be those which took place in Galatia about 113,
including perhaps that of Antioch (A.D. 115: Dio 68. 25).

The eighth satire seems to have been written not very long
after 100 A.D., for it speaks of the trial of Marius as recent
(*cum tenues nuper Marius discinxerit Afros*, v. 120).   And the
same remark applies, as I have said, to the first satire.

The fourth satire purports at least to have been written not
very long after Domitian's death, and the same may be said
of the second.   The lines (29–30) *qualis erat nuper tragico
pollutus adulter Concubitu, qui tunc leges revocabat amaras*, &c.
can hardly have been written in Domitian's life-time.   While
the expression (v. 160) *modo captas Orcadas et minima con-
tentos nocte Britannos* shows that the memory of Agricola's
British campaigns was still fresh in the writer's memory.

We have thus obtained definite marks of time from about
96 to 127 A.D.   It should be added that the first, third, fourth,
eighth and tenth satires contain vivid reminiscences of Nero's
reign [1], while Otho figures in the second.   These reminiscences
suggest that Juvenal was, during Nero's reign (54–68 A. D.), of
an age to be keenly alive to what was going on in Rome.

[1] e.g. 1. 155 Tigellinus: 3. 116 Barea (66 A.D.) : 3. 251 Corbulo: 8.
211–212 Seneca and Nero.

Let us now proceed to consider another source of evidence. There is no doubt that Juvenal and Martial were on terms of intimate friendship[1], and Martial died, at about the age of sixty, in 101 or 102 A.D. In the twenty-fourth poem of his seventh book Martial says *Cum Iuvenale meo quae me committere temptas, Quid non audebis, perfida lingua, loqui? Te fingente nefas Pyladen odisset Orestes, Thesea Pirithoi destituisset amor : Tu Siculos fratres et maius nomen Atridas, Et Ledae poteras dissociare genus.* In the same book we have an epigram (91) addressed to Juvenal himself, *De nostro facunde tibi Iuvenalis agello Saturnalicias mittimus, ecce, nuces.* The date of Martial's seventh book is 92 A.D.[2] At that time he knows Juvenal intimately and calls him *facundus.* This word has been taken as implying that Martial only knew of him as a teacher of rhetoric: but such a limitation is not necessary. *Facundus* is by writers of this period applied to eloquent writers as well as eloquent speakers or declaimers : Horace *A. P.* 41 *Cui lecta potenter erit res, Nec facundia deseret hunc nec lucidus ordo.* Statius *Silv.* 1. 4. 28–30 *seu plana solutis Cum struis orsa modis, seu cum tibi dulcis in artum Cogitur, et nostras curat facundia leges* (whether you write prose or poetry) : Martial 5. 30. 3 *facundia scaena Catulli* (of Catullus as a writer of mimes): 14. 185 *facundi Maronis* : a strong instance, as Vergil was notoriously a bad speaker. Quint. 8. 1. 3 *in Tito Livio, mirae facundiae viro, putat inesse Pollio Asinius quandam Patavinitatem.* There is nothing, then, to stand in the way of supposing that Martial knew of Juvenal as a writer in 92 A.D.

The only other allusion to Juvenal is in Martial's twelfth book (18), written in 101 or 102 A.D. *Dum tu forsitan inquietus erras Clamosa, Iuvenalis, in Subura,* &c.

---

[1] One of the biographies (3) notices the fact: *Romam cum veniret et Martialem suum non videret.*

[2] Martial's epigrams are dated by Friedländer as follows: Books I and II, 85–86 A.D.: III, 87-88: IV, published December 88; V, autumn 89: VI, 90 (summer or autumn): VII, VIII, 92, 93: IX, X (1st edition), 94–96 (December): X (2nd edition) 98; XI, 96; XII, 101.

The intimacy between Juvenal and Martial need not, of course, of itself exclude the supposition that Juvenal was much the younger man. But taking the evidence as a whole, I doubt whether it is necessary to suppose that there was a difference of more than ten years between the ages of the two poets. One very remarkable circumstance, which so far as I know has not been fully considered by the writers on this subject, seems to me to show that Martial and Juvenal must have been intimate not only as men, but as writers: that they sympathized in their views of literature and saw a good deal of each other's literary work. The circumstance to which I allude is the remarkable correspondence between Martial's epigrams and the satires of Juvenal, a correspondence apparent not only in their view of literature, but in the subjects they treat, the persons they mention, their language and expression, and their general tone. This consideration is always of great importance when we have to deal with the history of Latin literature. The correspondence I allude to points to one of two conclusions: either that Juvenal, writing some twenty years after Martial's death, took a pleasure in imitating his friend's poetry: or that like Calvus and Catullus, Vergil and Horace, Martial and Juvenal were much in each other's confidence, working and it may almost be said thinking together.

Before pronouncing in favour of one or the other conclusion, it may be well to quote the following passages:

(1) Their view of literature.

Martial 4. 49 *Nescit, crede mihi, quid sint epigrammata, Flacce, Qui tantum lusus ista iocosque vocat. Ille magis ludit, qui scribit prandia saevi Tereos, aut cenam, crude Thyesta, tuam, Aut puero liquidas aptantem Daedalon alas, Pascentem Siculas aut Polyphemon oves. A nostris procul est omnis vensica libellis, Musa nec insano syrmate nostra tumet. ' Illa tamen laudant omnes, mirantur, adorant' : Confiteor: laudant illa, sed ista legunt.*

Martial 8. 3. 17 *Scribant ista graves nimium nimiumque severi, Quos media miseros nocte lucerna videt. At tu Romano*

lepidus sale tinge libellos: Agnoscat mores vita legatque suos.
Angusta cantare licet videaris avena, Dum tua multorum vincat
avena tubas.

Martial 10. 4 *Qui legis Oedipodem caligantemque Thyesten,*
Colchidas et Scyllas, quid nisi monstra legis? Quid tibi raptus
Hylas, quid Parthenopaeus et Attis, Quid tibi dormitor proderit
Endymion? Exutusve puer pinnis labentibus, aut qui Odit
amatrices Hermaphroditus aquas? Quid te vana iuvant miserae
ludibria cartae? Hoc lege, quod possit dicere vita, Meum est.
Non hic Centauros, non Gorgonas Harpyiasque Invenies: homi-
nem pagina nostra sapit.

Juvenal 1. 52 *Haec ego non agitem? sed quid magis?*
Heracleas Aut Diomedeas aut mugitum labyrinthi Et mare per-
cussum puero fabrumque volantem? 85 Quicquid agunt homines,
votum timor ira voluptas Gaudia discursus nostri farrago li-
belli est.

(2) Subjects treated.

Philosophical debauchees.

Martial 1. 24 *Aspicis incomptis illum, Deciane, capillis,*
Cuius et ipse times triste supercilium, Qui loquitur Curios,
adsertoresque Camillos: Nolito fronti credere, nupsit heri.

12. 42 *Barbatus rigido nupsit Callistratus Afro,* &c.

7. 58. 7 *Quaere aliquem Curios semper Fabiosque loquentem,*
Hirsutum et dura rusticitate trucem: Invenies: sed habet tristis
quoque turba cinaedos: Difficile est vero nubere, Galla, viro.

9. 27. 6 *Curios, Camillos, Quinctios, Numas, Ancos, Et quid-*
quid umquam legimus pilosorum Loqueris sonasque grandibus
minax verbis, Et cum theatris saeculoque rixaris. Occurrit
aliquis inter ista si draucus, &c.

9. 47 *Democritos, Zenonas, inexplicitosque Platonas Quid-*
quid et hirsutis squalet imaginibus, Sic quasi Pythagorae lo-
queris successor et heres, Praependet sane nec tibi barba
minor, &c.

Juvenal 2. 1 foll. *Ultra Sauromatas fugere hinc libet et*
glacialem Oceanum, quotiens aliquid de moribus audent, Qui
Curios simulant et Bacchanalia vivunt. Indocti primum;

quamquam plena omnia gypso Chrysippi invenias, nam perfec-
tissimus horum est, Si quis Aristotelen similem vel Pittacon emit,
Et iubet archetypos pluteum servare Cleanthas. Frontis nulla
fides: quis enim non vicus abundat Tristibus obscenis? castigas
turpia, cum sis Inter Socraticos notissima fossa cinaedos. His-
pida membra quidem, &c.

2. 129 *traditur ecce viro clarus genere atque opibus vir,* &c.
Neglect of the liberal professions by their proper patrons.

Martial 1. 107 *Saepe mihi dicis, Luci carissime Iuli, ' Scribe*
aliquid magnum : desidiosus homo es': Otia da nobis, sed
qualia fecerat olim Maecenas Flacco Vergilioque suo : Condere
victuras temptem per saecula curas Et nomen flammis eripuisse
meum. In steriles nolunt campos iuga ferra iuvenci: Pingue
solum lassat, sed iuvat ipse labor.

4. 46 *Saturnalia divitem Sabellum Fecerunt: merito tumet*
Sabellus, Nec quenquam putat esse praedicatque Inter causidicos
beatiorem. Hos fastus animosque dat Sabello Farris semodius
fabaeque fresae, Et turis piperisque tres selibrae, &c.

3. 38 *Quae te causa trahit vel quae fiducia Romam, Sexte?*
aut quid speras aut petis inde, refer. ' Causas' inquis 'agam
Cicerone disertior ipso, Atque erit in triplici par mihi nemo foro.'
Egit Atestinus causas et Civis ; utrumque Noras, sed neutri,
pensio tota fuit. ' Si nihil hinc veniet, pangentur carmina nobis ;
Audieris, dices esse Maronis opus.' Insanis: omnes gelidis
quicunque lacernis Sunt ibi, Nasones Vergiliosque vides. ' Atria
magna colam.' Vix tres aut quattuor ista Res aluit, pallet
cetera turba fame. ' Quid faciam, suade : nam certum est vivere
Romae.' Si bonus es, casu vivere, Sexte, potes.

5. 16. 11 *Sed non et veteres contenti laude fuerunt, Cum*
minimum vati munus Alexis erat.

8. 56. 5 *Sint Maecenates, non derunt, Flacce, Marones,* &c.

8. 82. 5 *Fer vates, Auguste, tuos : nos gloria dulcis, Nos tua*
cura prior deliciaeque sumus.

The whole of the seventh satire of Juvenal might be taken
as an illustration of these lines ; see especially the lines 1–12 :
53–70 : 105–123.

The vulgar and niggardly patron: perhaps the individual referred to by Pliny Ep. 2. 6 [1].

Martial 3. 49 *Veientana mihi misces, ubi Massica potas: olfacere haec malo pocula quam bibere* [2].

3. 60 *Cum vocer ad cenam, non iam venalis ut ante, Cur mihi non eadem, quae tibi, cena datur? Ostrea tu sumis stagno saturata Lucrino, Sugitur inciso mitulus ore mihi. Sunt tibi boleti, fungos ego sumo suillos: Res tibi cum rhombo est, at mihi cum sparulo,* &c.

12. 36 *Libras quattuor, aut duas amico Algentemque togam brevemque laenam,* &c. *Pisones Senecasque Memmiosque Et Crispos mihi redde, sed priores,* &c.

Juvenal 5. 30–110 may again be taken as a companion picture to all these sketches.

The unsociable gourmand.

Martial 7. 59 *Non cenat sine apro noster, Tite, Caecilianus. Bellum convivam Caecilianus habet.*

Juvenal 1. 140 *quanta est gula, quae sibi totos Ponat apros, animal propter convivia natum!*

The man who burns his own house for the sake of the contributions made for him after the disaster.

Martial 3. 52 *Empta domus fuerat tibi, Tongiliane, ducentis: Abstulit hanc nimium casus in urbe frequens. Conlatum est deciens. Rogo, non potes ipse videri Incendisse tuam, Tongiliane, domum?*

Juvenal 3. 220 *Meliora et plura reponit Persicus, orborum lautissimus, et merito iam Suspectus, tamquam ipse suas incenderit aedes.*

---

[1] *Longum est altius repetere, nec refert quem ad modum acciderit, ut homo minime familiaris cenarem apud quendam, ut sibi videbatur, lautum et diligentem, ut mihi, sordidum simul et sumptuosum. Nam sibi et paucis opima quaedam, ceteris vilia et minuta ponebat. Vina etiam parvis lagunculis in tria genera discripserat, non ut potestas eligendi, sed ne ius esset recusandi, aliud sibi et nobis, aliud minoribus amicis (nam gradatim amicos habet) aliud suis nostrisque libertis.* Pliny's second book of letters is dated between 97 and 100 A.D.

[2] See also Martial 1. 20; 2. 43; 4. 85; 6. 11.

Life at Rome.

Martial 4. 5 *Vir bonus et pauper linguaque et pectore verus Quid tibi vis, urbem qui, Fabiane, petis ?   Qui nec leno potes nec comissator haberi, Nec pavidos tristi voce citare reos : Nec potes uxorem cari corrumpere amici, Nec potes algentes arrigere ad vetulas,* &c.

Juvenal 1. 38 *optima summi Nunc via processus, vetulae vensica beatae :* 55 *cum leno accipiat moechi bona.*

3. 41–50 *Quid Romae faciam ? mentiri nescio, librum Si malus est, nequeo laudare et poscere, motus Astrorum ignoro, funus promittere patris Nec volo nec possum, ranarum viscera nunquam Inspexi, ferre ad nuptam quae mittit adulter Quae mandat, norunt alii,* &c.

Rome and the country.

Martial 12. 57 *Cur saepe sicci parva rura Nomenti Laremque villae sordidum petam, quaeris,* &c.

Compare Juvenal 3. 239 foll.

Women and their habits.

Martial 6. 6 *Comoedi sunt tres, sed amat tua Paula, Luperce, Quattuor : et κωφὸν Paula πρόσωπον amat.*

Juvenal 6. 73 *Solvitur his magno comoedi fibula.*

Martial 6. 7 *Iulia lex populis ex quo, Faustine, renata est, Atque intrare domos iussa Pudicitia est, Aut minus aut certe non plus tricesima lux est, Et nubit decimo iam Telesilla viro. Quae nubit totiens, non nubit : adultera lege est : Offendor moecha simpliciore minus.*

Juvenal 6. 224 *Imperat ergo viro, set mox haec regna relinquit, Permutatque domos et flammea conterit, inde Avolat et spreti repetit vestigia lecti.   Ornatas paulo ante fores, pendentia linquit Vela domus et adhuc virides in limine ramos. Sic crescit numerus, sic fiunt octo mariti Quinque per autumnos, titulo res digna sepulchri.*

Martial 7. 67. 4 *(Philaenis) Harpasto quoque subligata ludit Et flavescit haphe, gravesque draucis Halteras facili rotat lacerto,* &c.

Juvenal 6. 246 *Endromidas Tyrias et femineum ceroma Quis*

nescit, vel quis non vidit vulnera pali? &c. ib. 420 *magno gaudet sudare tumultu Cum lassata gravi ceciderunt bracchia massa,* &c.

Martial 10. 68 *Cum tibi non Ephesos, nec sit Rhodos aut Mytilene, Sed domus in vico, Laelia, patricio, Deque coloratis nunquam lita mater Etruscis, Durus Aricina de regione pater;* Κύριέ μου, μέλι μου, ψυχή μου *congeris usque, Pro pudor! Hersiliae civis et Egeriae. Lectulus has voces, nec lectulus audiat omnis,* &c.

Juvenal 6. 185 *Nam quid rancidius, quam quae se non putat ulla Formosam, nisi quae de Tusca Graecula facta est, De Sulmonensi mera Cecropis,* &c. . . . *Quotiens lascivum intervenit illud* Ζωή καὶ ψυχή, &c.

Martial 2. 66 *Unus de toto peccaverat orbe comarum Anulus, in certa non bene fixus acu. Hoc facinus Lalage, speculo quo viderat, ulta est, Et cecidit saevis icta Plecusa comis. Desine iam, Lalage, tristes ornare capillos,* &c.

Juvenal 6. 490 *Disponit crinem laceratis ipsa capillis Nuda umero Psecas infelix nudisque mamillis. Altior hic quare cincinnus? taurea punit Continuo flexi crimen facinusque capilli,* &c.

(3) Persons[1].

Thymele and Latinus: Martial 1. 4. 5 *qui Thymelen spectas derisoremque Latinum:* 5. 61. 11 *quam dignus eras alapis, Mariane, Latini.* 9. 28 (his epitaph). Juv. 1. 36; 6. 44.

Fronto: Mart. 1. 55; 5. 34: Juvenal 1. 12 *Frontonis platani.* Mommsen (*Index Plin.*) thinks this is possibly the consul of A.D. 96.

Chione: Mart. 1. 35. 7 al. Juv. 3. 136.

Pontia: Mart. 2. 34; 4. 43: Juv. 6. 638 (where see the *scholia*).

Tongilius: Mart. 2. 40, Juv. 7. 130.

Cordus the poet: Mart. 2. 57; 3. 15; 5. 23; 5. 26: Juv. 1. 2; 3. 208.

Pollio the singer: Mart. 3. 20. 18; 4. 61; 12. 12, Juv. 6. 387. 7. 176.

---

[1] I should perhaps have said names, as many of the names in Martial and Juvenal are doubtless fictitious. But even where this is the case, the coincidence is no less striking, and tells, though in a different way, in favour of my argument.

Paris the *pantomimus*, Mart. 11. 13, Juv. 6. 87.

Catullus the mime-writer: Mart. 5. 30, Juv. 8. 186; 13. 111.

Hamillus the schoolmaster: Mart. 7. 62, Juv. 10. 224.

Glaphyrus the flute-player : Mart. 4. 5. 8, Juv. 6. 77.

(4) Words and expressions.

Mart. 1. 20. 4 *boletum qualem Claudius edit edas.*   Juv. 5. 147 *boletus domino, sed quales Claudius edit,* &c.

Mart. 1. 76. 14 *steriles cathedras.*   Juv. 7. 203 *vanae sterilisque cathedrae.*

Mart. 1. 92. 9 *pasceris et nigrae solo nidore culinae.*   Juv. 5. 162 *captum te nidore suae putat ille culinae.*

Mart. 2. 1. 4 *hoc primum est, brevior quod mihi carta perit:* 10. 4. 7 *quid te vana iuvant miserae ludibria cartae ?*   Juv. 1. 18 *periturae parcere cartae.*

Mart. 2. 43. 9 *tu Libycos Indis suspendis dentibus orbes.* Juv. 11. 122 *latos nisi sustinet orbes Grande ebur.*

Mart. 4. 54. 1 *cui Tarpeias liceat contingere quercus.*   Juv. 6. 387 *an Capitolinam deberet Pollio quercum Sperare.*

Mart. 5. 44. 11 *antiquae venies ad ossa cenae.*   Juv. 8. 90 *ossa vides rerum vacuis exsucta medullis.*

Mart. 6. 50. 5 *Vis fieri dives, Bithynice ? conscius esto: Nil tibi vel minimum basia pura dabunt.*   Juv. 3. 49 *quis nunc diligitur nisi conscius,* &c.

Mart. 6. 60. 10 *victurus genium debet habere liber.*   Juv. 6. 562 *nemo mathematicus genium indemnatus habebit.*

Mart. 6. 71. 3 *tendere quae tremulum Pelian Hecubaeque maritum Posset ad Hectoreos sollicitata rogos.*   Juv. 6. 325 *quibus incendi iam frigidus aevo Laomedontiades et Nestoris hirnea possit.*

Mart. 8. 21. 3 *placidi numquid te pigra Bootae Plaustra vehunt ?*   Juv. 5. 23 *pigri serraca Bootae.*

Mart. 9. 35 *Scis quid in Arsacia Pacorus deliberet aula: Rhenanam numeras Sarmaticamque manum: Verba ducis Daci cartis mandata resignas, Victricem laurum quam venit ante vides: Scis quotiens Phario madeat Iove fusca Syene, Scis quota de Libyco litore puppis eat.*   Juv. 6. 402 *Haec eadem novit quid*

toto fiat in orbe, Quid Seres, quid Thraces agant . . . Instantem
regi Armenio Parthoque cometen Prima videt, &c.
  Mart. 9. 73. 9 *frange leves calamos, et scinde, Thalia, libellos.*
Juv. 7. 27 *frange miser calamos, vigilataque proelia dele.*
  Mart. 10. 25. 5 *nam cum dicatur tunica praesente molesta,*
&c. Juv. 8. 235 *quod liceat tunica punire molesta.*
  Mart. 13. 64. 1 *succumbit sterili frustra gallina marito.*
Juv. 3. 91 *quo mordetur gallina marito.*
  Mart. 10. 87. 10 *Cadmi municipes ferat lucernas:* 14. 114
Hanc tibi Cumanae rubicundam pulvere testae Municipem misit
casta Sibylla suam. Juv. 14. 271 *municipes Iovis advexisse*
lagonas.

  Two things should be observed with regard to these coincidences: first, that they are of a kind which points rather to
independent handling of the same themes by two intimate
friends than to imitation by the one of the other's work:
secondly, that they for the most part occur in the first nine
satires of Juvenal; the great majority, indeed, in the first
seven. The most natural conclusion is that during the greater
part of Domitian's reign Martial and Juvenal virtually worked
together. This inference would agree with the tradition of
the biographies that Juvenal was a professor of declamation
usque ad mediam aetatem. For supposing his youth to have
fallen in the reign of Nero and his death to have taken place
(say) 127 or 128 A.D., his *media aetas* would begin about 85,
not long before the publication of Martial's first two books.

  It does not follow, of course, because Juvenal had written
satire in Domitian's reign, and shown it to Martial and perhaps
to other friends[1], that he had published anything so early.
In their present form, at any rate, it is probable, if not certain,
that most of his satires are later than Domitian's death[2].

---

[1] As to Quintilian? who says (10. 1.94) *sunt (satirici) clari hodieque, et
qui olim nominabuntur.*

[2] Teuffel's solution is as follows (*Studien und Charakteristiken,* pp. 413
–415: pp. 538–40 in ed. 2, 1889). 'Dass Juvenal seine Satiren unter
Domitian nicht verfasst hat, sondern erst unter Traian, . . . geht aus seiner

I have said that many of the earlier satires are, in my
opinion, to be assigned to the later years of Domitian. It will
no doubt be asked whether the seventh satire, *Et spes et ratio
studiorum in Caesare tantum*, does not belong to the age of
Trajan or Hadrian. Undoubtedly this is the opinion of most
modern commentators, including Mr. Mayor[1]. But it is evident
that this hypothesis lands us in considerable difficulties. The
setting of the piece is, in any case, taken from the time of
Domitian, for Statius and Quintilian are spoken of as if alive,
and the good fortune of Quintilian, indeed, as quite recent
(189, *exempla novorum Fatorum transi*). But the commentators,
for some reason which I cannot comprehend, seem to have
an invincible repugnance to applying the line *Et spes et ratio*,
to Domitian. In no case is the saying truer than in that of
Domitian that the evil which men do lives after them. For the
crimes of his later years I am not attempting to apologize.
But it is only just to say that they were committed by a man
whom suspicion and terror had driven to the verge of frenzy.
Domitian was probably not a man of strong head, and it should
never be forgotten that the historians of his reign belonged to
the senatorial party. It is abundantly clear, however, even
from their evidence, that his administration of the empire was
that of a careful and conscientious ruler[2]. The provinces were

ersteren Satire . . . positiv hervor. . . ihr (i.e. der Satiren) Stoff die Zeit
des Domitian ist.'
 ‘ Perspektivisches Zeichnen scheint seine’ (Juvenal's) ‘ Sache nicht zu sein ;
die grössere künstlerische Ruhe, das Masshalten, die versöhnte Stimmung,
den weiteren Gesichtskreis und die epische Glätte, welche sich daraus hätte
ergeben sollen, dass es etwas Vergangenes, hinter ihm Liegendes ist, was
er schildert, hat er nicht eintreten lassen, sondern den gleichen Eifer
aufgewendet, wie wenn er noch mitten stünde in dieser grauenvollen Zeit
und jeden Augenblick dadurch zu leiden hätte. Ueberhaupt hat ihn jene
Differenz zwischen der Zeit, in welcher er schreibt, und der, welche er
darstellt, nicht viel Kopfzerbrechen gekostet ; er ignoriert sie einfach.'
 [1] [Friedländer (*Sittengeschichte* iii. 3. Appendix 5) considers that the introduction (vv. 1–21) of Satire vii was addressed to Hadrian, but was written
later than the bulk of the Satire.]
 [2] Suetonius, Domitian, 2 *simulavit et ipse mire modestiam, imprimisque*

well governed in his reign, and justice well administered. Profligate and cruel in private life, he yet showed in some of his legislation a real concern for humanity and public morals. Though himself an indifferent general, there is no evidence that he was not concerned to make good military appointments. That he had an honest intention to encourage literature, so far as to do so seemed compatible with the security of the Empire and the preservation of private morality, there can be no doubt. He took steps for the restoration of libraries and the copying of texts. The calumny of Suetonius, that he read nothing but the *commentarii* and *acta* of Tiberius, is refuted by the undoubted fact that he read Martial, and was indeed concerned to keep that brilliant writer within the bounds of decency. And if he read Martial he probably read Turnus and Statius. The *agon Capitolinus*[1], or five-yearly contest of artists and men of letters on the Capitol, and the

poeticae studium, tam insuetum antea sibi quam postea spretum et abiectum, recitavitque etiam publice . . . 4. Instituit et quinquennale certamen Capitolino Iovi triplex, musicum equestre gymnicum, et aliquanto plurium quam nunc est coronarum. Certabant enim et prosa oratione Graece Latineque, &c. . . . Celebrabat et in Albano quot annis Quinquatria Minervae, cui collegium instituerat, ex quo sorte ducti magisterio fungerentur ederentque eximias venationes et scaenicos ludos, superque oratorum ac poetarum certamina.

8. Ius diligenter et industrie dixit, plerumque et in foro pro tribunali extra ordinem : ambitiosas centum virorum sententias rescidit : recuperatores, ne se perfusoriis adsertionibus accommodarent, identidem admonuit : nummarios iudices cum suo quemque consilio notavit. Auctor et TR. PL. fuit aedilem sordidum repetundarum accusandi iudicesque in eum a senatu petendi. Magistratibus quoque urbicis provinciarumque praesidibus coercendis tantum curae adhibuit, ut neque modestiores unquam neque iustiores extiterint : e quibus plerosque post illum reos omnium criminum vidimus. Suscepta correctione morum licentiam theatralem promiscue in equite spectandi inhibuit: scripta famosa vulgoque edita, quibus primores viri ac feminae notabantur, abolevit, &c.

[1] Statius *Silvae* 3. 5. 28 : *tu me nitidis Albana prementem Dona comis, sanctoque indutum Caesaris auro*, &c., 4. 2. 66 *Cum modo Germanas acies, modo Daca sonantem Proelia, Palladio tua me manus induit auro*. 4. 5. 22 *hic mea carmina Regina bellorum virago Caesareo decoravit auro*: 5. 3. 228 *si per me serta tu'isses Caesarea donata manu*.

similar trials of skill at the emperor's Alban villa, no doubt must have done something to encourage poetry and rhetoric, even if we believe Pliny (*Paneg.* 54) that they resulted largely in flattery of the emperor.

To state the matter quite fairly, we should probably say that to encourage literature was an honourable tradition of the early empire. Here, as in politics, the *princeps* took upon himself the functions of the old aristocracy. There was no deliberate intention on the part of the emperors to crush the freedom of speech as such : a poet or orator was safe so long as he remained on neutral ground. None the less, of course, is it true that the springs of all nobler writing were gradually choked up, as the aristocracy declined from its ancient power, position, and independence. For the production of great works expansion of soul is necessary, nor could minds of high powers and sincere emotion be content with the hackneyed themes of mythology or the trivialities of social intercourse. But, after all, the main burden of Juvenal's seventh satire is not so much the encouragement of literature by the court as its neglect by the nobility, its natural patrons ; and this is a point upon which Martial, writing mostly under Domitian, insists with almost wearisome iteration. *Sint Maecenates, non derunt, Flacce, Marones,* and so on. If the satire under discussion is to be allowed to have any life and meaning it must surely be assigned to the reign of Domitian.

It remains to be asked whether there is any evidence that Juvenal was banished from Rome, and if so, when he was banished ? The fact is asserted by all the memoirs, though they differ as to the place of exile. I will now mention the only other evidence which seems to me to bear upon the point, and of this I must confess that little can be made. Juvenal was probably in Rome in the year 92 and 93, when Martial completed his seventh book, in which, as we have seen, he addresses Juvenal twice. It is, however, noteworthy that Martial does not again address Juvenal till the year 101, five years after Domitian's death. Can the reason of this be the absence

of the exile from Rome ? If so, it may well be that Juvenal
was one of the large number of persons whom the last years of
Domitian drove from the city and from Italy.

Let us now, leaving the question of chronology, endeavour
to form an idea of the social surroundings into which Juvenal
was born, and to examine whether his satires are a faithful
reflection of them.

It is not too much to say that modern city life on a large
scale, the highest development of European civilization in its
best and its worst forms, has its first example in the Rome
of the first century A. D. In the history of moral progress,
eighteen hundred years would sometimes appear to be a mere
cipher.

I am not, be it well understood, wishing to understate
the differences between ancient and modern life as a whole ;
but even taking all these into account, it remains true that
Rome was the first great capital city in Europe, exhibiting in
its society all the features of the struggle for wealth, that is, for
power and position, which is the main characteristic of modern
life when left at repose from war or revolution. The central
fact which should be grasped in looking at the Roman society
of the early Empire, as contrasted with that of the last two
centuries of the Republic, is the comparative instability of
its distinctions. The disorder, the want of public security
of the last period of the Commonwealth, had endangered commerce, and thus helped to maintain the landed aristocracy
in an assured position. With the Empire came peace, and
their chances to all and sundry. *Nunc patimur longae pacis
mala*, says Juvenal regretfully in his sixth satire (286). While
the aristocracy was wasting its strength in futile struggles with
the court, and many noble families were becoming impoverished,
the honest merchant and the unscrupulous adventurer, Roman,
Greek, or Oriental, were pushing to the front and using their
new social and political opportunities. The situation was
much aggravated by the existence of slavery. A peculiar
character was given at this time, and at Rome, to this curse of

the ancient world.   Quantities of slaves of all known nations
and all characters were brought, from one reason or another, to
Rome.   Their disproportionate number tended, in one respect,
to alleviate their condition and prospects.   Emancipation was
easy and common.   It let loose upon society a number of
persons who had lived, and meant to live, by their wits, often
not inconsiderable, men who had done and suffered everything,
with the vices of slavery and without the virtues of freedom,
supple, serviceable, wicked.   'A serving-man, proud in heart
and in mind, that curled my hair, wore gloves in my cap,
served the lust of my mistress's heart and did the act of
darkness with her : swore as many oaths as I spake words,
and broke them in the sweet face of heaven : one that slept in
the contriving of lust and waked to do it.   Wine loved
I deeply, dice dearly, and in woman out-paramoured the Turk.
False of heart, light of ear, bloody of hand ; hog in sloth, fox
in stealth, wolf in greediness, dog in madness, lion in prey.'

In Shakespeare's portrait we seem to recognize the coarser
forms of the Calvisius Sabinus (Sen. *Ep.* 27. 5 foll.) the Hostius
Quadra (Sen. *N. Q.* 1. 16) the Zoilus and the Trimalchio of
Seneca, Martial, and Petronius ; men for whom the court,
in case of need, had its favours, ladies their commissions, men
of letters their filthiest verses.   The traditions of Italian man-
liness and dignity were violated at every turn by the influx
of foreign vice and the shamelessness of foreign adventure.
The mere presence of the Orientals irritated and alarmed
Roman feeling.   The hunt for wealth, the rush from step
to step of the social ladder, was fierce and undisguised [1].   There
was no end to the accumulation of large fortunes and the
formation of immense landed estates.   The desire of pleasure
gratified itself by every refinement of luxury ; the multitude of
slaves gave facilities for the gratification of every form of lust.

---

[1] Schol. Iuv. 5. 3 *Sarmentus . . . incertum libertus an servus, plurimis
forma et urbanitate promeritis eo fiduciae venit ut pro equite Romano ageret,
decuriam quoque quaestoriam compararet.*   See especially Pliny *H. N.* 33
§§ 32-34.

*Impudicitia in ingenuo probrum est, in servo necessitas, in li-
berto officium,* is an opinion quoted by the elder Seneca. A
loosening of the older social conventionalities began even in
the circles of the Roman nobility, who sometimes for their own
gratification, sometimes to please the court, would forget the
proprieties of a former day and turn actors, gladiators, charioteers.
Women enjoyed their share of the general freedom, and while
the more serious among them plunged into literature or law, or
became devotees of some foreign religion, others patronized
actors and gladiators, or pursued other and more questionable
forms of an emancipated life. Meanwhile the life of the
capital exercised its irresistible attraction upon the provinces.
Men streamed to Rome, with hopes, more or less slender, of
making a livelihood by honest means. They might succeed,
and make a name in literature or politics ; they might fail, and
become the restless and degraded dependents of one or more of
the great houses.

This is the dark side of the picture ; what is there to set
against it ? This century, if characterized by the beginning of
remarkable social changes, saw also the beginning of a religious
and moral evolution no less remarkable. In the upper and
better educated class philosophy and the higher culture were
producing considerable moral results. Philosophy and religion
are in this unfortunate, that while their practical manifestations
in ordinary life are often unrecognized even by honest observers,
any clever cynic can detect their counterfeit. Philosophy also,
as Bernays has well pointed out, lay in the ancient world under
a peculiar disadvantage. It was for the most part revolutionary
and opposed to the existing forms of social life. *Postremo nemo
aegrotus quicquam somniat Tam infandum, quod non aliquis dicat
philosophus,* is the verdict of healthy Roman common sense as
expressed in Varro's *Saturae (Eumenides* fr. 6). No doubt, as
the social evolution implied in the change from Greek to
Roman life worked itself gradually on, the antagonism became
less pronounced. The organization of the Roman empire was,
to a certain extent, a realization of the Stoical ideal ; at any

rate, it had broken down the conception of isolated city life, and substituted for it the conception of a larger society. An active performance of the duties of a citizen was not inconsistent— far from it—with the profession of a Stoic or Academician. None the less had the philosophic profession, as a whole, a strong tendency, at the period which we are considering, to isolate its followers if not from the duties, at least from the interests of ordinary life, and devote them to the contemplation of an ideal morality. Stoicism, the most influential theory in the first century, had a pronounced influence in this direction. That philosophers of any independence of character were looked upon with suspicion both by the government and by society lay in the nature of things[1]. *Errare mihi videntur,* says Seneca (*Epist.* 73. 1), *qui existimant philosophiae fideliter deditos contumaces esse et refractarios, contemptores magistratuum et regum eorumve per quos publica administrantur.* The prejudice extended to men who professed to represent a sound and common-sense view of educated life and conduct, men like Quintilian, Martial, and Juvenal. These could only see that there were not a few hypocrites among the professors of philosophy (Quint. 12. 3. 2, Sen. *Ep.* 29. 2, Juv. and Mart. ll. cc.).

If philosophy was doing much to hold a lofty ideal of life before the eyes of those among the cultivated classes whose intellect and moral sense were capable of accepting its teaching, Judaism found its way from the Jewish quarters into the great houses, and was popular, nay, even fashionable, among rich and high-born ladies. But of the great revolution which was silently preparing itself among the lower orders, binding together the poor and oppressed into a new society, with principles of conduct, a mode and object of worship, and hopes for the future unknown or imperfectly known before, the upper classes, in Rome at any rate, knew nothing. Christianity was to them no more than a form of Judaism.

---

[1] Seneca *Epist.* 5. 2 *Satis ipsum nomen philosophiae, etiamsi modeste tractatur, invidiosum est . . . Intus omnia dissimilia sint: frons populo conveniat.*

In the presence of social phenomena so absorbingly interesting, what is Juvenal's attitude? Are his pictures of contemporary life to be trusted? Does he, in his character of moralist,
represent the highest effort of contemporary thought?

In a sense in which Juvenal did not intend the words,
difficile erat saturam non scribere. The *satura* was not properly
an attack on vice and folly, though Juvenal did his best to
encourage the idea that it was, but a sketch of life and character.
The Romans had a natural aptitude for this kind of writing,
not because they were more spiteful than the Greeks, but
because they had a larger sphere of experience, and a greater
knowledge of the *ars vivendi.* At the time which we are now
considering, the artist had abundance of materials, nor is it
surprising that during these years two eminent poets, Martial
and Juvenal, refused to have anything to say to the old
mythologies, and turned to real life for their models. Turnus,
a third excellent writer of the time and a satirist like Juvenal,
has been so unfortunate as to leave to posterity nothing but his
name, which is coupled with that of Juvenal by Rutilius Nama-
tianus (1. 603). Martial (11. 10) says of him *Contulit ad saturas
ingentia pectora Turnus :* and again (7. 97. 8) *Turni nobilibus
libellis.*

Juvenal was the native of a country town, Aquinum, and
had been brought up in the house of a rich *libertinus,* whether
as his son or fosterchild is unknown. In position he exactly
resembled his contemporary Turnus, who, if we may believe a
notice preserved in Valla's *scholia* to Juvenal 1. 20, attained
great influence in the courts of Titus and Vespasian. He
seems to have been in Rome from his childhood upwards (3. 84
nostra infantia, &c.). Thus, though an Italian by birth, he was
a Roman by education, and as a consequence became a Roman
in sympathies and antipathies. Several passages show that for
some time at least he was a *cliens,* in the later sense of the
word, that is, a poor dependent on great houses : 1. 99 *iubet
a praecone vocari Ipsos Troiugenas, nam vexant limen et ipsi
Nobiscum ;* 3. 187 *praestare tributa clientes Cogimur, et cultis*

augere peculia servis: and so Mart. 12. 18 *Dum tu forsitan inquietus erras,* &c.

The statement of the memoirs, that Juvenal practised declamation till middle age, is abundantly confirmed by the tone of his compositions. The touch of the *declamator* is every-where. There is no need, with Ribbeck (*Der echte und unechte Iuvenal*) to separate the declamatory satires, such as the tenth, from the rest[1]. Some pieces evidently contain several rhetorical *loci* or passages of description well tricked out and loosely strung together. Such are, for instance, the picture of Otho 2. 99–109 : of Eppia, 6. 82 foll. : of Messalina, 6. 114 foll.: of Lateranus, 8. 146 : the verses on Cicero, Marius, and the Decii 8. 231–268 : on Seianus, 10. 56 foll., and others in the same satire. The composition again is sometimes that of a rhetor-ician, loose, inharmonious, inconsistent. The first satire is a series of incoherent complaints : *unde illae lacrimae?* A married impotent, an athletic lady, a barber rich enough to challenge the fortunes of all the patricians : the Egyptian Crispinus with his ring, the lawyer Matho in his litter: the infamous will-hunter, the robber of his ward, the plunderer of the provinces : the pander husband, the low-born spendthrift, the forger, the poisoner ; all these are hurried together in no intelligible order, and with the same introductory *cum hoc fiat,* and the same conclusion in several variations *non scribam saturam?* Then at v. 81 the satire seems to open again and promise a description of various vices, but instead of this we have an elaborate complaint, extending over many lines, of the poverty of the nobility, with a description of the hardships of a client. The ill-proportioned piece concludes with a promise to write against the dead, and the dead are to be (if we are to suppose any coherence at all in the peroration) those who lived before the days of Nero. Yet the satire in another passage (*exul ab octava,* &c.) purports to have been written after 100 A.D.

[1] Teuffel's answer to Ribbeck (*Studien und Charakteristiken,* p. 414, p.539 in ed. 2) is well worth reading.

Juvenal's most elaborate effort is the sixth satire. A very brief analysis of the first part of this celebrated piece will discover the badness of its composition, 1–59 : Do not think of marriage, few women being both chaste and fair : 60–113 do not look for a wife in the theatre : all ladies prefer actors and gladiators : 114–135 Messalina's habits are described : 135–160 no men love their wives, but only their wives' fortune or beauty : 161–183 a perfect wife would be intolerable : 184–199 it is very bad in a lady to talk Greek : 200–224 a wife is always a tyrant: 225–230 she will marry as often as she likes : 231–241 the daughter-in-law is corrupted by the mother-in-law : 242–245 there is a woman in every lawsuit : 246–267 ladies are often very fond of gymnastics : and so on, and so on.

In fact, with all its brilliancy of execution in detail, the piece, as far as composition is concerned, is a mere chamber of horrors. The main theme, that it is madness to marry because a good wife cannot be found, is not so much worked out as illustrated by a series of pictures quite unconnected, and arguments sometimes inconsistent. The gist of the argument seems to be that women are either very bad or very good, or too learned, or too athletic ; but in truth there is no argument properly so called, but a string of sketches, which give the impression of having been drawn not from a wide observation of life, but from particular and notorious cases. An instance of Juvenal's desire to produce effect at the expense of consistency is to be found in his treatment of the passion of women for athletics and for law, in the second and in the sixth satires. In the second satire, where his object is to exalt women at the expense of men, Favonia is made to say *luctantur paucae, comedunt colyphia paucae : Numquid nos agimus causas, civilia iura Novimus ?* &c. But in the sixth satire (242 foll., 246 foll., 352 foll.) a directly opposite impression is conveyed.

Rhetoric, as Matthew Arnold well says, is always inconsistent, and this is the inconsistency of the rhetorician. A corresponding unreality tinges many of Juvenal's utterances as a moralist. We have seen that in the first satire he expends much the same amount of indignation on the *nouveau riche* of a barber as on the most abandoned criminals, and that the grievances of the poor client, perhaps his own grievances, occupy a place out of all proportion to their moral importance. Still more strikingly conspicuous is this perversity of judgement in the second and eighth satires [1]. In the eighth, after some hundred and fifty verses of excellent quality in all respects, Juvenal strikes off into an indignant tirade against the nobleman who is too fond of horses, the nobleman who acts on the stage, and the crimes of Nero: which are, it would seem, his murders of his mother and his relations; and, as a climax, his love of music and the drama. Are we reading De Quincey's *Art of Murder?* or is further evidence needed that Juvenal is only half a moralist, that irritation against social improprieties is almost as strong an element of his invective as genuine anger against vice? That with such a point of view he should have no theory of life but that of the most superficial common sense, that he should see little in philosophy but a solemn imposture, is only natural (14. 120)[2]. Nemesis overtakes him, however: he has nothing to say against slavery nor against the games of the amphitheatre, though Seneca (see *Epist.* 7 and 47) completely condemns them.

Nor can this capriciousness be defended on the ground that Juvenal is not a moralist but a humorist. If he falls short of the simple philosophical elevation of Persius, he is equally incapable of the light and plastic touch of Petronius. From Juvenal we hear what people on particular occasions have done; but we know nothing of their personality; he cannot draw a character, he cannot laugh. Think of Juvenal's Virro and

---

[1] In the second (v. 143), after mentioning a case of unnatural vice, he goes on *Vicit et hoc monstrum tunicati fuscina Gracchi, Lustravitque fugam,* &c.

[2] It is interesting to compare this satire with Seneca's forty-fourth epistle.

then of Petronius's Trimalchio ; the one is a figure cut out in
paper, the other a living man. The inconsistencies of the
sixth satire might be defended in a humorist ; he would be in
his right in saying that a licentious wife or an over-virtuous
wife are equally objectionable. But this ground is not open to
the moralist, who is bound to defend virtue against all cavil.

In fact, Juvenal is at his best not when he is lashing vice,
but when he is in the vein of grave and simple moral expostulation. The tenth satire is perhaps too declamatory to be
taken as a specimen of his best work : the thirteenth and fourteenth are better, defaced by none of the faults which I have
mentioned, and carrying the reader along from point to point
with sweetness and dignity.

The style of Juvenal, the influence of which is so familiar
in modern literature, is, so far as we know, new in satire.
While Persius imitates Horace, and makes at least a clumsy
attempt to preserve the form of a dialogue, Juvenal, in most of
his pieces, throws this entirely aside, and casts his ideas into
the mould of the Vergilian epic. *Fingimus haec altum satira*
sumente coturnum Scilicet, et finem egressi legemque priorum
Grande Sophocleo carmen bacchamur hiatu Montibus ignotum
Rutulis caeloque Latino (6. 634). Taking these words out of
their context, we might accept them as a description of Juvenal's manner, which, like all we know of the man, is elevated,
serious, and unbending. He is a perfect master of his
metre, a perfect master of expression within the limits of his
ideas. But his ideas, and the way in which he marshals
them, are those of the poetical declaimer, not of the poet.
Facit indignatio versum : verses, yes ; but not poetry. It
would be difficult to quote from Juvenal one really poetical
line. But he is a great metrist, a master of points, a rhetorician
inspired by the love of his calling. His arrangement is often
bad : it is his glittering language which arrests attention. It is
this, far more than the coherence or truthfulness of his workmanship, which has won and will maintain his position in
literature. There is a genuine and passionate rhetoric which

seems almost to reach the strain of poetry ; this is the gift of
Juvenal, which we should do ill to underrate.   But we should
do equally ill to mistake it for anything higher than it really is,
or to put too much confidence in a writer honest indeed, but
soured by poverty and disappointed ambition, who, with
whatever brilliancy of detail, does not pass beyond the bounds
of a somewhat narrow experience, mingles righteous anger with
much personal irritation, and gives, after all, an exaggerated
picture of a peculiar phase of ancient life.

[NOTE TO PAGE 118.

The ancient lives of Juvenal have been collected by Julius Dürr, *Das Leben
Juvenals* (Ulm, 1888).

It may perhaps save trouble to print here the unpublished life of Juvenal
to which Mr. Nettleship alludes on p. 118, though it is of no real value, being
almost identical with Jahn's third life, still more so with Dürr's IV A. It
occurs on the first page of MS. Canon. Lat. xxxvii :—

Iuuenalis iste Aquinas fuit i. de Aquino oppido temporibus Claudii Neronis
imperatoris: prima aetate siluit : in media fere aetate declamauit ; unde
quasi diu tacens ab indignatione cepit, dicens ' semper ego auditor tantum.'
Idem fecit quoddam in Paridem pantomimum, qui tunc apud imperatorem
plurimum poterat (?) : hac de causa venit in suspitionem quasi ipsius imperatoris tempora notasset. Sicque sub autentu militiae pulsus est urbe : ita
tristitia et languore periit.]

VI.

THE STUDY OF LATIN GRAMMAR AMONG THE ROMANS IN THE FIRST CENTURY A.D.[1]

('JOURNAL OF PHILOLOGY,' VOL. XV. (1886).)

———•••———

THE history of Latin Grammar in antiquity demands a new chapter in the record of Latin literature. The seven volumes of Keil's edition of the *Grammatici Latini* appear to contain a large number of independent grammatical treatises, which bear different names, and are often quoted as the works of independent authors. A nearer study of them soon reveals the fact that they consist, in large part, of matter nearly or quite identical ; that the same rules, lists, and instances served as the stock in trade of a great number of different professors at various times and in distant places : and that the whole mass might probably be so sifted as to reduce the bulk of original work to a comparatively small amount, and enable us to refer it to the authorship of probably less than a dozen scholars, none of them later than the age of the Antonines.

The work of analysis will certainly be tedious beyond expression, but it will be worth going through, and indeed must be gone through before the history of Latin literature is complete. I can personally claim to have done no more than attempt an

---

[1] [Prof. Nettleship left a few notes for the revision of this essay, but they were far too fragmentary for another hand to use.]

account of the labours of Verrius Flaccus, and make a beginning in the way of investigating the sources of Gellius's *Noctes Atticae* and the *De Compendiosa Doctrina* of Nonius. The present essay will be devoted to an extension of these enquiries. It may fairly be said of this troublesome piece of research, as Quintilian says of grammar in general, *plus habet operis quam ostentationis.* As far as I know, there is no continuous work in which the subject is dealt with with anything like thorough‑ness. Much has been done towards the investigation of particular points by several scholars in Germany, as by Alfred Schottmüller in his monograph *De C. Plinii libris grammaticis,* by Casimir Morawski's *Quaestiones Quintilianeae* and analysis of the first part of Charisius's *Ars Grammatica,* by H. F. Neumann's essay *De Plinii Dubii Sermonis Libris Cha‑risii et Prisciani fontibus,* and by Schlitte *De Plinii Secundi Studiis Grammaticis* (Nordhausen, 1883). These treatises, none of which exceed the length of an ordinary dissertation for the degree of doctor of philosophy, are, with some German reviews upon them, the only aids which I have been able to procure [1].

It will perhaps be convenient that I should divide my subject into two parts ; giving, in the first place, a short account of the scholars who wrote upon grammar during this period, with a sketch of their works, and in the second place en‑deavouring to ascertain the contents of these works, and mark the progress of the science, if any, recorded in them.

I. It would be impossible to gain anything like an intelligent idea of the progress of grammatical study in the first century without taking notice of the labours of Marcus Terentius Varro, on which, to a large extent, though perhaps not to so large an extent as has sometimes been supposed, the work of succeeding scholars was based.

Varro, then, composed neither a regular *Ars Grammatica,* nor a lexicon. But he treated *grammatica* as one of the

[1] Dr. J. W. Beck has kindly presented the writer with his *Quaestiones Novae de M. Valerio Probo* (Groningen, 1886) since these sheets were sent to press. See p. 169 *n.*

nine *disciplinae*, or stages of the ordinary educational *curriculum*, translating the word γραμματική by *litteratura*, a term fairly equivalent to our word *philology* when used in the wider sense. Of *litteratura* or γραμματική Varro took the broader view which was the inheritance of the Alexandrian tradition. He defined it as consisting of four parts, reading, interpretation, correction, and criticism : *lectio, enarratio, emendatio, iudicium.* His book is known to have included also a treatment (*a*) of the alphabet, (*b*) of parts of speech, of which he recognized four, (*c*) of pronouns, (*d*) of local adverbs or prepositions. And it can hardly be doubted that he must also have handled the subject of nouns and verbs.

Besides the *Disciplinae*, which was more or less an educational handbook, Varro was the author of several fuller and more valuable treatises.

(1) The *De Lingua Latina*, in twenty-five books, only a few of which remain. This was a comprehensive work on the Latin language, including discussions on etymology, gender, case-formation, comparison of adjectives, conjugation of verbs, and the collocation of words in forming sentences.

(2) *De Sermone Latino. Lingua* means language, *sermo* language in a connected form : in other words, *lingua* is language, *sermo* is usage. The treatise of Varro consisted of five books, which discussed orthography, accent, quantity, metre, and the various styles of prose composition.

(3) *De Antiquitate Litterarum ;* probably one of his earliest works, treating of the origin and history of the Latin alphabet.

(4) *De Origine Linguae Latinae ;* probably a discussion of the connexion between the Greek and Latin languages.

(5) *De Similitudine Verborum.* Of this only a single fragment remains, and the same must be said of

(6) *De Utilitate Sermonis.*

Two other important works belonging to the last years of the republic must be mentioned, the *Commentarii Grammatici* of Nigidius Figulus, and the *De Analogia* of Julius Caesar. The first was a work in some thirty books, which according to

Gellius, who has preserved some fragments of it, was prevented by its style from becoming popular, or even as widely known as the writings of Varro. Julius Caesar's treatise *De Analogia* consisted of two books, the first of which dealt with the alphabet [1] and with words [2]: the second with irregularities of inflection in nouns and verbs.

We have now arrived at the Augustan age. The first work which meets us here is the lexicon (*De Verborum Significatu*) of Verrius Flaccus, a contemporary of Livy. Of this work and its author I have already given an account in my *Essays in Latin Literature*. Verrius also wrote a work *De Orthographia*, of which I shall have occasion to speak further on.

Of M. Pomponius Marcellus, a scholar of the age of Tiberius, I believe that nothing is known but what Suetonius tells us in the twenty-second chapter of his *De Grammaticis* [3]. Originally a boxer, and one must presume a slave, he for some reason or other turned his attention to scholarship, and became a very severe critic of the Latin of his contemporaries. He informed Tiberius that though he could confer the franchise upon human beings, to confer it upon words was out of his power. We must suppose from the account given us by Suetonius—and this I believe is all we have—that he made his livelihood by practice at the bar and teaching grammar: that he wrote anything there is no evidence.

I come next to a figure notable for a time in Roman society

---

[1] Pompeius in Keil's *Grammatici Latini* 5. p. 108.

[2] Gellius I. 10.

[3] *M. Pomponius Marcellus, sermonis Latini exactor molestissimus, in advocatione quadam (nam interdum et causas agebat) soloecismum ab adversario factum usque adeo arguere perseveravit, quoad Cassius Severus, interpellatis iudicibus, dilationem petiit, ut litigator suus alium grammaticum adhiberet: 'quando non putat is cum adversario de iure sibi, sed de soloecismo controversiam futuram.' Hic idem, cum ex oratione Tiberium reprehendisset, adfirmante Ateio Capitone, et esse illud Latinum, et si non esset futurum certe iam inde, ' Mentitur,' inquit, ' Capito ; tu enim, Caesar, civitatem dare potes hominibus, verbo non potes.' Pugilem olim fuisse Asinius Gallus hoc in cum epigrammate ostendit : ' Qui caput ad laevam didicit, glossemata nobis Praecipit : os nullum, vel potius pugilis.'*

and ever afterwards in the history of Latin Grammar, that of Remmius Palaemon of Vicenza [1]. This vain, arrogant, talented, luxurious and immoral man was born, it is probable, during the last years of Augustus's reign. He was originally a slave, by trade a weaver, and learned the rudiments of literature while accompanying his master's son to and from school. Having obtained his freedom, he took to teaching grammar at Rome. Although there was no vice with which he was not commonly charged, although both Tiberius and Claudius openly stated that he was the last man to whom the education of youth ought to be committed, his long memory, his readiness as a speaker, and his power of extemporizing verses, enabled him to distance all his competitors. Nor was his school his only source of emolument, though it brought him in £4000 a year. He made a considerable profit from clothes-shops, and succeeded to a marvel in the cultivation of the vine.

Palaemon's *Ars Grammatica*, or handbook of grammar, seems to have been the first exclusively scholastic treatise on Latin Grammar. For the section on *Grammatica* in Varro's *Disciplinae* was, in all probability, no more a school-book than Freund's *Triennium Philologicum*, or Iwan Müller's *Handbuch der klassischen Philologie*. Varro and Verrius Flaccus had taken the trouble to collect stores of material; our able pedagogue knew how to turn their labours to his own profit. Nor was he in the least grateful to the scholar who was no doubt indirectly responsible for much of his success. Terentius Varro he called a pig, and boasted that letters had been born and would die with himself.

The *Ars* of Palaemon, which gained its author considerable celebrity in his day, contained, as we learn from Juvenal, rules for correct speaking, instances from ancient poets, and chapters on barbarism and solecism [2]. When it was published is not

---

[1] Suetonius *De Grammaticis* 23.

[2] Juvenal 6. 452 *Odi Hanc ego, quae repetit volvitque Palaemonis artem, Servata semper lege et ratione loquendi, Nec curanda viris opicae castigat amicae Verba: soloecismum liceat fecisse marito.* Ib. 7. 215.

known, but for a reason which I will mention below I think it probable that the date fell between 67 and 77 A. D.

I now proceed to mention the eight books of the elder Pliny entitled *Dubii Sermonis*, an expression which may be paraphrased *On Irregularities in Formation*. This work was written in the last years of Nero's reign, when, as the younger Pliny puts it [1], the atmosphere of despotism made it dangerous to pursue any free or manly branch of study. It had been published for ten years when Pliny, in 77 A.D., was writing the Preface to his Natural History [2]; and it had excited some opposition among the philosophers of all the principal sects. The *Ars Grammatica* attributed to Pliny by Priscian and Gregory of Tours is, it can hardly be doubted after all the labour expended on the point by recent scholars, the same work as the *Dubii Sermonis*.

I must finally mention the man who was probably the best scholar of the century, M. Valerius Probus of Berytus in Syria. This remarkable man took up the study of scholarship, if we may believe Suetonius, only after failing to succeed in the military profession. The study of the ancient authors—and such was the self-confidence of the Augustan writers and their immediate successors that Cicero, Lucretius, Catullus, and Varro were reckoned and perhaps half-despised as ancients long before the century had run its course—soon began to languish at Rome. But these writers maintained their reputation out of Italy, and the curiosity of Probus was awakened by reading some of them with a provincial lecturer. The study of these authors inspired him to go on to others, and regardless of the fact that the pains he was spending were likely to gain him nothing but discredit, he determined to devote his life to the emendation, punctuation, and explanation of ancient texts. He appears to have paid especial attention to Terence, Lucretius, Vergil and Horace [3]. He published but little of importance

---

[1] *Epist.* 3. 5. 5.   [2] *H. N.* Praef. § 28.

[3] Suetonius *De Viris Illustribus*, p. 138 (Reifferscheid) : *Probus illas (notas) in Vergilio et Horatio et Lucretio apposuit, ut in Homero Aristarchus.*

during his lifetime, but left a considerable posthumous work in the shape of a *Silva Observationum Sermonis Antiqui*, or miscellaneous collection of ancient usage ; and also a book *De inaequalitate consuetudinis*. He was alive in 88 A. D., but his merits had been recognized at Rome some thirty years before [1].

II. So much upon the external history of grammatical study during this period. We have now to enter upon the more difficult and interesting part of our task, and endeavour to ascertain approximately what were the contents and character of the various works just mentioned.

Much of the treatise of Verrius Flaccus *De Orthographia* can be recovered from the books *De Orthographia* of Terentius Scaurus and Velius Longus [2], who wrote under Trajan and Hadrian, and from the seventh, with part of the fourth, chapters of Quintilian's first book. This statement I am, of course, bound to make good ; and must ask for the patient attention of the reader while I develop a somewhat tedious argument.

The treatises of Terentius Scaurus and Velius Longus on orthography are so generally similar that they may almost certainly be referred to a common authority. Now we have already seen that Varro had a disquisition on orthography in his *De Sermone Latino*. But, so far as we can infer from the remaining fragments of this work, Varro treated the subject incidentally only, as a branch of Latin usage. He does not seem to have written any special work on correct spelling. Nor, again, is it at all likely that Scaurus and Longus had direct recourse to this section of the *De Sermone Latino*. They often, indeed, mention Varro, but as an authority of whom they are independent, and from whom they are quite ready to differ. And their range of quotations includes Vergil, which Varro, who died in 27 B. C., could hardly have done.

It is next to be observed that the authority followed by Scaurus and Longus must have been more ancient than

---

[1] Conington's Vergil, vol. 1. 4th edition, p. lxiv.

[2] Keil *Grammatici Latini* vol. 7 : the following references to Scaurus and Longus are to the pages of that volume.

Quintilian. For it is impossible to read the fourth and the seventh chapters of Quintilian's first book side by side with Longus and Scaurus *De Orthographia* without noticing the remarkable correspondences between them. Let me exhibit these in detail, by printing Quintilian in the text, and the parallel passages from Longus, Scaurus and Paulus in the notes :

Quintil. I. 4.

§§ 7, 8. *Desintne aliquae nobis necessariae litterae, non cum Graeca scribimus (tum enim ab iis duas mutuamur) sed proprie in Latinis, ut in his 'servus' et 'vulgus' aeolicum digamma*[1] *desideratur, et medius est quidam 'u' et 'i' litterae sonus: non enim sic 'optimum' dicimus ut 'opimum*[2].'

§ 9. *An rursus aliae redundent (praeter illam adspirationis notam, quae si necessaria est etiam contrariam sibi poscit), ut k, quae et ipsa quorundam nominum nota est, et q, cuius similis effectu specieque, nisi quod paulum a nostris obliquatur, coppa apud Graecos nunc tantum in numero manet*[3], *et nostrarum ultima, qua tam carere potuimus, quam psi non quaerimus*[4].

[1] Scaurus p. 12 Keil *quia antiqui per ' uo ' scripserint... ignorantes eam praepositam vocali consonantis vice fungi et poni pro ea littera que sit* f : so Longus 58.

[2] Longus 49 *ut iam in ambiguitatem cadat, utrum per i quaedam debeant dici an per u, ut est optumus maximus. In quibus adnotandum antiquum sermonem plenioris soni fuisse, et, ut ait Cicero, rusticanum, atque illis fere placuisse per u talia scribere et enuntiare. Erravere autem grammatici, qui putaverunt superlativa per u enuntiari. Ut enim concedamus illis in optimo, in maximo, in pulcherrimo, in iustissimo, quid facient in his nominibus in quibus aeque manet eadem quaestio superlatione sublata, manubiae an manibiae, libido an lubido?* See ib. 67, quoted below, p. 156, note 3.

[3] Scaurus 14 foll. *K quidam supervacuam esse litteram iudicaverunt, quoniam vice illius fungi satis C posset...* 15 *Q littera aeque retenta est propter notas...* 16 *Unde et Graeci coppa, quod pro hac ponebant, omiserunt, postquam usu quoque, quod auxilio eius litterae non indigebant, supervacuum visum est :* comp. Longus 53.

Scaurus 23 *Primum illud respondemus, H esse litteram, &c.* Comp. Longus 52, 53, who concludes on the whole that *h* is a letter. This was denied by Varro: see Priscian *Inst.* I. 16 (Keil *Gramm.* 2. 13).

[4] Longus 50 *Z lingua Latina non agnoscit.*

§ 10. *At quae ut vocales iunguntur aut unam longam faciunt, ut veteres scripserunt, qui geminatione earum velut apice utebantur*[1]*, aut duas, nisi quis putat etiam ex tribus vocalibus syllabam fieri, si non aliquae officio consonantium fungantur.*

§ 11. *Littera i sibi insidit: 'coniicit' enim est ab illo 'iacit,' et u, quomodo nunc scribitur 'vulgus' et 'servus.' Sciat etiam Ciceroni placuisse 'aiio Maiiamque' geminata i scribere; quod si est, etiam iungetur ut consonans*[2]*.*

§ 12. *Quare discat puer, quid in litteris proprium, quid commune, quae cum quibus cognatio: nec miretur cur ex 'scamno' fiat 'scabillum,' aut a pinno, quod est acutum, securis utrimque habens aciem 'bipennis*[3]*.'*

§ 13. *Ut Valesii et Fusii in Valerios Furiosque venerunt, ita arbos labos vapos etiam et clamos ac lases et asae fuerunt*[4]*.*

§ 14. *Atque ipsa s littera ab his nominibus in quibusdam ipsa alteri successit: nam 'mertare' atque 'pultare' dicebant*[5]*: quin 'fordeum faedosque' pro aspiratione f ut simili littera utentes*[6]*:*

§ 15. *Sed b quoque in locum aliarum dedimus aliquando,*

---

[1] Scaurus 18 *Accius geminatis vocalibus scribi natura longas syllabas voluit, cum alioqui adiecto vel sublato apice longitudinis et brevitatis nota posset ostendi.* Comp. Longus 55.

[2] Longus 54 *Cicero videtur auditu emensus scriptionem, qui et Aiiacem et Maiiam per duo i scribenda existimavit: quidam unum esse animadvertunt...Inde crescit ista geminatio, et incipit per tria i scribi coiiicit, ut prima syllaba sit coi, sequentes duo iicit.*

Ib. 58 *Cum per o (volgus et servos) scriberent, per u tamen enuntiabant.* Comp. Scaurus 12.

[3] Scaurus 14 *B cum p et m consentit, quoniam origo eorum non sine labore coniuncto ore respondet... Et alii scamillum, alii scabillum dicunt.*

[4] Paulus p. 23 M.: Scaurus 13 and 23: Longus 69 and 73.

[5] Paulus 81 *exfuti effusi, ut mertat pro mersat.* 124 *mertat pro mersat dicebant.*

[6] Paulus 84 *'faedum' antiqui dicebant pro 'haedo,' 'folus' pro 'holere,' 'fostim' pro 'hoste,' 'fostiam' pro 'hostia.'* Scaurus 11 *ubi illi f litteram posuerunt, nos h substituimus, ut quod illi 'fordeum' dicebant nos 'hordeum,' 'fariolum' quem nos 'hariolum,' similiter 'faedum' quem nunc nos 'haedum' dicimus.* Comp. ib. 13 and 23: Longus 69.

unde 'Burrus' et 'Bruges' et 'Belena[1]*.'* (? Read *ballena* from Paul. 31, *ballenam* : . . . *hanc illi* φάλαιναν *dicebant antiqui consuetudine, qua* πύρρον *burrum,* πύξον *buxum dicebant.) Nec non eadem fecit ex 'duello' 'bellum,' unde Duelios quidam dicere Belios ausi*[2].

§ 16. *Quid 'stlocum stlitesque*[3]*'?*

Quid d litterae cum t quaedam cognatio[4] *?*

Quid o atque u permutatae invicem? ut 'Hecoba' et 'notrix,' 'Culcides' et 'Pulixena' scriberentur, ac ne in Graecis id tantum notetur, 'dederont' et 'probaveront[5]*.'*

§ 17. *Quid? non e quoque i loco fuit? 'Menerva' et 'leber' et 'magester' et 'Diove Victore,' non 'Diovi Victori*[6]*.'*

Quintilian 1. 7.

§ 4. *Putaverunt illa quoque servanda discrimina, ut 'ex' praepositionem, si verbum sequeretur 'specto,' adiecta secundae syllabae s littera, si 'pecto,' remota scriberemus*[7].

§ 5. *Illa quoque servata est a multis differentia, ut 'ad' cum esset praepositio, d litteram, cum autem coniunctio, t acciperet*[8].

---

[1] Paul. 31 '*Burrum*' *dicebant antiqui quod nunc dicimus* '*rufum*. Scaurus 14 *quem Graeci* Πυρρίαν *nos* '*Byrriam,*' *et quem nos* '*Pyrrhum*' *antiqui* '*Burrum,*' &c.

[2] Paul. 66 *duellum bellum*.

[3] Paulus 312 *ea consuetudine qua* '*stlocum*' *pro* '*locum*' *et* '*stlitem*' *pro* '*litem*' *dicebant*.

[4] Scaurus 11 and Longus 69 notice this, instancing the necessary distinction between *ad* and *at*. See note 8.

[5] Longus 49 (after quoting Verrius Flaccus he proceeds, probably from Varro) *Apud nos quoque antiqui ostendunt, qui aeque confusas o et u litteras habuere. Nam* '*consol*' *scribebatur per o, cum legeretur per u, consul. Unde in multis etiam nominibus variae sunt scripturae, ut fontes funtes, frondes frundes.* Comp. Pliny ap. Prisc. *Inst.* 1. 35, Keil p. 26, 27.

[6] Longus 73 discusses *delerus* and *delirus, fesiae* and *feseae*. Paul. 12 notices *loeber* and *loebertas* for *liber, libertas*.

[7] Longus 63 *In eo quod est expectatus duplicem scriptionem quidam esse voluerunt*. (But the distinction is a different one from Quintilian's.)

[8] Scaurus 11 : Longus 61, 62, 69. See note 4.

'*Cum,*' *si tempus significaret, per q et m, si comitem, per c ac duas sequentes scriberetur*[1].

§ 6. *Frigidiora his alia, ut '*quidquid*' c quartum haberet, ne interrogare bis videremur*[2], *et quotidie, non cotidie, ut si quot diebus*[3].

§ 7. *Quaeri solet, in scribendo praepositiones sonum, quem iunctae efficiunt, an quem separatae, observare conveniat, ut cum dico '*obtinuit*' : secundam enim b litteram ratio poscit, aures magis audiunt p*[4].

§ 10. *K quidem in nullis verbis utendum puto nisi quae significat, etiam ut sola ponatur*[5].

§ 15. *Diutius duravit ut e et i iungendis eadem ratione qua Graeci* ει *uterentur: ea casibus numerisque discreta est, ut Lucilius praecipit*

> *iam puerei venere : e postremum facito atque i*
> *ut pueri plures fiant :*

ac deinceps idem

> *mendaci furique addes e, cum dare furi*
> *iusseris*[6].

---

[1] Caper Keil *Gramm.* vol. 7 p. 95.   [2] Caper 95.

[3] Longus 79 (*Existimo*) *illos vitiose et dicere et scribere, qui potius per quo quotidie dicunt, quam per co cotidie. . . . Non enim est a quoto die quotidie dictum, sed a continenti die cotidie tractum.*

[4] Longus 64 '*Ob*' *praepositio interdum . . . ad eam litteram transit, a qua sequens vox incipit, ut est* '*offulsit,*' '*ommutuit*' : *item et si p sequatur, ut* '*opposuit.*'

[5] Longus 53 *Qui k expellunt, notam dicunt esse magis quam litteram, qua significamus kalumniam kaput kalendas.* Comp. Scaurus 15.

[6] Longus 55, 56 *Hic quaeritur etiam an per e et i quaedam debeant scribi secundum consuetudinem Graecam. Non nulli enim ea quae producerentur sic scripserunt, alii contenti fuerunt huic productioni i longam aut notam dedisse. Alii vero, quorum est item Lucilius, varie scriptitaverunt, siquidem in iis quae producerentur alia per i longam, alia per e et i notaverunt, velut differentia quaedam separantes, ut cum diceremus '*viri,*' si essent plures, per e et i scriberemus, si vero esset unius viri, per i notaremus Et Lucilius in nono*

> '*iam puerei venere,*' *e postremum facito atque i,*
> *ut puerei plures fiant, i si facis solum,*
> '*pupilli,*' '*pueri,*' '*Lucili,*' *hoc unius fiet.*

Quod quidem cum supervacuum est, ... tum incommodum aliquando.

§ 18. *Ae syllabam, cuius secundam nunc e litteram ponimus, varie per a et i efferebant ; quidam semper ut Graeci, quidam singulariter tantum, cum in dativum vel genetivum casum incidissent, unde 'pictai vestis' et 'aquai' Vergilius amantissimus vetustatis carminibus inseruit. In eisdem plurali numero e utebantur, 'hi Sullae Galbae'.'*

§ 20. *Quid quod Ciceronis temporibus paulumque infra, fere quotiens s littera media vocalium longarum vel subiecta longis esset, geminabatur? ut 'caussae' 'cassus' 'divissiones' : quomodo et ipsum et Vergilium quoque scripsisse manus eorum docent*[2]*. . . . Etiam 'optimus maximus,' ut mediam i litteram, quae veteribus u fuerat, acciperent, Gai primum Caesaris inscriptione traditur factum*[3].

§ 23. *Quid? non Cato Censorius 'dicam' et 'faciam' 'dicem' et 'faciem' scripsit*[4]*, eundemque in ceteris, quae similiter cadunt, modum tenuit?*

§ 26. *Nostri praeceptores 'servum cervumque' u et o litteris scripserunt, quia subiecta sibi vocalis in unum sonum coalescere et confundi nequiret: nunc u gemina scribuntur ea ratione quam*

---

item

'*hoc illi factum est uni,' tenue hoc facies i :*
'*haec illei fecere,' adde e, ut pinguius fiat.*
. . . *Hoc mihi videtur supervacaneae esse observationis.*

[1] Paulus 25 *Ae syllabam antiqui Graeca consuetudine per ai scribebant, ut 'aulai,' 'Musai.'* Pompeius, Keil 5 p. 297 '*Aulai medio'. . .una syllaba in duas divisa est. Legite Verrium Flaccum et Catonem, et ibi invenietis.*

Longus 57 *Illud etiam adnotandum circa i litteram est, quod ea quae nos per ae antiqui per ai scriptitaverunt, ut 'Iuliai' 'Claudiai.' hac scriptione voluerunt esse differentiam, ut pluralis quidem numeri nominativus casus per a et e scriberetur, genetivus vero singularis per a et i.* Comp. Scaurus 16.

[2] Scaurus 21 *Causam item a multis scio per duo s scribi, &c.*

[3] Longus 67 *Varie etiam scriptitatum est mancupium aucupium manibiae, siquidem C. Caesar per i scripsit, ut apparet ex titulis ipsius, at Augustus per u, ut testes sunt eius inscriptiones.*

[4] Paulus 72 '*dice*' (? *dicem*) *pro 'dicam' antiqui posuere.*

reddidi. . . . Nec inutiliter Claudius aeolicam illam ad hos usus litteram adiecerat[1].

§ 27. *Illud nunc melius, quod 'cui' tribus quas posui litteris enotamus, in quo pueris nobis ad pinguem sane sonum qu et oi utebantur, tantum ut ab illo 'qui' distingueretur*[2].

§ 28. *'Gaius' C littera significatur, quae inversa mulierem declarat*[3].

Now we know of no special treatise on orthography older than Quintilian, except that of Verrius Flaccus. And of one of the notes quoted above, that on *pictai vestis* from the Aeneid, it is nearly certain that it cannot be from Varro, while Pompeius in the passage cited tells us that it came from Verrius; indeed a note very like it is preserved by Paulus p. 25. Moreover two other notes, that on *dicem, faciem,* for *dicam, faciam,* and that on *Gaius,* occur in the epitome of Verrius's lexicon; and this, as we have seen, is the case with many of the notes in the fourth chapter. May we not then pronounce almost with certainty that in Quintilian, Scaurus, and Longus we have part at least of the treatise of Verrius *De Orthographia?*

If I am right in referring these parallel or identical notes to Verrius, it is not impossible to state with some precision what was the nature of his book. That it was largely based on the researches of Varro is evident: and if we may trust Pompeius, Verrius must have also used the *grammatici libelli* of Valerius Cato. *Legite Verrium et Catonem, et ibi invenietis*[4]. It discussed the various changes of letters as known to the history

---

[1] Scaurus 12. Longus 58 *Aeque ab iisdem 'equus' per v et o scriptus est, et quaeritur utrum per unum u an per duo debent scribi. Sed priusquam de hoc loquamur, v litteram digamma esse interdum non tantum in his debemus animadvertere, &c.*

[2] Longus 76 *Itaque audimus quosdam plena oi syllaba dicere 'quoi' et 'hoic' pro 'cui' et 'huic,' quod multo vitiosius est, quam si tenuitatem y litterae custodirent. Est autem ubi pinguitudo u litterae decentius servatur.* Comp. ib. 72.

[3] Longus 53 *C conversum, quo Gaia significatur . . . Gaias enim generaliter a specie omnes mulieres accipere voluerunt.* Comp. Paulus 95 fin.

[4] See above, p. 156, note 1.

of the Latin language, and their variations in contemporary writing. While Verrius must have derived much of his information from Varro's *De Sermone Latino* and *De Antiquitate Litterarum*, his book was probably more systematic than anything which Varro had written; it was, with equal probability, written in no spirit of servile adhesion to Varro's opinions; and it included, of course, instances of the usage of authors later than those quoted by him.

Let us now pass to the consideration of Pliny's work entitled *Dubii Sermonis*. We know that this consisted of eight books, *libri* as the younger Pliny calls them, *libelli* in the modest phraseology of their author.

A considerable number of notes, bearing Pliny's name, are quoted by the later grammarians, and a great deal more has almost certainly been taken from Pliny without acknowledgment. I hope to make it probable, also, that parts of the early chapters of Quintilian's first book (1. 5. § 54—1. 6. § 28) are based on the same authority.

It may be certainly inferred, from the remains of Pliny's treatise which have come down to us, that it covered a very wide field. It embraced the consideration (*a*) of letters, their changes and pronunciation; (*b*) of nouns, their gender, declension, and forms of derivation; (*c*) of the article and pronoun; (*d*) of verbs, active, passive, and deponent, with questions about their irregular formation; (*e*) of prepositions and their usage; (*f*) of conjunctions; (*g*) of solecism and barbarism. Nor was it a mere collection of lists. We owe to Pliny more than one successful or unsuccessful attempt to frame a grammatical terminology. He reckoned the gerunds *dicendi dicendo*, &c., as adverbs[1]. He applied to the comparative adverbs such as *magis* and *potius* the terms *relativae ad aliquid*. He seems[2] to have invented the phrase *nomina facientia* for the primary forms of nouns as opposed to their

---

[1] So Dionysius Thrax (Uhlig p. 85) called ἀναγνωστέον, γραπτέον, πλευστέον &c. ἐπιρρήματα θετικά.

[2] Charisius *Inst.* 1. 16 (Keil *Gramm.* 1. p. 118).

derivatives. He is probably responsible for the use of *arti-culus* in the sense of the definite article (Probus *Inst.* Keil *Gramm.* 4. p. 133). He was careful, when he could, to point out a difference of meaning coincident with a difference of form, as, e.g. when he remarks that *vertex* means height (*immanem vim impetus*) and *vortex* a whirlpool (Charis. p. 88 Keil), or that *auguro* means to have a presentiment, *auguror* to take the auguries.

We know from his own statement that the book excited the opposition of the philosophers. Why this was the case we can to a certain extent conjecture with probability ; and here again I must ask for the reader's attention to a somewhat complicated argument.

The fourth chapter of Quintilian's first book, and the fifth as far as § 54, includes, as I shall endeavour to show further on, the main chapters of an *Ars Grammatica ;* and indeed at the end of § 54, Quintilian seems to take leave of grammar altogether. He then proceeds to consider the question of words, provincial, Gallic, Spanish and Greek, simple and compound, literal and metaphorical. Thus the fifth chapter ends, and the sixth is a dissertation on *sermo* or usage, con-sidered under four heads, that of *ratio* or reason, including *analogia* and *etymologia*, antiquity, authority, and custom.

Now this division is not the same as that adopted by Varro in his *De Sermone Latino.* According to Varro, *sermo* de-pended on *natura, analogia, consuetudo, auctoritas*[1]. Again, Varro is expressly attacked by Quintilian in his remarks upon etymology. The authority for this section then can hardly be Varro, but must be some later writer.

It is not probable that this writer was the same as the author of the fourth chapter, and the fifth down to § 54. For Quintilian, in several instances, repeats, in a different con-nexion, remarks which he has already made there, without any sufficient notification of the fact. This looks as if he were, in the later of the two passages, borrowing or adapting from another treatise which partially covered the same ground.

---

[1] Diomedes in Keil *Gramm.* I. p. 439.

There is good reason for supposing that this treatise was Pliny's *Dubii Sermonis.* Several of Quintilian's remarks coincide exactly with notes quoted from that work by later grammarians. Thus in 1. 5 § 63 his observation on the declension of such words as *Dido, Calypso—neque enim iam Calypsonem dixerim ut Iunonem, quamquam secutus antiquos C. Caesar utitur hac ratione declinandi. Sed auctoritatem consuetudo superavit*—agrees nearly with what Pliny says in Charisius (p. 127 Keil), *consuetudinem facere hanc Calypso, hanc Io, hanc Allecto.* Again, Quintilian lays stress on the gender of the diminutive as a test of the gender of the principal noun (1. 6 § 6). So Pompeius (p. 164 Keil) tells us of Pliny, *Ait Plinius Secundus secutus Varronem, quando dubitamus principale genus, redeamus ad deminutionem.* We may compare Quintilian's remarks on *lepus* and *lupus* with those of Charisius p. 135, which are in all probability Pliny's. In 1. 6 § 15 Quintilian notices *Albanus* and *Albensis* as a double form from *Alba,* and this observation Pompeius (p. 144) quotes from Pliny. In § 17 he laughs at persons who insist on saying *tribunale* for *tribunal.* So Charisius p. 62, in a context full of material taken from Pliny, says *quod tamen consuetudine extorqueri non potuit, quin vectigal et cervical et capital et tribunal animalque contempta ratione dicamus.* I would also call attention to the constant appeal of Charisius in this part of his compilation to *ratio,* known to be a favourite principle with Pliny [1].

To return then to the point of this argumentation. We know that Pliny was fond of appealing to *ratio* and *consuetudo;* and that he recognized *veterum licentia* and *veterum dignitas,* or antiquity, as an element in the explanation of usage (Charis. p. 118). Whether he reckoned *natura* as a positive principle

---

[1] See the quotations from Pliny ap. Charis. p. 116 foll. : and comp. Charis. p. 79, *Plinius quoque Dubii Sermonis V adicit esse quidem rationem per duo i scribendi, sed multa iam consuetudine superari. Ratio* was opposed to *auctoritas* by Verrius Flaccus *in Epistulis :* Servius on Aen. 8. 423.

active in the formation of words is not certain: all that we
know is that he spoke of an irrational expression as violating
natura (Servius on Donatus Keil 4 p. 444, Pompeius p. 283).
On the other hand we know that Quintilian describes *sermo* or
usage as depending on *ratio, vetustas, auctoritas*, and *consuetudo.* Now if other important remarks in this chapter of
Quintilian can be shown to come from Pliny, is it too much
to infer that it is to Pliny that Quintilian owes his fourfold
division? And if this is so, the reason will appear why Pliny
feared the contradiction of the philosophers. For while Varro,
following his favourite Stoics, allowed a large field to *natura*
and *analogia*, and (as in duty bound) distinguished between
auctoritas and *consuetudo*, Pliny probably expunged *natura*,
introduced *ratio*, which he made to include *analogia* and
etymologia, and *vetustas*, a head which should have been
distributed between *consuetudo* and *auctoritas*. It is small
blame to the philosophers if they were expected to rise up
in arms against a division like this.

The authorities upon which the work was mainly based
were Caesar's two books *De Analogia*, the various writings
of Varro, and the lexicon and grammatical treatises of Verrius
Flaccus. These authorities Pliny used with respect, but in
no spirit of servile repetition. It is probable that in philosophical grasp (if indeed such an expression can be used
in reference to any Latin writer) he fell behind Varro; but
his collections of instances would of course include later
authors than those accessible to the latter, and would bring
to light changes which had crept in since his time.

What was the arrangement of the work, what subjects were
treated in each of its eight divisions, cannot be exactly
ascertained. We know that the sixth book, largely used by
Julius Romanus in the age of the Antonines in his work
De Analogia, contained lists of words whose case-forms were
uncertain. In all probability these were arranged, as they
had been by Julius Caesar, according to the endings of· the
nominative case. For Quintilian, in the Plinian passage

quoted above (1. 6. 4), recognizes this, the *comparatio similium in extremis maxime syllabis,* as one of the guides for the grammarian. Whether this arrangement was further subordinated to an alphabetical one, as by Julius Romanus and later authors, is uncertain [1].

From the fifth book Charisius (p. 79) preserves a quotation relating to the doubling of *i* in the genitives of words ending in *-ius* : from the second a distinction is cited between *clipeus* and *clupeus* (with a notice of the doubtful gender) and a remark on the postposition of *cum* in *nobiscum, tecum,* &c.

That the subject of gender was treated early in the work is probable, from the fact that Quintilian treats it early in his sixth chapter. He also, it may be observed, takes the question of analogy in declension late, which coincides with the fact that the quotations on this subject in Julius Romanus mostly come from the sixth book.

If I were to be allowed to conjecture roughly what was the order of Pliny's eight books, I should suppose it may have been as follows :

1. Alphabet and words (Priscian Inst. 1. 34, Keil 2. p. 26 ; Quint. 1. 5. 54 foll.).

2. Substantives doubtful in form, gender, and meaning (but Priscian quotes a doubtful gender from lib. 1.).

3. Pronouns.

4. Verbs : doubtful conjugation, doubtful voice.

5. Cases of nouns.

6. Question of analogy in doubtful declension.

7. Adverbs.

8. Prepositions and conjunctions.

It may be that the lists of adverbs and conjunctions given by Diomedes and Charisius come ultimately from Pliny, though there is no direct evidence for this statement.

It is in any case morally certain that much of Nonius's third book (*De Indiscretis Generibus*) and of his seventh and

---

[1] It may be observed that Martianus Capella, in the chapter on *analogia* in his third book (§ 290 foll.), treats nouns in much the same way.

tenth books on verbs comes ultimately from Pliny: perhaps the same may also be said of his eleventh book on adverbs. And the crowd of later grammarians, whose writing is for the most part mere scissors and paste work badly cut out and put together, are in large parts of their treatises greatly indebted to him. The same must be said of the later authors of lists of synonyms, or as they were called *differentiae*: for nothing is more characteristic of Pliny than the attempt to show that differences of grammatical form often cover differences of meaning.

I now come to the *Ars Grammatica* of Remmius Palaemon. We have already seen that he was the author of an *Ars Grammatica*, that is a manual of grammar, not a philosophical treatise on usage and word-formation. What was the nature of this book?

A scholar named Palaemon is not unfrequently quoted by the later grammarians. Charis. p. 225-6 (= Diom. p. 415) cites him on the subject of conjunctions: Charis. p. 231 (roughly = Diom. 409) on prepositions, and soon afterwards on the various usages of prepositions (essentially = Diom. 411 foll.).

Schottmüller[1] has made a very curious observation with regard to the pages of Charisius (225 foll.) which treat of conjunctions and those (p. 231 foll.) on prepositions. It is that before hypothetical instances (such as *cum dico* as example of *cum* with indicative) Charisius in these places mostly uses *velut* instead of *ut*, or *ut puta*: and as Palaemon's name is mentioned in the neighbourhood, he jumps to the conclusion that this use of *velut* is a sure test of the presence of quotations from Palaemon. Applying this test to other passages in Charisius, he vindicates to Palaemon all in which *velut* is found in this connection. Some other passages in Charisius he claims for Palaemon on other grounds.

But the Palaemon of Charisius and Diomedes is not, in Schottmüller's opinion, the Remmius Palaemon of Quintilian and Juvenal. He is a late grammarian of the age of Sidonius Apollinaris (A. D. 450). The arguments for this position are

(1) The Palaemon of the grammarians sometimes quotes

---

[1] *De Plini secundi libris grammaticis diss.* (Leipzig, 1858) p. 22.

Pliny. Now Remmius Palaemon died before the publication of Pliny's preface to the Natural History (77 A.D.) and Pliny must have mentioned his *Ars Grammatica* had it been written after the publication of his own book *Dubii Sermonis*, that is, had it been written between 67 and 77 A.D. It must therefore have been written before 67, and consequently Remmius Palaemon could not have quoted Pliny.

(2) Quintilian (1. 4. 20) mentions Palaemon as a second Aristarchus (Schottmüller p. 28 *cum Aristarchis comparat*): a compliment which would be quite out of place as applied to the author of the very weak remarks which are attributed by the later grammarians to Palaemon.

I propose to take the last point first, and to argue that there is no valid reason why the Palaemon of the grammarians should not be identified with the Palaemon of Quintilian.

Quintilian, it may be observed, does not really speak of Palaemon as a second Aristarchus, but says merely that he followed Aristarchus in making eight parts of speech: *ut Aristarchus et nostra aetate Palaemon.*

This argument being disposed of, let us now consider whether there is any necessity that Palaemon's *Ars Grammatica* should have been written before, and not after, Pliny's *Dubii Sermonis*. Pliny says that he has waited in vain for the grammarians to attack his book. But supposing Palaemon to have meantime written a book friendly to Pliny, why should the latter mention him as hostile? What objection is there to supposing that the *Ars* of Palaemon was partly based upon the collections made in the *Dubii Sermonis*, and that Palaemon may really, as he is represented in the grammarians as doing, have quoted Pliny?

Again, the definitions and remarks attributed to Palaemon by Charisius and Diomedes are by no means those of an incompetent writer. The passage on conjunctions (Charis. 225-6 = Diomedes 415) is very sound work, and so is a good deal of the dissertation on prepositions in Charis. 231-2. Indeed it must be added that the notes on this

subject in Diomedes p. 411–413, which only differ from
those in Charisius as an older and better draft differs from
a later and inferior one, must also be from Palaemon, and
that they show not only good sense but learning. They are
probably due to Pliny[1] and ultimately to Verrius Flaccus.

Supposing then that they come from Remmius Palaemon,
can Schottmüller's test of the use of *velut* be applied to detect
his hand in other passages?

While I admit the oddness of the phenomenon to which
Schottmüller has called attention, I doubt whether he draws
the right inference from it. For the same passages from
Palaemon (or depending mainly upon him) are quoted more
than once by both Charisius and Diomedes, but where Charisius uses *velut*, Diomedes uses *ut*. This we find to be the
case if we compare the passage on conjunctions as given by
the two grammarians (Charis. p. 225–6, Diomedes p. 415):
and again if we compare the chapter on the usages of prepositions (Charis. p. 232, Diom. 411) where Diomedes gives
fragments of a much fuller version than that of which Charisius,
perhaps, abridges the whole.

I suppose then that the use of *velut* is a sign, not of
Palaemon's hand, but of some late redactor using old material
and putting his own mark upon it.

Assuming then that the Palaemon of the grammarians is the
real Palaemon, we infer that he wrote fully upon prepositions
and conjunctions, and (at least in his account of prepositions)
may have been indebted directly to Pliny and indirectly to
Verrius Flaccus. Priscian tells us further (Inst. 1. 47, Keil 2.
p. 35) that he called the ψιλή or soft breathing *exilis*: and
from Quintilian we learn that he recognized eight parts of
speech and no more.

But can we not learn more than this from Quintilian about
Remmius Palaemon?

I have before observed that the part of Quintilian's first
book which begins 1. 4. 1 and ends 1. 5. 54 contains in an

[1] See Audax, Keil *Grammatici* 7 p. 355.

abridged and adapted form much of what might well have
been found in an *Ars Grammatica.* 1. 4. §§ 2–17 treat of
letters : §§ 18–21 of the parts of speech : §§ 22–26 of nouns
and cases : §§ 26–29 of the verb: 1. 5. §§ 5–33 of *barbarismus* : §§ 34–54 of *soloecismus* : and at this point Quintilian
bids adieu to grammar.

That Quintilian had some technical treatise before him, the
rules of which he throws into literary form, may be assumed as
almost certain : have we any means of deciding who its author was?

No careful reader of Quintilian can fail to observe that
these sections go over, in part, the same ground as is again
traversed in chapters 6 and 7, and at the same time that
Quintilian takes hardly any notice of the fact.

The authority cannot be Varro.   For to Varro, as we saw,
grammatica or *litteratura* included *lectio enarratio emendatio*
and *iudicium.*   To Quintilian (1. 4. 2) it is no more than *recte
loquendi scientia* and *poetarum enarratio* : the schoolmaster has
driven the philosopher away, or put him in the background—
*enarrationem praecedit emendata lectio, et mixtum his omnibus
iudicium est*[1].   Again, Quintilian or his authority does not
accept Varro's theory about the letter *h* (comp. 1. 5. 20 with
Cassiodorius Keil 7. p. 153).   Accent is by Quintilian (1.
5. 22) called *tenor*, to Varro it is *prosodia* : nor is Quintilian's treatment of accentuation at all like Varro's (Sergius on
Donatus Keil 4. p. 528 foll.).   Varro called the ablative *sextus
casus* (Diomedes 302) :   Quintilian is disposed to divide it into
two, making the instrumental a *septimus casus.*   Nor again are we
reading Pliny in these sections.   This is proved by the fact
that the definition of *barbarismus* given by Pliny is different
from Quintilian's.   Quintilian accepts on the whole the theory
which reappears very often in the later grammarians, that
barbarismus is a mistake in a single word (*quod fit in singulis
verbis vitium*), *soloecismus* a faulty combination of words
expressed or implied, which may be committed in one or

---

[1] [Professor Nettleship marked this argument as doubtful in his copy
of this essay as printed in the Journal of Philology].

more words, but never in a word isolated from its expressed or implied context: 1. 5. 38 *sit aliquando in uno verbo, numquam in solo verbo.* Now Pliny made quite a different distinction: *barbarismus* was what violated *natura*, *soloecismus* what offended against rule (Pompeius 283). What this meant we may perhaps gather from Pompeius's remark (p. 290), *cum per naturam nemo dicat scalam, nemo dicat quadrigam, sine dubio barbarismi sunt.* Quint. 1. 5. 16 says it may seem absurd to apply the term *barbarismus* to mistakes such as *scala scopa* for *scalae scopae*: but had he been adapting from Pliny, is it conceivable that he would not have mentioned Pliny's theory of nature and art as applied to barbarism and solecism?

If Quintilian, then, is in these sections consulting neither Varro nor Pliny, it is most probable that he had the *Ars* of Remmius Palaemon before him.

There is some positive evidence to help us here.

Quintilian 1. 4. 27 uses the word *qualitas* for mood: so again 1. 5. 41 *modos sive cui status eos dici seu qualitates placet.* This term seems to have been used by Palaemon. Charisius 226 and Diomedes in his corresponding section, a passage which, as we have seen, comes essentially from Palaemon, says *superest ut dicamus quae coniunctio cui qualitati iungatur*: and so *subiunctiva, finitiva qualitas* Charis. 263.

Remmius Palaemon, if we may believe the Scholia on Juv. 6. 452, was Quintilian's master: what more likely, then, than that Quintilian should give him the place of honour in his grammatical dissertation?

And I may finally observe that the sketch of *Ars Grammatica* which Quintilian gives, as a system beginning with *recte loquendi scientia*, ending with *soloecismus*, and including especially the explanation of poets, coincides exactly with Juvenal's description of Palaemon's work: *Odi Hanc ego, quae repetit volvitque Palaemonis artem, Servata semper lege et ratione loquendi, Nec curanda viris opicae castigat amicae Verba: soloecismum liceat fecisse marito* (6. 452). There it is, all of it: rules, poetry, and solecism.

If I am right then in supposing that these sections of Quintilian are no more than a literary adaptation of the principal parts of Palaemon's *Ars Grammatica*, I may proceed to state what seem to have been the main characteristics of that work, and to make a few observations on its influence upon the later writers of *Artes Grammaticae.*

The first part consisted of a dissertation on the alphabet and the combination and changes of letters. As almost all of this coincides closely with the treatises on *Orthographia* of Velius Longus and Terentius Scaurus on the one hand, and with notes in Festus or Paulus on the other, it is highly probable that it was taken by Palaemon from Verrius Flaccus *De Orthographia* : a work which as we have seen was, in all likelihood, partly transcribed by Quintilian in his seventh chapter. After letters came syllables : Quint. 1. 4. 17. Palaemon (after Dionysius Thrax) made eight parts of speech, not distinguishing *appellatio* or *vocabulum* from *nomen*[1]. He divided substantives according to their genders, not omitting to inquire into the etymology of such substantives as had passed into *cognomina*. He in all probability distinguished the uses of the ablative proper from those of the same form used instrumentally or otherwise—the *septimus casus*. He discussed the half verbal half nominal nature of the participle, the impersonal use of the passive, and the passive after nouns of cognate signification. The supines he called participial, while remarking that the form of the passive supine resembled that of some adverbs. Finally he gave a very full treatment to the various kinds of *barbarismus* and *soloecismus.*

Whether or no it be admitted that Palaemon was the author of the treatise which Quintilian was consulting, there can be no doubt that that treatise was the foundation of large parts of the later *Artes.* All the later grammarians adopt Palaemon's eight parts of speech. Many are kindly disposed to the seventh case : the discussions on participles and impersonal passives and supines recur in fuller or shorter forms ;

[1] The distinction is given from Scaurus by Diomedes, 320.

and the doctrine of *barbarismus* and *soloecismus* is expounded on the same principles, but with differing degrees of fulness, in many *Artes.* Quintilian's authority may, on this point, be best studied in Pompeius and Consentius[1].

The sum of my conclusions with regard to the grammatical chapters of Quintilian's first book is, then, as follows. The fourth chapter, and the fifth as far as § 54, is a rough literary adaptation of the *Ars Grammatica* of Remmius Palaemon. Chapter 5. § 54 to 56. § 27 is probably from Pliny's *Dubii Sermonis.* §§ 28–38 of the same chapter, on etymology, is partly directed against Varro, partly against etymological writers and their science in general. It is impossible to point out any particular authority for these sections, which may well represent no more than the general recollections which Quintilian had carried away from lectures and from his own reading. The seventh chapter, on orthography, from § 1 to § 28, is taken or adapted from the *De Orthographia* of Verrius Flaccus.

Of the *Silva Observationum Sermonis Antiqui*[2] written by

---

[1] Pompeius, p. 284, foll., Consentius, Keil 5. p. 386, foll.

[2] The main contentions of Dr. Beck's excellent essay (see p. 146*n*) on Probus are as follows : (1) That the *Silva Observationum Sermonis Antiqui,* attributed by Suetonius to Valerius Probus, was not a work composed by that scholar, but a collection of the notes taken home by the young men who had conversed with him. (2) That Probus was not the author of any regular grammatical treatise, but only left behind him a few *obiter dicta* on grammatical points. (3) That in several places where Priscian professes, and has hitherto been supposed, to be quoting Valerius Probus, he is really quoting Diomedes: and that this is sometimes true also of other grammarians. (4) That, in consequence, the grammatical observations usually attributed to Valerius Probus must be assigned to other scholars, and, in particular, to Pliny.

Dr. Beck's second proposition will probably not be disputed : but I am not so sceptical as he is as to the *Silva Observationum,* and the relics of this work generally supposed to have been preserved by Diomedes and Priscian. It may be, of course, that Probus did not himself entitle his book *Silva Observationum Sermonis Antiqui,* though it has been generally assumed that he did. Gellius, it is true, never mentions such a book when he quotes Probus; but Gellius's method of quotation is so unsatisfactory that little can be made of his evidence one way or the other. On the whole, there seems to me to be nothing in the evidence to disprove the existence of

Valerius Probus little can be said positively except that it was the work of a pure scholar, untinctured by any philosophical theories perfectly or imperfectly apprehended. It was a collection of apparently irregular usages taken from ancient authors : and undoubtedly it must have covered much the same ground as Pliny's *Dubii Sermonis*. Its general character can be inferred from what remains of it in the grammatical books of Nonius Marcellus, which I hope I have shown (in my essays prefixed to the first volume of Conington's Virgil) are based upon Pliny and Probus. It may indeed be said that these two authors are responsible for most of the notes on irregularities in conjugation or declension which meet us in the later grammarians.

The conclusion to which my argument points is that the main outlines of the traditional Latin grammar, such as we find it in the numerous, but often identical, expositions which bear the various names of the later grammarians—Charisius, Diomedes, Pompeius, Donatus, Cledonius and others, were drawn in the first century A.D. The rules and arrangement

such a work, whatever its title. Suetonius's words, *reliquit autem non mediocrem silvam,* &c., seem to point to more than a mere collection of notes.

I am unable to agree with Dr. Beck as to the quotations in Priscian and Diomedes. I grant, of course, that the Probus of Priscian is, in a great many cases, not Valerius, but the Probus of the *Instituta Artium*. I still think, however, that when Priscian quotes, with the name of Probus, specimens of really ancient Latin usage, it is not unreasonable to suppose that they come from Valerius : especially as those quotations are exactly what one would have expected from a miscellaneous collection of ancient usages. Nor do I see any sufficient reason for supposing that Probus, in Priscian, is ever a mistake for Diomedes. Not only does Priscian quote Diomedes more than once by name, but in the important section on verbs (Diomedes, p. 347, foll. Keil) where the two grammarians go over the same ground, and partly with the same instances, Priscian is fuller than Diomedes, and adopts a different method of arrangement. The impression left on my mind is that both authors are, very likely at second or third hand, consulting the same authority, very probably Caper, who was himself using the collections of Probus and Pliny. A comparison of Diomedes and Priscian with Nonius will, I think, be found to bear out this conclusion.

of the conventional *Ars Grammatica*, such as was used and taught during the later empire by the professors in the large cities, were in all probability, in most cases, those of Remmius Palaemon. The instances were mostly supplied by scholars of the age of Hadrian and the Antonines, who drew their information largely from Pliny and Valerius Probus.

The grammatical studies of the first century A.D., when compared with those of the last century of the republic, exhibit, in some respects, the same character as the other literary work of the same period. There is more system, more effort after compilation and arrangement, but less freedom, less grasp, and altogether a narrower sphere of ideas. Pliny's researches are inspired by a philosophy more hasty and commonplace than that which Varro had adopted from the Stoics, and Verrius, Palaemon, and Probus write without any philosophy at all. Again, the scientific impulse is checked by the requirements of practical necessity. The passion for correct speaking and writing is strong in the upper class, and is instilled into the boy from his earliest school-days; just as it is the fashion in literature, whether in prose or verse, to hunt for choice expressions and telling points. With the increase of wealth and population at Rome the demand for education increases. A boxer like Pomponius Marcellus, a weaver like Remmius Palaemon, find teaching grammar a profitable occupation. Scholarship is one of the dozen accomplishments of the *Graeculus esuriens*, and Juvenal's complaint that the schoolmaster is badly paid shows only that the market was overstocked The modern scholar may lament this degeneracy, and bitterly regret the loss of Varro's encyclopaedic treatises; but he must remember that but for the educationists and scholars of this period he might have lost much even of what he seems to have, and have been left ignorant of the very existence of the Latin studies in philology, one of the most remarkable and interesting intellectual efforts of the ancient world.

VII.

ON THE PRESENT RELATIONS BETWEEN CLASSICAL RESEARCH AND CLASSICAL EDUCATION IN ENGLAND[1].

No acquisition of modern times is more remarkable than the nearer realization of the unity of spirit which pervades all research. Among a multitude of labourers in various fields of knowledge, there is a consciousness of a common aim, a common method, a common inspiration. This consciousness is no mere abstraction, but a living reality ; the active pursuit of truth is a bond as strong as the bond of charity. And, while the widely-spreading love of truth is forming a new element of union among men, the objects of knowledge themselves are discovering more and more of their inner harmonies as their laws are read and verified by fresh experience. No branch of knowledge can now be seriously studied in isolation, or without a view to its actual or possible connexion with other branches, and the ultimate discovery of the simple principles underlying them all. This fact is obvious in the sphere of the humanities as well as in that of the natural sciences. Histories are studied for the sake of knowing history, languages for the sake of knowing language ; and the studies of language and history are seen to be

[1 Originally printed in *Essays on the Endowment of Research* by various writers (London, 1876): essay X, pp. 244-268. Some of Mr. Nettleship's criticisms are naturally less true now than in 1876.]

inseparably connected. Unities only guessed at or wrongly imagined before are disclosing themselves in their true aspect under the light of the comparative method. In this view it cannot be said of any ascertained set of facts that it is unfruitful or unworthy of further examination, or of any philosophical system, that it is final.

It is of the essence of a liberal education that it should stand in constant relation to the advance of knowledge. Research and discovery are the processes by which truth is directly acquired; education is the preparation of the mind for its reception, and the creation of a truth-loving habit. The two lines of activity, though one is subordinate to the other, are in their nature inseparable. In practice, however, a clear line of distinction, familiar in common parlance and opinion, is rightly drawn between the functions of education and of research. The ends of education are practical and immediate, those of research speculative and remote. Education is mainly concerned with the imparting of elementary and essential knowledge, scientific investigation with the discovery of new truths, the importance or unimportance of which is not immediately present to the investigator. It is a teacher's first duty to consider the mind of his pupil, and whether his communication is suited to its condition; it is the first duty of a person engaged in research to consider what new materials, what new combination of old materials, what new hypothesis, are available for the progress of knowledge under his hand. This difference of pure and applied truth exists in all branches of education and knowledge, mathematical, classical, or scientific.

Men engaged in the cultivation of the natural sciences are fully aware that, although the spheres of education and of discovery are distinct, the two pursuits have a living and perpetual relation to each other which can never be lost sight of without detriment to both. The progress of science is so rapid, and the interest excited by it so absorbing, that the work of education is being continually modified by it. It is im possible for a teacher of one of the natural sciences to hold aloof from the progress of discovery. But in the case of classical study it is hardly too much to say that, in England, the connexion between education and research has been, as far as popular feeling and opinion is concerned, almost wholly lost sight of. A great deal of the best educational ability of this country is absorbed in the teaching of classics; but the number of persons in England who are engaged in, or seriously interested in, classical learning is out of all proportion small, and the importance of that learning is hardly acknowledged, or at least not acknowledged at all as clearly as the duty of scientific research is by scientific men. There is an unmistakeable tendency among Englishmen, whether engaged in education or not, to regard classical research as an unproductive pursuit, a pleasure of the few rather than a labour serviceable to the many. ' Many,' says Professor Mayor, ' who live by teaching the classics, affect to despise them [1].'

Without entering into the perplexing questions connected with the present distribution of endowments, or asking whether any other possible distribution would have the effect of reviving a love for the higher scholarship, I propose to notice some of the causes and some of the results of the present indifference to learning, and to suggest means by which some advance might be made towards restoring the proper relation between classical research and classical education.

Among the causes of the phenomenon under consideration, one of the most obvious and important is the idea that the field of classics is practically worked out. The masterpieces of classical literature have long been familiar to the cultivated classes among us, and have formed the staple of our liberal education. Enough, it may be thought, is known of these immortal monuments and of their practical value to us. With the general outline of ancient life we are so familiar that we may fairly dispense with the trouble of adding new and minute touches to a picture already sufficiently restored. The

---

[1] Preface to his *Bibliographical Clue to Roman Literature.*

age of discoveries in classical literature is past; the spirit of discovery has gone elsewhere, to animate new labourers in new regions of unexplored wealth.

Though the facts of the case are far otherwise, though (to say nothing of the new position in which comparative philology has placed the Greek and Latin languages) there is an amount of work, practically infinite, yet to be done before we can know all that is to be known of the ancient world, and though every succeeding generation brings its own lights to the reading of antiquity, reasoning like this is plausible enough to weigh strongly with many able and practical minds. But there are other reasons which co-operate with it to prejudice against the cause of classical learning not only many whose life lies outside the educational profession, but many also of the classicists themselves, both at our schools and at our universities.

The vocation of a scholar is often wrongly conceived. The classical authors are rightly studied, in great part, as models of style, but in England we have been too tenacious of this point of view. Boys are set to imitate in their own verses the poetry of Sophocles and Euripides, of Virgil, Ovid, and Horace, and in their prose the eloquence of Demosthenes and Cicero. A few succeed, to a certain extent, in the difficult task, win the name of scholars, and keep it mainly on the strength of their skill in Greek and Latin writing. The element of taste is undoubtedly an essential element in scholarship, but far too great a prominence has been given to it in common English opinion. It is forgotten that for the making of a scholar, more manly qualities are required; grasp of mind, power of dealing with materials, historical insight; and scholarship and scholars suffer by the forgetting. The rhetorical side of classical education may be justly insisted on with boys, but it has unfortunately become our habit to apply the same method to men, and to continue too exclusively at the universities a training only suited to schools. One result has been that the words 'scholarship' and 'scholar' often convey, in popular language, little or no idea of research, but imply chiefly the power of manipulating the Greek and Latin languages, or translating them into English.

I have touched so far only upon habits of thought and language; but there are also important conditions in the life of English schools and universities which tend to foster our forgetfulness of the importance of classical study.

The English nation has adopted the habit of sending boys, when possible, from home to be taught and trained at the large boarding schools which, it may be roughly said, have now the monopoly of our higher education. The system is expensive and exclusive, and it might at first sight be supposed that it would favour the cultivation of learning and of studious habits among the masters of our great schools, who are able, as a rule, if fairly successful in their profession, to live in easy circumstances, and to enjoy some three months' holiday every year. But the case is in reality different. The duties of a 'house-master' at an English school are in themselves so absorbing and exacting as to leave him little, if any, leisure for reading. He has to provide for some thirty or thirty-five boys, to care for their instruction, to attend to their discipline, to sympathize with their various needs. He has but few hours in the week to himself, and cannot even call his evenings his own. The old system of *laissez-faire* which was tolerated by public opinion a generation ago is now generally, and it may be hoped for ever, abandoned, and the master of a 'house' at one of our large schools must attend to the moral, physical, and mental welfare of his boys, at the expense of failing in his profession. It is hardly surprising that, after their monotonous and absorbing duties, schoolmasters should often when the holidays come round, leave their books for a 'complete change,' and hurry to games or mountain air for recreation.

Again, the mere fact that the boys attending the great English schools live together for most of the year with little or no society but their own creates among them a well-defined boyish tradition, code of morals, and general habit of mind, which is strong in proportion to the position which the school occupies in the eye of the public, and to the length of time during which it has maintained that position. This boyish public opinion is sometimes of great strength, and not without its influence upon the masters, who in many cases have been public school boys themselves, and are therefore in sympathy with it. There is now a far better understanding than formerly between boys and masters, far more effort on the part of the masters to enter into the feelings and even into the pursuits of boys, far more endeavour to make learning attractive to them and to vary the subjects of study with their varying aptitudes. The modern English master is not an easy-going isolated pedant, but a member of an active community, whose aims, habit of mind, and tone of thought he makes his own. The familiar moral and social type of character developed by the English public schools is, in many respects, a high and manly type, but it is on the whole unfavourable to the cultivation of learning, and to sympathy with it. The work done is regarded less as an end in itself than as a means of strengthening the minds, and above all the characters, of the boys. This is as it should be, regarding the matter from the boys' side ; but a broader view is required for the masters, otherwise their work becomes so much task-work, a medley of isolated and second-hand results having no living interest or connexion with the great body of knowledge.

Such, then, are the conditions of life in our great schools as to make the thorough pursuit of learning, in any branch of knowledge, extremely difficult ; in general, indeed, impossible. But in the universities, it may be supposed, with larger opportunities and abundance of leisure, the pursuit of learning is actively carried on. It can hardly be said that the routine work either of professors or college tutors is onerous or absorbing, when they enjoy more than six months' vacation every year. There is plenty of time for research at the universities, which are its natural homes.

The very idea of a university is that of a place where all the great branches of knowledge are taught and cultivated, and where students and teachers are united, if not by a common system of thought embracing all their studies, at least by a common method and common ends.

With all their advantages, however, it cannot be said that the English universities implant in their students either a love of research or a knowledge of its methods. Men leave them with their minds liberalized and expanded, and with a sense of having gone through a course of mental gymnastic which has trained and tested their powers, and braced them for active life. But it may be doubted whether an average first-class man at Oxford or Cambridge has, as a rule, any clear conception of the principles and procedure of classical research. He has read and mastered the contents of a considerable number of classical books, and (at least at Oxford) has acquired a tincture of modern philosophical culture, and a ready power of expressing himself on paper. But his knowledge has been gained almost entirely in the form of results, and with the directly practical aim of succeeding in the examinations and assuring him a good start in life. He has been taught in the main by young men, who hand on the tradition in which they have been reared themselves, and whose method is more popular, because more practically useful, than that of older and more experienced teachers. In short, the attitude of the students and the teachers at the universities towards the subjects of study has a tendency to become professional rather than scientific. Knowledge is worked up and dealt out for the purposes of the market, not pursued and communicated as a life-giving means of culture.

It is easier to dwell upon a fact now so generally acknowledged as this than to point out its causes or suggest remedies for it. It is not uncommon to lay the whole blame on the examination system, and no doubt this has much to answer for. At Oxford (of which alone I am able to speak at first-hand), a definite course of reading is prescribed to the classical student, which occupies him from the beginning to the end of his career, leaving him no time for following his own inclination in the choice of a branch of study[1]. It follows that no lectures which travel out of the ordinary beat are likely to obtain many listeners. The noble idea of *Lehrfreiheit* and *Studienfreiheit*, familiar to the Germans, is unknown to us, and, as a consequence, little also is known of the continuous quickening contact between the minds of the teacher and the taught which is the result of the effective love of knowledge pursued by the one and communicated to the other. The conditions of the examination system at Oxford not only make it almost an impossibility for the professors (the natural representatives of learning) to obtain large classes, but go far to prevent the college tutors from giving thorough courses of lectures. The whole tendency of the system is towards summarizing and shortening, towards the communication of results, not the training in method. It cannot be said that classical philology is at all represented as it should be in the Oxford *curriculum*. For the first public examination, in which men are examined in the language of parts of certain classical books, is a boyish proceeding, in which the rudiments of the higher scholarship have but little part; while the university scholarships are for the most part awarded, and necessarily awarded, for sagacity and rhetorical skill rather than for width and depth of knowledge or mastery of materials. It cannot be otherwise, when no time is left for the acquirement of knowledge.

At Cambridge a far greater freedom in the choice of classical study is, in terms at least, allowed than at Oxford. The theory is that a man is examined in Greek and Latin

---

[1] It is true that recent legislation at Oxford allows the reading of certain voluntary or 'extra' subjects. But the mass of compulsory work is so great that this freedom is, so far as philology goes, in practice illusory, and that the higher scholarship is not taught in the ordinary courses of lectures. [More recent legislation has tended considerably in the direction desired by Mr. Nettleship.]

without limitation to particular books. Such a system, while it necessitates wide reading, must also leave considerable time for special study. And it is, I think, the case that Cambridge men have, as a rule, a more thorough knowledge of the Greek and Latin languages than Oxford men, and a clearer idea of the methods of classical research. If less accomplished rhetoricians, they have received a more solid grounding in the elements of scholarship. But at Cambridge also I believe (I cannot speak from actual knowledge), that the rigidly competitive character of the examination has of late had a tendency to throw the teaching more and more into the hands of private tutors, and to give it a more practical and professional complexion; while the importance attached to Greek and Latin composition compels the bulk of the men who read for honours, to spend much time on writing which might be more profitably given to reading.

There is no doubt that a well organized system of examinations is, in its essence, the enemy of research. The more its organization is improved, the more must the examination tend to narrow the field of knowledge both for teacher and taught, the more must it exact of the memory and the knack of rapid composition, the more time must it demand, the less must it encourage creative and original power. Yet I cannot agree with those who are inclined to lay upon the examination system alone the dearth of learning in our universities. The classical examinations might go on much as they now do, and much time would still be left to the college tutors for original work, which, though it might not have any direct bearing on their lectures, would naturally be interesting in itself, and would indirectly strengthen their teaching efforts. It is not so much the examinations which are at fault as our ready acquiescence in the necessary evils which attend them. We make ourselves their willing slaves, and then blame them for their despotism over us. There is no inherent necessity for this. Examinations are probably, as things now are, an essential part of the machinery of education, and they have, no doubt, though in a somewhat mechanical way, helped materially to diffuse the elements of knowledge, and to diminish habits of idleness and dissipation among the students. It does not follow that they should be allowed to narrow the aims of the teaching body. The comparative barrenness of our universities in original work appears to be rather attributable to that general want of speculative interest which is characteristic of Englishmen. Our mode of dealing with examinations is probably no more than a symptom of a deeply seated and long inherited tendency.

If this be so, why, it may be asked, indulge in fruitless complaints? If the English universities, with all their opportunities, have ceased to be the living centres of learning and research, if recent reforms have only ended in producing an increased amount of activity and industry in the appropriation of knowledge for practical purposes, why endeavour to stem the tide of which we can do no more than mark the advance? Our national character, it may be thought, has insensibly set its stamp upon our national education; we have got what we want, not the best thing, it may be, but the best thing for us; we do not produce, and do not wish to produce, scholars, but educated men, furnished with so much of liberal culture as will enable them to win and to maintain their position in life and in society, or to succeed better in any practical pursuit in which they may engage; this, whether expressed or not, is our deliberate aim. We like acting better than thinking or writing, or making discoveries; practical activity, success in all our pursuits, professional or disinterested, selfish or philanthropic—*hae tibi erunt artes.*

This ought we to do, and not to leave the other undone. Mere energy and activity, divorced from the thought of principles and wider aims, must in the long run waste itself. Our so-called practical habit of mind is the cause of a great defect in our conception both of education and of learning. It may be worth while to notice some of the evils which result from this defect, for one at least of the conditions of health is a recognition of the disadvantages of an unhealthy state.

One marked result of the neglect of classical learning in England is the isolation of learned men both among themselves and from the body of the educational profession. Learning and research are furthered, more than by anything else, by combination; but of combination for classical research we have in England little or nothing. There is undoubtedly in this country, within and without the universities, a respectable body of learned men, but the want of concert between them, and the indifference with which their labours are regarded by the general public, are a serious discouragement both to those who have chosen the career of learning and to those who are aspiring to enter upon it. Learned men are isolated, again, from the educational profession as a body. The conditions of life in our leading schools, as I endeavoured to describe them above, tend to concentrate the attention of masters more and more upon questions of morals and discipline, and the qualifications for a classical teacher in a good school, though they naturally include 'scholarship,' or in other words, the attainment of a high classical degree at a university, do not include the intention to pursue any branch of study. And this is true, as a rule, of head masters, as well as of assistant masters. Head masters are now so occupied with the duties of administration, that it would be impossible for them to imitate Arnold's combination of knowledge with practical power. No one would now dream of expecting a 'History of Rome' from the head master of an English public school. The cause of learning has thus, to a great extent, lost the sympathies and interest of the very men whose co-operation, owing to their position and influence throughout the country, would be most serviceable to it. Again, the defect under consideration leaves marked traces in the general character of our learned literature. No systematic instruction is given at Oxford or, I believe, at Cambridge, in the methods of classical research; there is little concert between university professors and students (before or after taking their degree) for the object of common labour and co-operation in the solution of outlying philological problems. If a man wishes to make himself a thorough scholar, he must go to Germany and learn method there, and improve by his efforts on what he has learned. Meanwhile, there is no lack of new classical books in England. Some of these have a quasi-literary character, and are written *animi causa*, as a sign of the author's interest in the subject; many are educational and intended, directly or indirectly, for school purposes, or for service in examinations. Too much of the scholarship displayed in both classes of books is of an amateur cast. It must be so, for a scholar is not trained to know clearly what he intends to do when he sits down to edit a Greek or Latin book. He has been left entirely in the dark as to the principles of diplomatic criticism, and has never even been made intimately familiar with the proceeding of any great scholar in his greatest works.

The dearth of really original work is as remarkable as the number of our school books. The staple of the classical education given at Oxford, for instance, has long been the study of Aristotle and Plato and of Greek and Roman history; yet no considerable work has appeared at Oxford in recent times on the philosophy of Aristotle as a whole, or upon Herodotus or Thucydides, or Livy, or Tacitus.

The unhappy divorce of learning from teaching is also the cause of much of the confusion of aim and idea with regard to classical knowledge and education which is manifest both in the minds of educationists and of the general public. So long as the classical literature was generally thought to contain the best things that could be known, there was no difficulty in maintaining it as the staple of a liberal education. It cannot be said, however, at the present time, that the Greek and Latin books have now the paramount claim which they once had to dominate our schools and universities. This is a fact which students of natural science and of modern languages have naturally, in the discussion of the rival claims of the ancient and modern learning, been ready enough to seize upon, and, so far as the parallel claims of their own studies are concerned, they may be considered to have had the best of the argument. But the defenders of classical education have put themselves at a disadvantage by not thoroughly recognizing and insisting upon the fact that, while the classical literatures retain their intrinsic, though not their paramount, value, they have won a new place for consideration as an important part of the growing organism of knowledge. Classical teachers have regarded their subject too exclusively as a means of training, or of information, or of enjoyment, forgetting that like any other branch of knowledge it requires fresh and constant cultivation, that the field of classical research is in no sense worked out, that even for the greatest and best known works of the ancients much remains to be done in the way of criticism and interpretation, while the field of the late Greek and Latin has much fresh store to yield; that fresh discoveries of coins and inscriptions and works of art are almost daily throwing new light on obscure points of ancient life and history; that the comparative study of languages has given to every detail of Greek and Latin grammar a possible interest and importance that it never had before; that the comparative study of syntax is only in its infancy; that the comparative study of institutions is making ever fresh demands upon the students of Greek and Roman law and antiquities. When it is fully recognized that classical study is an essential part of the growing body of knowledge, and of paramount importance as the key to a great chapter of human history (*humani nihil alienum*), it will matter little on what other grounds it may be commended or disparaged. Classical students will have a clear aim and a hope of fruit, and the spirit of languor and compromise will disappear [1].

[1] In his Inaugural Lecture on the Academical Study of Latin (published in the first volume of his *Miscellaneous Writings*) Conington has the

It is time to ask whether there are any practical ways of meeting the evils complained of. It is difficult enough to

following observations, which I venture to quote as suggested by considerations parallel to those upon which I have been dwelling :—

' There are, I know, persons to whom the enumeration of the obstacles to the understanding of the classics suggests regretful, if not contemptuous, feelings. They lament the waste of labour spent, not in the discovery of the unknown, but in the recovery of the lost, and make light of divinations of truth which the unrolling of a single new manuscript may supersede or disprove. The complaint is the same which is put so epigrammatically by the author of *Hudibras* where he says of Time and his daughter Truth :

> 'Twas he that put her in the pit
> Before he pulled her out of it.

I need hardly say that, if valid at all, it is valid, as Butler doubtless intended it, against all historical research. There, as here, we have the spectacle of human thought toiling painfully to repair the losses caused by human thoughtlessness as well as by the unavoidable chances of time ; there, as here, the utmost that can be done may disappear before the contradiction or the fuller affirmation of an accidental discovery. But is the case so different as regards other parts of knowledge ? Is not the attainment of all intellectual truth a labour which might have conceivably been spared to us, nay, which doubtless would have been spared had the mere possession and enjoyment of truth been the end which we were meant to compass? Even the very word enjoyment, so used, implies a misconception. The intellect enjoys truth, not by simply contemplating it but by feeding on it, by assimilating it, and thus making it instrumental to the perception of further truth, which in its turn ministers to other and higher realizations. The toil of getting and the joy of using are not, as in other things, separate, but identical ; if distinguishable in common speech it is only as we may choose to distinguish parts of a process which is really uniform and indivisible. . . . Whoever may complain of the difficulties which beset the pursuit of classical scholarship, assuredly it will not be the scholar himself. He knows it is precisely by means of these difficulties that he is made perfect in his work. . . . It is nothing to him that his time has often to be spent on minute and seemingly trivial points, for he feels that the smaller is to be estimated by the standard of the greater, and that in accepting his calling he has accepted a duty, more or less defined, to everything that appertains to it. The task of recovering a lost word or illusion is not resented as a gratuitous hardship but embraced as a welcome boon, which compels the student, as it were, to enter the author's laboratory, not as a spectator but as a fellow-worker, and rewards the restoration with something of the same delight which must have attended the original invention. It is his labour that he has to go down among those who have long been dead ; but there is a conscious

suggest any means of counteracting an inveterate tendency which can only be fully met by the arising of a new spirit. There are, however, methods of bringing classical education and research into closer relation, which might, without any violent or sweeping changes, be adopted with some success both at schools and universities.

Something more might perhaps be done, even at our large boarding schools, than is done at present. Our system of classical teaching might be, to a certain extent, adapted to a broader point of view. There is no reason why the fact that the classical languages and literature are monuments of a great period of history should ever be forgotten by teachers of classics, and there are ways of leading boys up to this aspect. Boys are now kept at school till within two years of manhood, and the older and abler among them are capable of some appreciation of principles. The reading in the higher classes might be so arranged as to involve, as far as possible, the study of contemporaneous authors. Thus Sophocles might be read side by side with Herodotus, Thucydides with Euripides and Aristophanes, Cicero and Caesar with Catullus and Lucretius, Vergil and Horace with Livy, Tacitus and the younger Pliny and Seneca with Juvenal. Boys would thus be accustomed to regard their authors not only as models of style and storehouses of grammatical construction, but as representatives of their time. And, as the texts of most of the Greek and Latin authors, whether of the best periods or otherwise, are now accessible in a cheap form in the Teubner series, boys might be encouraged to form select libraries of these authors and guided to a method of reading them, as far as possible, in chronological order. Much has been done and much more might still be done in the way of illustrating ancient life by casts and photographs. In these

pleasure in every step of the way, and it is his glory that he can break their sleep and revive them, that he can make them drink the blood of life and speak living words, that he can endow them, if not with the gift of prophecy, at least with the human power of memory.'

and in other ways the foundation of an historical point of
view and of a living interest in antiquity might be laid in
a boy's mind, and this in itself would be an incentive, if not
to study, at least to sympathy with it.

It cannot, however, be expected that, while the boarding-
house system is in virtual possession of the field of the higher
education, original study will, to any great extent, be pursued
by schoolmasters. It may be that the present state of things
will for a long time remain unsuperseded, and even unchal-
lenged; but there are solid reasons for hoping that a system
of day schools may in time grow up strong enough to rival the
great boarding schools in the estimation of the public. There
are considerations bearing on this question which can hardly
fail, in the long run, to force themselves upon the attention
of the country. The existence of good day schools in our
large towns, whether for classical or for modern education,
would be an incalculable benefit to the English people. It
would materially cheapen the higher education and render
it accessible to a far greater number than at present. Thousands would be brought under humanizing influences who
are now out of their reach. The stiffness, unkindliness, and
pedantry of our present social distinctions would to a great
extent disappear, for there is no leveller like culture. It
would no longer be considered the natural and obvious thing
that parents should send their sons from home and home
influences to become, from their early boyhood, the citizens
of a new society. I mention these patent facts in passing
only to show that an arrangement which would be favourable
to study among schoolmasters would be also, in respects
far more important, a national benefit. That the day-school
system would be comparatively favourable to study, as it has
proved to be in Germany, need hardly be pointed out. It
would relieve the masters of the load of anxious and responsible work which is inseparable from the care of a house.

School work can of course be only preparatory, but a more
thorough initiation into the interpretation of ancient life and

the methods of classical study may be expected at the universities. I suppose that the Cambridge system, if worked with reasonable flexibility, would allow of all the freedom that is desirable. But at Oxford the claims of the examinations, for which a definite set of books is prescribed, are so exacting as practically to leave no room for lectures in the higher scholarship. I am not complaining of the main principle on which the Oxford final examination is based; there is no hardship, there are even great advantages, in compelling a classical student to read Plato and Aristotle, Herodotus and Thucydides. A prescription of this kind acts as a check upon vagaries, and secures to the student a thorough knowledge of important books. But the demands of the examination should not be, as they are at present, so rigid as to leave no time for the formation of voluntary classes in which instruction might be given in the rudiments of criticism. Such classes would in all probability never be large, nor would they attract the ablest among the students. But they would provide, it may fairly be said, for the wants of a reasonable number of men with a taste for criticism and a capacity for contributing something original towards it, who now are left almost entirely without guidance. In these voluntary classes tutors might give a general introduction to the principles of philological evidence, whether derived from manuscripts or inscriptions, using manuscripts, where such are available, for illustration (even inferior manuscripts would be very serviceable in this way where good ones are not accessible); or the student might be taken carefully through some great work of criticism such as Bentley's *Horace* or *Manilius*, or Madvig's *De Finibus*, the tutor calling special attention to the method of the critic, its strong and its weak points; or some important period in the history of scholarship (a subject almost entirely ignored by Oxford men) might be studied.

No such distinction should be drawn between the form and the matter of classical writings as is now drawn at Oxford, where the students are taken first through a preliminary course of poetry and oratory, and are afterwards introduced to the historians and philosophers, reading, for instance, for the first public examination Demosthenes and Cicero and Homer and Virgil, and for the second Thucydides and Livy and Aristotle and Plato. This arrangement not only makes the first year of the student's Oxford life a mere continuation of his school work, but prevents him from taking any view of classical literature as a whole.

The comparative study of languages should be begun at the universities not (as now at Oxford) by the reading of *compendia* or notes from lectures, but by learning the rudiments of Sanskrit.

Students of philology, after they have completed their university course, should be invited by the professors to co-operate with them in original work, or to undertake original work of their own. Or they should at least be directed how to set about such work, if it be their wish to undertake it.

Suggestions of this kind (and there are doubtless many others which will occur to minds more fertile than my own) might be acted upon without materially modifying the principles on which the course of studies at our universities is based. They require for their application no more than an increased elasticity in the examination system, with which, in its main features, I should not propose to interfere. I suppose that the demands of the examinations are nowhere more rigorous than at Oxford; but even there, if the mass of compulsory work were diminished, and a real freedom given to learn and to teach subjects falling outside the prescribed course, there would be little difficulty in communicating, to those interested in the matter, the elements of philological method, and removing from the Oxford system what no one interested in classical antiquity can but regard as a glaring defect. I am pleading for a kind of instruction with which I suppose all serious teachers and students of the natural sciences to be familiar, and which is indeed inseparable from the progressive pursuit of any branch of knowledge whatever.

Classical study can maintain itself as a living element of knowledge, but not as a patchwork of accomplishments. The revival of learning in England requires the aid not of genius, but of ordinary ability and good will. Singleness of aim among even a few like-minded persons can accomplish much, and it is to be hoped that the importance of research to education, its efficacy in strengthening the individual character of the student, and the general indirect influence of learning in preventing the degeneration of literature, will soon be recognized not by a few but by many. In resources of all kinds, endowments, leisure, opportunities, our universities are exceptionally rich. Much has been done to remove the old restrictions which prevented free access to these resources; the duty remains of employing them fruitfully, and adding a new element of well-being to the national life of England.

VIII.

THE MORAL INFLUENCE OF LITERATURE[1].

———◦•◦———

In choosing this subject for an evening lecture, I need hardly say that I had no thought of attempting to exhaust it; still less did I suppose that I had anything new to say. An hour is a very short time to give to a great subject on which much has already been said and written. On the other hand, a great subject has this advantage over a small one, that it invites more attention and stimulates more interest, and thus the points to which one can attract notice in a short time are more likely to remain in the memory, and suggest reflection afterwards.

(1) It is hardly superfluous to ask—What is literature? We are apt to think of literature as the contents of books, and books as an affair of ink and paper, half, if not altogether, dead; something removed from the real life of the world. And no doubt it is true that a mere knowledge of books is not the same as a knowledge of life and of the world; it is not the same thing, and it is a very inadequate substitute for it. But look at the matter a little more closely, and one sees that the line is drawn too rigidly. For books are, after all, nothing more or less than voices speaking to us—not the voices merely of our own friends and contemporaries, but of a long line of past

---

[1] [A Lecture delivered at Toynbee Hall, October, 1889: published, with Essay IX, by Percival & Co., London, 1890.]

generations; human life that has escaped the grave, still appealing to us for our homage, our love, our sympathy, our condemnation, or our abhorrence. Literature is a voice; and what is there that its message does not contain if we will listen?

But we must add a word more Literature is the voice of those who can speak. The addition means something. The writer of books is one who has the gift of utterance. Not by any means, on that account, a greater or better man than his fellows; for some of the greatest men—Socrates, for instance, and Cromwell—were comparatively inarticulate, and thousands of others who have taken a great part in making social and political history have died without leaving a word behind them. There is a great deal of life which never finds its way into books or speeches at all. But the gift of utterance is a special talent, sometimes associated with greater qualities, sometimes not so; sometimes even bound up with mean qualities, and depending apparently on a defect of moral nature. Great powers of imagination are usually connected with great powers of expression; but imaginative genius, as every one knows, does not always carry with it what is generally understood to be a sound moral constitution.

Literature, then, being, in its length and breadth, the voice of those who are more able to speak addressing those who are less able, the moral effect of their message must depend on what they have to say; and this, again, must depend on the moral force that is in them, and the degree in which it has moved them to speak. Their gift of utterance may be inseparably linked with some weakness or defect of nature; and thus it may happen—indeed, very often it does happen—that the literature of a particular generation gives but an inadequate idea of the best part of its life.

(2) We are talking, somewhat too glibly perhaps, about morality and moral force. So, at the risk of being tedious, I must define the sense in which I am going to use the words in this lecture. I will say then at once that by morality I do

not mean the mere passive obedience which we render to law and social prescription. If the be-all and end-all of life were summed up in the one duty of doing what we were told by the powers ruling in the state or in society; if our whole aim were to live, not in conscious and active sympathy with the natural principles out of which law and prescription have in the long run arisen, but in a mere enforced conformity to law and prescription, we should have a society like that of ancient Sparta or the Geneva of Calvin. Literature would not be needed; the book of the law would be enough, and we should have accepted a dilemma like that attributed to the Mohammedan conqueror of Alexandria, 'If these writings of the Greeks agree with the book of God, they are useless and need not be preserved; if they disagree, they are pernicious and ought to be destroyed.' This feeling still exists widely, and always has existed, but it has been overruled by the instinct of moral and intellectual progress. For morality consists not in an imposed but in a free conformity; in a free conformity to law and prescription so far as they are themselves based upon the moral impulse which has given them birth, and which they are there to protect.

I have no claim to speak as a philosopher, and therefore this moral impulse may, for my present purpose, be defined as the spontaneous tendency which exists in human beings to live and act for each other's well-being. I am not concerned to go further than this, for my only object now is to lay stress on the fact that, in my opinion, no action can properly be called moral unless it is freely unselfish, done for the love of another without fear of punishment or hope of reward. If a man asks for a fee for not killing his father, his abstention from parricide cannot be called a moral act.

(3) What, then, are the principal and the most obvious manifestations of this natural or spontaneous tendency? Deep down in the laws of Nature herself is rooted the love of parent for child and child for parent; out of this, organized by custom and developed by the constant enlarging of the social sphere, has gradually arisen the social spirit which now more than ever

is felt around and among us, animating all the better part of modern life. On the active side of human life its work is evident, and need not be dwelt upon, especially in this place; on another side it has inspired the love of truth, the determination to hold fast to intellectual honesty, which is a far rarer and more difficult virtue, especially in a democratic society, than the practice of philanthropy.

(4) What, then, is the effect of literature in encouraging and developing this great social force?

I would answer, generally, that literature is powerful rather to encourage than to create moral action. For literature is in itself, to a large extent, produced by the moral impulse, and the stream cannot rise higher than its source. On the other hand, I believe that bad literature does not so much create vice as encourage it. I think that Milton was in the main right when he said that you may banish all objects of lust, and yet that you will not thereby make those chaste that are not so already; that Macaulay was in the main right when he said that men are not so much corrupted by books as by the course of the world. I know that there are many persons, better qualified than I am to speak on this matter, who would attribute to books a more powerful influence than I think they, on the whole, possess. My own belief is that bad literature, in the main, is created by the demand for it. 'Whatsoever from without goeth into a man, it cannot defile him; . . . that which proceedeth out of the man, that defileth the man.' If the bad book were not wanted, there would be no sale for it.

Not that this in any way lessens the responsibility of its author, whose conscience may one day be rudely awakened by the thought that he has been doing his best to encourage the forces of destruction.

(5) We are now naturally brought to consider what classes of literature have had, and are most likely to have, a direct effect in encouraging the moral impulse within us.

There is much literature the effect of which is good, but which may best be described as non-moral. I mean all such

writing as embodies the spirit of greatness and sublimity. The
greatest works, it must be said, are great; they are not moral.
The *Iliad* and *Odyssey*, the tragedies of Aeschylus, Sophocles,
and Euripides, the *Aeneid*, the *Divine Comedy*, the tragedies
of Shakespeare, the *Faust*,—these are creations of a scope and
grandeur which place them beyond any special human interest.
So far as the perceptions and imagination of man can, under
the limitations imposed upon him by the surroundings of his
time, compass the whole length, breadth, height, and depth of
his existence, can rise to its greatest capabilities and sound its
lowest baseness; not less than this is the measure of the power
which these monuments reveal. They are like Nature herself; we lose ourselves in them, are absorbed in awe and
wonder at the magnificent vision. The sense of elemental
power and beauty is borne in upon us; the sense of something all and more than all than we are. Many persons would,
I dare say, assert that the impression is a moral one. Ruskin,
for instance, is always endeavouring to impress upon us the
ethical bearings and meaning of art; and what is true of art, of
painting, or of music, is still truer of literature. I believe, however, that it is a mistake to identify the sphere of morals with
that of great art. The common sense of mankind refuses to
do so, and the course of life, as we observe it, supports the
common sense of mankind. We say commonly, 'He was
a great artist, and also a good man;' or, 'A great artist, but
not a good man.' But it is fair to say also that the study of
great art, and the absorption of life in it, whether the study be
creative or merely imitative, works negatively in the moral
direction. The condition of mind which is necessary to produce great works of art, or to study them with sympathy, is one
which is incompatible with baseness of intention, or a mean
absorption in petty interests. If such baseness be there, the
work will suffer: do we not feel this in the case of Byron?
Without charity, even genius becomes as sounding brass and
a tinkling cymbal.

It would seem, then, that while the study of great literature is good and ennobling, as drawing the mind upwards and bracing it to the consideration of sublimity and beauty, it cannot be said to have an actively moral effect. The same is true of the intellectual element in all works of art. By the intellectual element I mean not merely what may be called the intellectual contents, the intellectual significance, of such works, but the workmanship, the mechanical appliances by which such significance is brought home to us. Good workmanship is an absolute necessity to good literature. I only wish that English writers understood this as well as their French brethren. If Browning would have taken the trouble to write like Swinburne, how much more might he have done for us ! But workmanship is not a moral matter, except in so far as it requires a habit of mental concentration in the worker.

(6) It may seem as if I were excluding from the sphere of ethics the best things in literature—the writings to which we most naturally turn for relief and refreshment. But much is left, and I will speak first of a branch of literature which is not, perhaps, accessible to many, or at least not approached by them--the literature of philosophy, of history, of science, and of research in general.

I would observe, before going any further, that in my opinion knowledge is a moral force, and cannot be too clearly recognized as such ; and that consequently the acquisition and diffusion of knowledge is a duty, for the performance of which those who are able to devote themselves to it are seriously responsible. I am not speaking of the acquisition of knowledge pursued by individuals for their own pleasure, of the striving after culture for its own sake, of the intellectual life as a beautiful thing. These things may be good or not ; but they have a tendency to form intellectual epicures, and at best should probably be characterized as non-moral. I am speaking of the diffusion of knowledge—the spreading of the truth, so far as man can at any given time ascertain it, in its broad social effects, in its bearing on the life of nations. Now, I would wish to emphasize the fact that the pursuit of knowledge acts in more ways than one upon the character both of individuals and of peoples. To begin with, it sets before the individual the lofty ideal of harmonizing human life with fact, and thus improving and gladdening it in all its aspects and relations. This, throughout all the din and smoke of the thousand heart-rending conflicts which have stained the pages of history with blood, may be discerned to be the real end after which the great leaders of philosophical and religious thought have at all times and in all places been striving. Need I speak of the discipline and qualities necessary to the right living of such a life? the renunciation of individual caprice; the training of the mind's eye to bear the light; the purity of motive; above all, the courage? As Goethe profoundly says, the most perilous service of all is the service of man.[1] Indeed, in a democratic society, with its tendency towards equality of condition and a uniform level of comfort, with its encouragement of sympathy and sentiment, I sometimes think that the virtue of intellectual honesty runs more danger of being sapped than in a ruder state of civilization. It is a good thing to love one's neighbour, but a bad thing to fear him; and we are constantly running the risk of regarding the truth of what we are saying less than the effect which we think it will produce. It is well for the philosopher, the historian, the savant, and the scholar to remember that he owes more, perhaps, to posterity than to his contemporaries.

But there is another way in which morality is effected by knowledge. Cruelty is born, to a large extent, of fear, and everything which tends to diminish fear tends to diminish cruelty. Now, of all the agencies which diminish fear, knowledge is perhaps the most powerful. In the great struggle in which mankind is perpetually engaged with Nature, it is the progress of knowledge which enables him to win for himself, inch by inch, a freer and stronger position, to gain constantly

---

[1] ' Willst du viele befrei'n, so wag' es vielen zu dienen ;
Wie gefährlich das sei, willst du es wissen? Versuch's.'
(*Epigramme* (1790), 51.)

new points of vantage, from which the light that he has with
him shines further, and the shadows that have been terrifying
him vanish into nothingness.   His new acquisition is not to be
measured only by the advance he has made in material prosperity, in inventive power, in the command of new mechanical
appliances for bringing ease and comfort to his outer life.   He
has won something better than this, namely, a surer apprehension of the laws of his own existence, a knowledge which acts
as a force conservative of the conditions which maintain life,
and as a force destructive of the conditions which impair it;
which dissolves the antagonisms and hatreds born of terror, and
acts in conformity with all the great charitable powers out of
which Nature, even without the aid of widely extended knowledge, is ceaselessly active in building up human society.

(7) Philosophy, the highest of all forms of literature,
represents the highest endeavour of the human spirit after
knowledge.   The study of philosophy, then, in the works of its
greatest masters, is, of all the intellectual aids to moral life, the
most effective.   There is nothing like it for bracing the mind,
for raising it upwards, for realizing that mastery over circumstance which the spirit of man has always claimed as its
birthright.   Will it be said that theology does this better than
philosophy?   I would answer that the comparison is mistaken;
that theology, so far as it is true, is no more than philosophy
assuming a special character and attitude under special
historical conditions.   Will it be said, again, that philosophy
necessarily leads to pessimism?   If so, it is a partial philosophy,
an imperfect synthesis.

(8) The course of history shows that this is no piece of
a priori dogmatism.   What are the great moral forces upon
which European civilization, as we know it, is founded?   The
answer would be, I suppose, the system of social ethics derived from the Jews, improved and extended by Christianity,
and the intellectual impulse derived from the Greeks.   But
this answer, though true in the main, is put in a form which
somewhat misrepresents the facts.

We owe to the Greeks, as well as to Christianity, much of our ordinary ethics. No doubt the most striking and obvious characteristic of Greek literature is its presentation to us of great personalities or types of humanity—Achilles, Empedocles, Pericles, Socrates, Aristotle, Alexander. We think of Greek society as imperfect on the political and moral side, and as giving us examples rather of individual power and harmonious self-development. This judgment is partial, as being based mainly on our reading of the great classical monuments of Greek literature. We forget the schools of the philosophers, which for the three centuries before the Christian era kept up an unbroken tradition of healthy moral practice in the face of an imperfectly instructed society, and developed ideas which on the one hand came into fruitful contact with the religious doctrines of the Jews, and on the other hand inspired a new and inner life into the developed social and political organization of the Roman empire.

(9) Seldom, if ever, has philosophy and the spirit of progressive intellectual inquiry been more fruitfully alive than during those three centuries. Much was done in them, not merely in the way of gathering literary knowledge and advancing physical science, but in consolidating the foundations of moral conduct. Yet, when all is said, there is wanting in Greek literature, as a whole, the element of sweetness and wholeness which meets us in that of the Jews. I am sorry to say that I am no Hebrew scholar, and have, therefore, no right to speak of the Old Testament, except as an ordinary reader might speak of it. But I think that even a superficial reader of the Hebrew prophets must be struck with the fact that they appeal to a people which knows and understands, in a special manner, the sanctity of family ties, the love of father and mother, wife and child. The wife is not a nonentity in the household, but the husband's love is for her, body and soul. How beautiful is the constant image under which the God of the Hebrews is represented as the lover and the husband of His people ! ' Thus wast thou decked with gold and silver ;

and thy raiment was of fine linen, and silk, and broidered work ;
thou didst eat fine flour, and honey, and oil : and thou wast
exceeding beautiful, and thou didst prosper unto royal estate.
And thy renown went forth among the nations for thy beauty :
for it was perfect, through the majesty which I had put upon
thee, saith the Lord God. . . . Thou hast built thy lofty place
at every head of the way, and hast made thy beauty an
abomination. . . . How weak is thine heart, saith the Lord
God, seeing that thou doest all these things ! . . . A wife that
committeth adultery ! that taketh strangers instead of her
husband ! . . . Nevertheless I will remember My covenant
with thee in the days of thy youth, and I will establish unto
thee an everlasting covenant [1].'   Can Greek or Latin literature
show anything like this ?

Or, again, will you find, in Greek and Latin literature, such
sympathy for the poor and suffering as is expressed over and
over again in the Hebrew prophets and psalms ?   ' Hear this,
O ye that would swallow up the needy, and cause the poor of
the land to fail, saying, When will the new moon be gone, that
we may sell corn ? and the sabbath, that we may set forth
wheat ? making the ephah small, and the shekel great, and
dealing falsely with balances of deceit ; that we may buy the
poor for silver, and the needy for a pair of shoes, and sell the
refuse of the wheat ?   The Lord hath sworn by the excellency
of Jacob, Surely I will never forget any of their works.   Shall
not the land tremble for this, and every one mourn that
dwelleth therein [2] ? '

(10) A national literature is the offspring of the national life,
and its moral influence will be strong in proportion to the
moral forces which are the spring of that life.   The position
which the Bible has held as a religious book, as an inspired
record of events, and as an oracle of conduct, has varied in
past times among different Churches, and will continue to vary
as fresh light is thrown by scholarship upon its historical
narratives, and upon the true meaning of its moral and religious

---

[1] Ezek. xvi. 13, 14, 25, 30, 32, 60. (R.V.)   [2] Amos viii. 4-8.

utterances. Its real influence, however, will not be impaired
so long as it is apparent that large portions of it, at least, are
based upon a clearer apprehension of the univeral laws of
moral progress than existed among any nation of antiquity
except the Jews. So long as this is admitted, all questions
affecting the date and authorship of particular books will, however they are determined, produce no effect upon the ethical
position of the Bible. The value of the historical record may
be differently estimated; the value of the moral record does
not depend on time, place, or writer.

(11) To pass from the Bible to works of modern fiction may
seem to you a piece of unpardonable bathos. But one can
hardly exaggerate, nowadays, the power for good or evil which
is exercised by the novelist. The Ten Commandments, the
Catechisms, even the Sermon on the Mount, are learned by
heart and forgotten, or, if the words are not forgotten, they
become conventional and cease to convey an effective meaning.
But the influence of novels pervades the whole of modern
society in its length and breadth. Children are brought up
upon stories ; the majority of women, when they have leisure
for reading, devote it to reading works of fiction. I have
heard it said that in England alone a new novel is written for
every day in the year ; in a single year some three hundred and
fifty romances.

Let us try to lay our finger upon the main objects which
a novelist should aim at securing, if his books are to have
a genuine moral effect. I assume what is taken for granted in
France, and ought to be taken for granted in England, that he
spends the utmost pains on his workmanship. His writing
should, then, if there is anything in what has been said already,
be based upon the great foundations of moral life, and follow
their lines. In other words, it should be animated by two
spirits—the spirit of truth, and the spirit of charity. If these
are present in full measure, two subordinate results will follow :
the work will be pure, and it will be noble. If they are
present in imperfect measure, or, to put the same thing in

a simpler form, if the writer is thinking of himself more than of his readers, of his own gain or his own intellectual gratification, the work will be less pure and less noble ; the whole effect being, of course, in all cases, proportionate to the genius of the writer.

By truth I do not mean what is called realism, and by charity I do not mean sentiment.   M. Zola and his followers profess to describe human life exactly as it is, or nearly as it is, for, after all, no novelist will ever be able to describe everything.   I may be wrong, but I confess that Zola appears to me to have missed his mark.   If you are to describe life as it really is, you must take note of its heights as well as its depths, and you must have a firm hold, in your intellect and imagination, of the organic connexion between them, of the wonderful correlation of moral forces which human life everywhere exhibits.   You must be ideal as well as real, to use two phrases of which one gets somewhat weary.   The ideal is, after all, nothing outside us. It is the highest and best of what is within us.   *The kingdom of God is within you.*   What do we know of the possibilities of human effort, of the life of hero or saint or martyr, unless it be from what the hero and saint and martyr have actually thought, imagined, and done, and from the sympathetic echo which their thoughts, imaginations, and deeds awaken in our own breasts ?   It is the constant absorption of the lower elements of life into the higher, the reality of both in their mutual relàtion, that is the real theme of the novelist.   A novel need not be impure because it is true ; it is impure only if it reveal the fact that, in the novelist's own mind, the baser elements are the more real.

I find it impossible to read much of Zola, because of what seems to me the want of proportion in his view of human society.   This want of proportion is destructive of beauty, and is, therefore, a literary as well as a moral blemish ; in short, Zola's realism is not only a crime but an error.   On the other hand, Balzac appears to me to be a realist of the right kind, because, with all his grasp of the lower side of life, he never loses sight of its sublime possibilities. He regards man as a living whole, not as a headless galvanized body. The same may, I think, be said of Thackeray, who no doubt would have written with even greater truth and freedom than he has done had he not stood too much in awe of the susceptibilities of his English public. What could give a more terrible picture of the gaunt realities of wickedness than the following passage from ' A Gambler's Death,' in the *Paris Sketch-Book ?*—

'We sallied forth, and speedily arrived at the hotel which Attwood inhabited still. He had occupied, for a time, very fine apartments in this house ; and it was only on arriving there that day, that we found he had been gradually driven from his magnificent suite of rooms *au premier* to a little chamber on the fifth story. We mounted, and found him. It was a little shabby room, with a few articles of rickety furniture, and a bed in an alcove ; the light from the one window was falling full upon the bed and the body. Jack was dressed in a fine lawn shirt ; he had kept it, poor fellow, *to die in ;* for in all his drawers and cupboards there was not a single article of clothing ; he had pawned everything by which he could raise a penny— desk, books, dressing-case, and clothes ; and not a single half-penny was found in his possession.

' He was lying as I have drawn him, one hand on his breast, the other falling towards the ground. There was an expression of perfect calm on the face, and no mark of blood to stain the side towards the light. On the other side, however, there was a great pool of black blood, and in it the pistol ; it looked more like a toy than a weapon to take away the life of this vigorous young man. In his forehead, at the side, was a small black wound ; Jack's life had passed through it ; it was little bigger than a mole.

' " Regardez un peu," said the landlady, " messieurs, il m'a gâté trois matelas, et il me doit quarante-quatre francs."

' This was all his epitaph : he had spoilt three mattresses, and owed the landlady four-and-forty francs. In the whole world there was not a soul to love him or lament him. . . .

'Beside Jack's bed, on his little *table de nuit* lay the remains of his last meal, and an open letter, which we read. It was from one of his suspicious acquaintances of former days, and ran thus—

'" Où es-tu, cher Jack ? *why you not come and see me ?* tu me dois de l'argent, entends-tu ? un chapeau, une cachemire, *a box of the Play.* Viens demain soir, je t'attendrai *at eight o'clock,* Passages des Panoramas. *My Sir is at his country.*

'" Adieu à demain,

' " FIFINE.

' " Samedi."

'I shuddered as I walked through this very Passage des Panoramas in the evening. The girl was there, pacing to and fro, and looking into the countenance of every passer-by, to recognize Attwood. *Adieu à demain* — there was a dreadful meaning in the words, which the writer of them little knew.'

What can be more real, and yet what could suggest more to the imagination or more profoundly stir the moral emotions? Let us for a moment pause, and see what Thackeray can be in his mood of exquisite tenderness. I quote the end of the tenth chapter of the second volume of *The Newcomes.*

'Clive sees the carriage drive away after Miss Newcome has entered it without once looking up to the window where he stands. When it is gone he goes to the opposite windows of the salon, which are open towards the garden. The chapel music begins to play from the convent next door. As he hears it he sinks down, his head on his hands.

'*Enter Madame de Florac. (She goes to him with anxious looks.)* What hast thou, my child ? Hast thou spoken ?

'*Clive (very steadily).* Yes.

'*Madame de F.* And she loves thee ? I know she loves thee.

'*Clive.* You hear the organ of the convent ?

'*Madame de F.* Qu'as-tu ?

'*Clive.* I might as well hope to marry one of the sisters

of yonder convent, dear lady. (*He sinks down again, and she kisses him.*)

' *Clive.* I never had a mother, but you seem like one.

' *Madame de F.* Mon fils ! Oh, mon fils ! '

Thackeray is true and tender ; pure, therefore, and noble.

To speak of Dickens is hardly necessary, for I think he is better known, certainly he is better understood than Thackeray, who veils his great qualities under a kind of aristocratic reserve. I would only say that if there be any novelist of genius anywhere whose work is based upon charity, upon love for his kind, sympathy for the weak, the healthy worship of goodness, it is Dickens. The fantastic, grotesque, unreal, theatrical element in him will be forgiven by posterity for this. I know no work of his in which the real mind and heart of the man is more plainly revealed than in that strange story of 'The Haunted Man,' printed among his *Christmas Books.* It is the tale of a man who, over-sensitive and with an over-mastering memory, obtains from a spirit the power of forgetting all his past recollections. With this power he loses, also, all his power to sympathize with suffering ; the springs of his moral nature are broken, and he blights the moral nature of others. ' " Give me back *myself !* " exclaimed Redlaw like a madman. " I am infected ! I am infectious ! I am charged with poison for my own mind, and the minds of all mankind. Where I felt interest, compassion, sympathy, I am turning into stone. Selfishness and ingratitude spring up in my blighted footsteps. I am only so much less base than the wretches whom I make so, that in the moment of their transformation I can hate them.' "

Had I not prosed long enough, I might have said a few words on the great living Russian novelist, Count Leo Tolstoi. The applause with which you receive his name shows me that you are familiar with his books, and this fact of itself relieves me of the necessity of talking long. I will therefore only say this—that the greatness of Tolstoi seems to me to consist in his almost unique combination of a prosaic grasp of common facts and everyday life with an extraordinary strength of moral vision.   By the aid of this vision Tolstoi beholds our ordinary life elevated, transformed, glorified.   He is not only a great artist (I mean in the wider sense, for his workmanship is defective), but a moralist of profound spiritual insight, who has steeped his mind and heart in the teaching of the New Testament.   I would call your attention especially to the view which he is always either propounding or suggesting, that it is often not until the approach of death that the true relations of things are borne in upon us.   Read the account of the illness and death of the Prince André, in *War and Peace*, and say whether the moral imagination of man has ever risen higher.   Then his powerful apprehension and interpretation of the old truth, that in the simple service of his fellow-men lies a man's only lasting happiness—how beautifully is it repeated and enforced, more especially in his later allegories !   His notion of a return to a primitive communistic life, in which wealth-hunting and war and violence, and with them literature and science, should cease, is, I suppose, more easily comprehensible when we remember that the village communities of Russia have, in times past, approached a certain way towards its realization.   To an inhabitant of Western Europe, with its highly developed city life and the consequent complexity of its civilization, Tolstoi's idea must appear a dream.   But there are dreams and dreams, and from Tolstoi's dreams one would rather not awake.

(12) Can literature, in these its aspects, be made an instrument of moral education for the numberless children whom we are daily teaching to read, but providing with very little direction what to read ?   I was much struck with a suggestion of Lord Armstrong's, made, I think, some months ago in one of the magazines, that two hours or so every week should be set aside in elementary schools for the reading of good novels to the children.   To say nothing of such writers as Hood and Dickens, English literature is singularly rich in good works of fiction.   Could not two hours a week in elementary

schools be spared (say) from the analysis of sentences, or the geography of Siberia, to the reading aloud, by the masters to their classes, of writers like Hood and Dickens? Such a lesson would, no doubt, not be disciplinary. But I believe that many children would remember all their lives long something of what they learned in it, and that is more than can be said for a great many lessons, the sole object of which is mental gymnastics.

In trying to recapitulate these scattered and inadequate remarks, I would say that what I have endeavoured to convey might be summed up in the observation that the moral force of a book is always in direct proportion to the moral force of its author. The works of Mill and Carlyle are moral forces; but how much greater do we feel the men to be than their books! The voice is much, but the speaker is more. This, and much more that I have said, is, I fear, a truism; but I am not without hope that you may feel what I remember once hearing said with regard to an obvious proposition, that 'though a truism, it is nevertheless true.'

IX.

CLASSICAL EDUCATION IN THE
PAST AND AT PRESENT[1].

I SHALL endeavour, in the few remarks which I am going
to make on this subject, to give some idea of the origin of
classical education, and the different character and position
which it has necessarily assumed, under the pressure of varying circumstances, at different periods of history. This may
perhaps make it easier to realize on what ground it stands
at present, and what services it can still render in modern
civilized communities.

The principle underlying the system of classical education
was originally this : that it was a good thing for a boy to
know the best literature, because the best literature would
furnish him not only with models of artistic composition,
but with words of practical wisdom which might aid him in
the realization of moral truth.

All educational material must be, from the nature of the
case, a small selection from the great mass of knowledge;
but the smaller this mass of knowledge is at any period, the
larger, of course, will be the proportion which the material
of education bears towards it. At the present time our great
difficulty lies in the vastness of the field around us. The

[¹ A lecture delivered before the Teachers' Guild, Oxford, November,
1889 : published, with Essay VIII, by Percival & Co., London, 1890.]

amount which can be known is infinite, but the limitations of each individual mind remain, and are likely to remain, what they always have been.

If we wish to find a people, and a period of history, which in this respect presented conditions almost diametrically opposed to those of our own day, we cannot do better than look at the Athenians in the early and middle parts of the fifth century B.C. It was among the Athenians, and at this time, that the principle of classical education first took root. It exhibited itself in a very simple form. An Athenian boy, for all his literature, learned his Homer and something of the best lyric poets. He had some, but not much, difficulty about the language; certainly not so much, I should imagine, as a modern English boy would have in learning Chaucer. We may realize this state of things by supposing that no English boy learned anything at school in the way of literature but certain passages of the Bible and Shakespeare, read, explained, and committed to memory.

A boy's literary education would probably, at this period of Athenian history, stop at this point; but if he were wealthy and wished to enter public life, it is very likely that he would, as a young man, get some further education in the art of public speaking. One can hardly exaggerate the importance of this art in classical antiquity. In all cities which had a republican constitution, and they were very numerous, it was absolutely necessary for a man who aspired to a leading position. The Sophists, as they are now called, were to a large extent professors of the art of persuasion. They taught the young speaker how to arrange his matter, to put his points, and to polish his style. The beautiful prose style which is one of the ornaments of Greek literature was, in great part, formed by the influence of these teachers and their pupils. Even historical prose was, to a considerable degree, moulded on the prose of the orators. The lessons of the Sophists, or teachers of speaking and such knowledge as bore on speaking, were partly lessons in the art of prose composition, and may so far be regarded as a part of literary, or what we should now call classical, education.

With the establishment of the Macedonian empire, and the extinction of freedom at Athens, another period in the history of classical education may be dated. Alexandria became the intellectual centre of Greek civilization. The Ptolemies founded great libraries there, and gathered round them savants and scholars from other parts of the world. The rich vein of genius which, from the time of Pindar and Aeschylus to that of Demosthenes and Plato, had been so fertile of great works, became exhausted. An age of scholars and savants succeeded the age of poets, historians, orators, and philosophers. Much great and lasting work was done in the third and second centuries B.C. The foundations of physical science and of criticism, literary and philological, were firmly laid. And it was in this period that literary education first began to assume the shape which it has worn ever since. It then became an education in a literature which, if not dead, belonged to the past, the spirit of which was extinct, and its form only to be restored by imitation.

Inseparably connected with this feature of classical study in the Alexandrian period is another; I mean the organization of literary and philological criticism into a system. It was necessary, on the one hand, to select from the large mass of good writing offered by the Athenian literature those works which seemed best suited for educational purposes. Accordingly we now find the masters of criticism, Aristophanes of Byzantium and his pupil Aristarchus, in the first half of the second century B.C., forming canons of the best poets, orators, and historians; canons which were in later times naturally enlarged or modified, but which, from that time to this, have exercised a great influence in the educational and even in the literary world. As the selection had to be made upon some principle or principles, it came to be thought part of the duty of a professor to give his higher classes something in the way of literary criticism; some remarks justifying the position which was assigned in the canon to the author they were reading. I grieve to say that one result of this was that bits of literary criticism were handed on unaltered from one master to another, and, we must suppose, epitomized and learned by heart by the pupils.

On the other hand, it was necessary that the selected authors should be read in good texts; and the necessity of forming and handing down such texts created the science of philological criticism. The professor was forced to ask, Can Homer, or Pindar, or Aeschylus, really have said this? If not, what did he say? If he said it, how is the usage to be explained? Commentaries thus began to be formed, parts of which have, in forms no doubt much abridged, and therefore very inadequate, survived to the present day.

It will be seen that classical education has now ceased to be the simple matter that it was in the time of Pericles. No author can now be taught without a considerable amount of professorial criticism, aesthetic and philological. The texts are encumbered with comment. The next change which takes place strengthens the inevitable tendency already begun.

Before the close of the third century B.C., a new political power had won a commanding position in the south of Europe. Italy under the lead of Rome had vanquished Carthage; Rome was thus becoming a great commercial centre, and was urging imperial pretensions; a collision between the Italian and the Macedonian empires was sooner or later inevitable. The Romans were as eager to submit to the Greeks in the field of letters as they were to conquer them in the field of battle. They had a great history behind them, a record of social and political achievement to which no city of Greece could show a parallel. They had literary records of all this, in their own national prose and poetry. But the Greeks had long been busy in the Italian cities—busy with the history and antiquities of Rome, eager to convince the Romans that their origin, and with it their religion and mythology, were Greek or Trojan—anything but what they really were. There was then no such thing as historical criticism, in the proper sense of the word. What there was was in the hands of the Greeks, whose writers were able and accomplished to a degree which no Italian could yet hope to attain. The Romans swallowed the lying tale, passively allowed their own mythology and antiquities to be corrupted, and left a legacy of endless difficulties to us unfortunate modern scholars. One can hardly blame them for this; and there is another point in their conduct for which they deserve nothing but praise. They recognized to the full the transcendent merits of the Greek literature, and set themselves, with genuine modesty, to learn from the Greek masters. Latin literature, as we have it, began with translations and adaptations from the Greek, and was at hardly any time wholly independent of Greek influence.

This important fact had an inevitable effect upon education. To learn Greek and understand Greek literature soon ·became an ambition of the wealthier classes in Italy, and in spite of much opposition on the part of some friends of the national language and literature, Greek had become, before the last century of the republic, a regular part of liberal education at Rome. To learn how to write Latin hexameters, boys learned the metre of Homer ; to master the principles of harmonious composition in prose, they wrote Greek prose exercises. Classical education had become bilingual. A new difficulty was added to it—that of mastering a foreign language and entering into the niceties and refinements of a foreign literature. By the end of the first century A.D., a canon of good Latin authors had been formed, and the phrase *classicus*, or *belonging to the first class*, was applied to those who were thought to deserve that position.

Literary education had now attained a fixed type, which, so far as I know, it retained for centuries. No doubt, with the decline of learning which set in after the beginning of the second century A.D., it degenerated in many schools into a mere getting up of fragments of literature and manuals of learning ; but the idea or principle remained the same. The masterpieces of literature were studied mainly as things of beauty, as models for style ; only secondarily as storehouses of thought or information. The conception was identical with that prevalent at Athens in the age of Pericles ; only the subject, with the manifold accretions of time, had become more complex and difficult.

To what extent the great writers of Greece and Rome were known and studied in the Middle Ages I am not competent to say ; but I suppose that the influence which they exercised upon thought and feeling cannot have been extensive, otherwise the Renaissance of the fifteenth century would have been a far less important phenomenon than it was. Or rather there would have been no Renaissance or new birth at all. What the fact really was we all know. The rediscovered literature of antiquity was regarded not only as a monument of beauty, but as a storehouse of moral and political wisdom, as containing the authentic basis of history and science, as revealing the possibilities of a free and humane life. Hence the passion, which the lapse of four centuries has not exhausted in the civilized world, for attaining a correct view of antiquity, for restoring its texts, piecing together its broken monuments, realizing the course of ancient history, living again in ancient thought and feeling.

The ardour of discovery which animated the scholars of the Renaissance and the Reformation was strong enough to give Greek and Latin literature a permanent place in education side by side with the Scriptures and the manuals of Christian doctrine. In this instance men acted, as they often do, upon the sound instinct which prompts them to embody in their life and action as many elements of good as they can, without inquiring whether those elements, if suffered each to attain its own development, might not turn out to be antagonistic, or even mutually exclusive.

The theory according to which the Greek and Latin classics were regarded as the main storehouse of human wisdom was a theory which, from its very nature, was doomed in the course of time to extinction. For, even supposing it to be true in its full extent, it is obvious that the lessons taught by the classics must, in the course of studying them, be absorbed into modern literature, and become part of the common stock of cultivated opinion. Since the Renaissance we find, accordingly, that this point of view has been gradually abandoned, and that two other aspects of the classics have come into prominence. I will term these two aspects the literary and the scientific respectively.

The literary aspect is that with which we are the most familiar in England, and which has also been dominant, I think, in France. But the recent history of classical education has been, I believe, different in France and in England. In France the Revolution dealt, for a time, a serious blow to the study of Greek in the public schools, and the literary study of Latin has served, hand in hand with that of French, as the main instrument for the culture of literary taste. In England we have fortunately had no revolution for two hundred years. Greek has never been banished from our schools; and the Greek as well as the Latin language and literature have been studied mainly as models of expression and composition; as a means of developing the literary feeling which was long regarded as a natural, if not necessary, characteristic of a cultivated Englishman.

By the scientific aspect of the classics I mean the view which regards them, not exclusively, or even mainly, as models of literary composition, but as historical documents, or material for reconstructing a truthful representation of ancient life in all its aspects, moral, religious, social, literary, and political. This view might, in the time of Scaliger have been called the French view, while the literary view was predominant in Italy. The more serious study of classical philosophy passed, however, with Scaliger, from France to Holland and, later on, from Holland to Germany. In Germany, for more now than a century, this field of intellectual labour has found many of its most illustrious representatives. It is this historical and philosophical tradition (for philology is really a subsidiary branch of history and philosophy), consolidated if not founded by the genius of Friedrich Wolf, which has formed the strength of classical study in Germany for a century past. Without an ideal so ennobling, the prodigious labour spent upon the classics in Germany could never have been maintained; it must have starved long ago for want of an adequate motive. I speak advisedly of an historical and philosophical *tradition*. We have had great scholars in England, but n progressive tradition of advancing knowledge. We honour our scholars, and found prizes and scholarships bearing their names; the results of their work are soon snapped up by teachers and examiners; but the spirit of their work—how many are found to cherish this, the most precious thing they had to bequeath, and to make it the animating principle of their own lives?

I suppose that few enlightened educationists in England would now contend that the Greek and Latin classics should form the exclusive, or almost exclusive, instrument of a liberal education. The field of knowledge has been immensely widened. Other literatures assert themselves as worthy of study side by side with those of ancient Greece and Italy. And, whether the literature be ancient or modern, few would now maintain that an education mainly or entirely literary ought to be the only kind of education encouraged by a great and civilized nation. The importance, now generally recognized, of physical science as the right means of training for some, perhaps for many, minds, is the great educational fact of to-day. My own opinion is of very little value in this matter. But I may perhaps say that I have no faith in a little science taught in classical schools, or a little Latin taught in scientific schools. I look forward to a time when the modern and the classical types of school shall be so separated as to ensure in each a training as thorough in its kind as was the best classical education of forty or fifty years ago. In the classical schools I would have the education as complete, as wide, and as simple as possible, so as to serve as a solid basis for future study, either in literature proper, or in history and philosophy.

No doubt such a separation of ancient and modern must result in a certain amount of rivalry between the two systems. And many, I dare say, are apprehensive that, what with the increasing prominence given to physical science, the growing mercantile spirit, and the depressingly low standard of literary taste among the large half-educated public which constitutes so large a part of all modern societies, the Greek and Latin classics will go to the wall. I do not share this apprehension. Classical education survived a serious attack on the part of the champions of 'useful knowledge' some sixty years ago. At present most enlightened educationists would probably say that we have not too little, but too much of it, in England. What is wanted is to ensure a larger variety in the subjects selected from the vast and increasing mass of knowledge for the purposes of serious mental training, and thus, as far as possible, confining the study of the Greek and Latin classics to those who are likely to profit by it. The ideal of education is that not a single mind should be thrown away upon a study for which it is unfit. The ideal of national culture is that not a single branch of valuable knowledge should be unrepresented in the national schools and universities. No reasonable man, probably, would desire that the study of the Greek and Latin classics should perish out of the land. They cannot, it is true, be any longer regarded as the chief storehouse of knowledge, or as furnishing us with absolute canons of composition and criticism. But the Agamemnon of Aeschylus is still the greatest tragedy that has ever been written; no amount of criticism and dissection will affect the commanding literary position of the Homeric poems; Pindar, Sophocles, Aristophanes, Demosthenes, Herodotus, Thucydides, Cicero, Tacitus, remain where they were. To say anything more of the classics in their literary aspect would be flat and affected. But there is another point on which, perhaps, I may be pardoned if I linger for a moment.

It must be remembered that the classics have still more than a merely literary function to perform. Greece was the mother not only of poetry and oratory, but—at least for the European world—of philosophy. And by philosophy I do not mean merely a succession of metaphysical and ethical systems, but the active love of knowledge, the search for truth. Will it be said that this spirit is not now as necessary an element in civilized human life as it ever was? In the long run it would almost appear as if it were mainly this which saves society from degeneracy and decay. The charitable instincts die out in an atmosphere of ignorance, for ignorance is the mother of terror and hatred. The free moral impulse which makes a man a man, which bids him love all good more than he fears death or pain—this is what was cherished in the Greek philosophic schools, the vital element, of which their metaphysical disputes were only the superficial manifestation. Even in the pale reflection of Greek philosophy which is presented in Latin philosophical writing, even in Cicero, you will find more of a temperate and manly love of truth than in the invectives of a Tertullian. This is an inheritance as precious as Greek art and literary form; nay, if the continuous life of the nations be regarded, an inheritance even more precious.

X.

AUTHORITY IN THE SPHERE OF
CONDUCT AND INTELLECT.

[INTERNATIONAL JOURNAL OF ETHICS, II. (1892) 217-231.]

————•+•————

Mr. LESLIE STEPHEN, in an article on ' Cardinal Newman's
Scepticism,' recently published in the *Nineteenth Century*
(1891, p. 188), says that the word 'authority' may mean
two different things. ' Authority, when I speak as a historian
or a man of science, is a name for evidence. Authority, as
used by a lawyer, is a name for coercion, whether physical or
moral.'

I propose to use the word 'authority' in the sense of the
power which, in the sphere of conduct, in the long run determines our practice, and in the sphere of intellect in the long
run determines our assent; admitting, at the same time, that
the two spheres are by no means always distinct in human life
as we know it.

It is not necessary for me to say a word on the importance
of this subject, either in itself or in reference to the present
time. Every one who observes human life at all must acknowledge that the desire for authoritative guidance is one
of the most universal desires which men experience and express; and that the feeling of loyalty or devotion to the
persons or institutions to whom, or to which, a man owes
anything of his better life is, of all feelings, one of the noblest

and the most commanding. This is true at all times and in all places, but at the present time the desire is felt to be especially urgent, because it is in so many cases unsatisfied. We live in a time of widely-diffused intellectual activity— widely-diffused, I say advisedly and with emphasis, rather than deep or penetrating. A main consequence of this fact is that there are as many claimants for authority as there are moral and intellectual aspirations demanding it.

The desire for authoritative guidance may be observed to exist in two different forms, and issue in two different results, according to the moral constitution of the persons anxious to satisfy it. In this relation, human beings may be roughly divided into two classes: those who are capable of forming convictions, and those who are not. This division does not, it need hardly be said, correspond with the line of mere intellectual cleavage; it is not a division into clever people and stupid people. The capacity of forming convictions is a sign of power, but not exactly of intellectual power. On the other hand, great intellectual capacity, great versatility of talent, and manifold insight into things, need not imply any faculty of forming a real conviction. These gifts may serve no purpose but that of intensifying a sceptical tendency.

The history of human thought and action varies as either of these types of mind has, at any given time, the predominance. To the former class are due, in large measure, the great and sincere and constructive movements which re-awaken the moral forces which inspire society and social life. The demand of those minds for authority is answered by the moral passion which moves them; the rule which they set up is the embodiment of their own love of truth. The latter class form their convictions, or what stands for their convictions, upon scepticism, and thus tend to look for and find their authority, or governing principle, in mere force. Nothing is true, they say or think; the human intellect is impotent; therefore, let the majority of mankind with its traditional institutions, its received opinions and conventions, be our deity.

Weary of reason, or disappointed at the results of its efforts, they fall back for guidance on the irrational elements in life.

It has long seemed to me that during the last quarter of a century we have been suffering under what I venture to call a disorder of this kind[1]. The intellectual tendency of this period has been towards laborious collection of facts in the special spheres of particular sciences, natural and historical. Little, if anything, however, of first-rate importance, even in effort and intention, has been produced in the way of comprehensive thinking. John Stuart Mill is dead; Lotze is dead; Herbert Spencer is an old man, and who is to succeed him? The tone of literature, where it is not merely dull or conventional or sentimental, is that of a moody pessimism, or, at best, a clever and impatient scepticism. The danger of a reaction against the true liberal spirit, by which I mean the spirit of free mental and moral effort, is a real one. In the highest of all spheres, that of morals and religion, we are now face to face with a tendency to rest in half-beliefs, to decry the effort of real thinking as a superannuated folly, to accept traditional opinions as if, because traditional, they represented accomplished facts; in short, to found a system of orthodoxy and conservatism upon scepticism and distrust.

Yet liberalism, or the movement in favour of mental and moral freedom, though not so powerfully represented in England as it was some thirty years ago, is no less vital in its essential characteristics. Its leading representatives at that time were John Stuart Mill and Thomas Carlyle. There were certain weaknesses or limitations in the teaching of both these great men which have tended to impair the permanency of its force. Neither, so far as I know, succeeded in giving

---

[1] This sceptical tendency seems to have begun, in the nineteenth century, with Joseph de Maistre, who characteristically opens his defence of the principle of authority with an attack upon Locke. But it has assumed various forms, and is very differently represented, for instance, by de Maistre, by John Henry Newman, and by recent popular writers such as W. H. Mallock.

a thoroughly satisfactory answer to the question which I am endeavouring to discuss.

Mill's contribution to the movement which he represented seems to have been twofold, lying partly in the moral force and concentration of the man himself, partly in his protest against existing authority in those cases in which it appeared to him to embody injustice. His *Essay on Liberty*, published in 1859, is a masterly exposition of his principles. It is a noble protest against the tyranny of society and legislation, but, as it stands, will seem incomplete to minds which require the statement of some positive principle which, whatever its embodiment, is to take the place of society and legislation.

Carlyle, who felt more strongly than Mill did where the weak side of contemporary liberalism lay, made a real attempt to set up a positive authority in the shape of the great men of history. Perhaps, if Mill had been asked the question, he would have answered that men ought to be content with the simple ' love of loving-kindness,' and to ask for no further light. This would probably have appeared to Carlyle an inadequate, if not a sentimental, answer. However this may be, there seems to be no doubt that Carlyle set himself seriously to inquire what had been the ruling force in human history, and to have found the answer in the characters and actions, much more the characters than the actions, of great men. But he executed his task in too crude and hasty a manner, and though, as I believe, he struck upon the right path, he did not succeed in satisfying his age. His action was too much confined to asserting the greatness of great men ; in what that greatness consisted, and where its permanent influence lay, he does not seem to me to have asked with sufficient seriousness.

In this brief and fragmentary article I shall make no pretence of treating the subject exhaustively, or even thoroughly. I shall attempt only so much as is possible to one who lives outside the serious study of philosophy, and who can do nothing but record his observations on the facts of modern civilized society as they have presented themselves to him. Starting from the point of view of liberalism, and speaking in complete sympathy with its principle and tendency, I would ask whether it is not possible, after all, for its representatives to take up a more positive ground than was occupied by the liberal philosopher of thirty years ago.   I shall first ask what are the chief existing seals of authority recognized by modern society in the spheres of conduct and intellect; and then inquire whether any common and permanent principle can be discovered which underlies them all.

Roughly speaking, one may distinguish four different kinds of authority, which, although mutually connected, and indeed inseparable, in fact, suggest convenient landmarks to guide us in the discussion.   These are (1) the authority of law, (2) the authority of religious bodies, (3) the authority of society or public opinion, (4) the authority of great men.

Do these various authorities rest upon any permanent principle? If so, on what? and why is the principle permanent?

I shall try to show, in answer, that the permanent element of authority, in all of them, is the moral feeling or conviction of the society which they affect; that where they are imperfect, or transitory, there they fall short of, or imperfectly represent, this moral feeling; that the authority of no one set of laws, of no one religious body, of no one society, of no one man, can be permanent; that at any given time the only absolute authority for the individual is his conscience, or his free moral conviction; but where this gives an uncertain answer, which it seldom does, recourse must be had to the moral feeling of mankind; or, failing that, to the moral feeling of the society to which he feels himself morally most nearly attached; that the cases of conflict, so arising, are inevitable, owing to the fact that the moral vision of every individual and every society is limited; but that the conflict is the means by which the moral force is asserting itself, and struggling for harmonious expression; that the conflict tends to a balance of moral forces and an ultimate agreement.

In all this I am obliged, for the mere sake of making way, to assume the liberty of using the words *morality, conscience,* and *freedom,* in their ordinary and popular sense ; and I shall also assume the truth of a theory, which is, of course, disputed, that the moral sense and moral action, whatever their ultimate origin, are, as they now exist, *sui generis,* and cannot be included in any other class of feeling or action, such as the desire for pleasure in any form, or the exercise of the reason [1].

(1) The authority of law is that with which we are all most immediately familiar. It may be said generally that law represents such part of social enactment and social demand as society allows to be carried openly into effect by physical force. You commit a robbery or forgery ; if detected, you are imprisoned ; you wrong your wife or your husband ; the law takes it out of your power to wrong them further ; you commit a murder, if detected, you are hanged. The court, the judge, the prison, the policeman, the scaffold, represent the power of law.

The spirit of liberalism has been generally adverse to the extension of the power of law into spheres where it is other than restrictive or preventive, and, on the whole, the spirit of liberalism may be said to have prevailed in modern states. Even in cases which appear to contradict this statement, in such cases as those of the English Factory Acts, Poor Law, Education Acts, Criminal Law Amendment Acts, and the like, enlightened legislators would probably argue that their aim was mainly if not entirely protective. The Factory and Vaccination Acts fairly admit of being represented as protective of life; the Criminal Law Amendment Act as protective of freedom. Legislation, such as that of which we have examples

[1] I might perhaps have used the word *social* for *moral,* but I prefer the older term, though the moral character of an act seems to me to consist entirely in its unselfishness. This is fully recognized in ordinary thought and language. An unselfish act is regarded as good or moral in the doer, though its consequences may be disastrous ; a selfish act may have excellent consequences, but no one calls it good or moral in the doer.

in the Poor Law and Compulsory Education Acts, does not, it is true, admit so easily of being viewed in this light; the wrong persons probably regard it as a preservative against barbarism and against revolution.

What is the permanent element in the authority of law? As regards conduct, its strength may be said generally to lie in its antiquity. I do not mean, of course, that a new law is not in many cases as binding as an old one. But I mean that society does not, as a rule, appeal to law—that is, to the employment of open force—unless the social demand for the employment of open force is, in the particular case, of long standing; and that the effectiveness of the law when thus appealed to is in direct proportion to the length of its standing. If a law is passed in satisfaction of a sudden or temporary demand, it soon ceases to be effective.

Those laws, the authority of which is most readily taken for granted in modern society, such laws, for instance, as secure the possession of private property and protect the institution of marriage, represent the social institutions, arrangements, and customs which can claim the highest antiquity. And they can claim the highest antiquity only because they represent the oldest moral feeling of the community, or, in other words, because they are the earliest creations of the moral force.

Still, confining ourselves to the sphere of conduct, we shall easily see that the very antiquity which gives law its strength may also be its weakest point. When the law is found to be at variance with the moral sense of the community, it will usually be found to be behind it. The law, for instance, has in times past imposed restrictions, as in the case of the exclusion of the Jews from Parliament, or the limitation of the right of voting for members of Parliament; the moral sense of the community demands and obtains their abolition. Or immoral institutions or customs, institutions or customs which in the long run are found to be injurious to society, have been allowed to exist in security—the slave trade, for instance, or the traffic in young girls. The moral sense of the community demands that the law should turn its arm against them. Or unjust institutions have been protected ; for instance, the husband's rights over the wife's property. The moral sense of the community demands and obtains the abolition of these rights. Thus law is continually being brought abreast of moral feeling, without the support of which the constable is powerless. It is then the general moral sense of society which gives to law its permanent authority. No prudent government will either try to resist a demand supported by this general moral sense, or force on legislation which, though in itself beneficial, is obviously in advance of it.

There is little to be said upon the influence of law in the sphere of intellect. In civilized states there are but few instances in which the law attempts to prescribe how men are to think. The tendency of civilization is to allow the law to meddle less and less with the intellectual life of society.

(2) At this point we pass, by an easy transition, to consider what elements of permanence there are in the authority of *religious bodies*. A religious body or a church is, so far as it can be, a theocracy. There are few, if any, churches which, if they had the power, would not extend their authority over the whole of human life. In modern times, the main difference between the secular authority and any religious authority is this, that while the law only imposes restrictions on conduct, the religious authority claims supremacy in the intellectual sphere as well. It says not only, ' This thou shalt do, and this thou shalt not do,' but also, ' This thou shalt believe, and this thou shalt not believe '—and this, from the very nature of the case, in the highest spheres attainable by human thought.

In matters of conduct, the churches generally represent a higher moral standard than that of the law, and this fact is one of the reasons, perhaps the most solid and respectable reason, of the perpetual conflict between church and state. The contest is, in Europe, as old as Christianity ; for, outside of the pale of Judaism, it was in Christianity that religion first embodied itself as a social force.   Leaving on one side all debatable points, we may confidently assert that the success of Christianity in its earlier stages was due to the fact that the Christians opposed an organized society, based upon ethical principles, to an imperfectly instructed government. The intellect of the Graeco-Roman world had not penetrated far enough to understand the necessity, or to attempt in practice the organization of social life.   Add to this the facts that the principles of political economy were not understood at all, that taxation was based upon wrong principles, and that scientific knowledge was not, to any great extent, applied to beneficent inventions, and it will be easily seen that the lot of the poor and of the slaves throughout the Roman empire was likely to be a hard one.   The Roman aristocracy had the genius for deciding cases of dispute between individuals, and their law is one of the greatest monuments of human intellectual effort.   They were masters of the machinery of organization, and their roads united into a whole the distant parts of their empire.   But they did not know how to improve life or bring it forward, and they were unequal to the problem of dealing with the poor and miserable.   It was to these first that Christianity, with its binding ordinances, based upon the ancient and indestructible laws of the moral nature, gave new life and new hopes.   Had its basis been any other, nothing could have saved it from perishing amid its errors and its dissensions.   It is hardly necessary to mention any among the thousand instances in which religious bodies in Europe, since the appearance of Christianity, have used their influence in destroying or modifying immoral customs and institutions.

It is the other pretension, the pretension to dictate to the intellect, which weakens the authority of religious bodies, and will, so long as it is effectively put forward, destroy the permanence of that authority.   A constant struggle, one of the most tragical of all struggles, has long gone on between the churches and the progressive intellect of mankind.   The conscience—I will not limit the term by saying the intellectual conscience—of the leading men imposes on them the duty of practising intellectual honesty, a virtue at all times rare, and in a democratic society perhaps the rarest of all. The conscience of the religious community has been taught that its practice is strictly dependent on certain beliefs. Hence the churches are continually tending to lapse into what is neither more nor less than an immoral position. They find themselves under the necessity either of expelling from their midst the men who have, so far as is possible to man, attained the truth, or are conscientiously trying to attain it, or of carrying on a hypocritical coquetry with error. Now, it is much easier for a society to make unavowed alterations in its theories than to change the form of its practice ; and the religious bodies accordingly, in view of their corporate interest, adopt, if they can, the former alternative. Thus the outward coherence of the society is maintained ; but at what a price ! At the price of keeping alive the rivalries and animosities of the various churches, and preventing the co-operation of good men, as though the forces of evil could be met with a divided front ; at the price, also, of attempting impossible compromise, debauching the reason, and helping on the ruin of the thinking power, the noblest gift, as its exercise is the noblest prerogative of mankind.

The religious life, to be of any value, must spring from the centre of a man's moral being, and absorb the whole of it. ' Mine own with usury ;' ' mine own ' includes the entirety of the loan. The religion which represents only a part of the man will die off, and perhaps corrupt the other part.

The conclusion to which these considerations seem to point is that, in the case of these moral questions, the importance of which can be immediately seen and generally grasped, the authority of the church is likely to be permanent ; but that in the sphere of speculation it will almost certainly be transitory. A strong and united organization may be necessary for moral as for political purposes ; but the wise course is to break it up when it has done the work for which it was called into existence. Even now a tendency may be observed towards a union in practical moral effort on the part of churches widely divided on points of doctrine.

(3) *The authority of society or of public opinion.* In modern Europe this is, or is tending to be, stronger than that of law and of the religious bodies. Society, on the whole, supports the open force which is the arm of the law, and adds to it a more formidable power, that of public opinion. Public opinion is dominant from end to end of human life, from the region of mere fashion to that of moral action, and even of intellectual belief. Its force can hardly be exaggerated. Say of an action, 'Cela ne se fait pas' ('we do not do that'), and it is doomed. This tremendous engine will become stronger as social conditions are more equalized, and what is called the democratic type of government develops itself. Let us inquire where the authority of public opinion is permanent, and where it is not, or should not be.

In the whole sphere of feeling, and of action which depends upon feeling, it is nearly irresistible; I had almost said absolutely irresistible, but for the fact that great men have at all times been found who could dare to stand up and face it. If public feeling allow it, you can put a man to lingering torture or a painful death. If public feeling forbid this, the man will probably be rescued by the mob, or vengeance will be taken upon his judges and executioners. In our own days we have seen that boycotting and its cruel sanctions may command, or seems to command, the respectful admiration of literary men.

The *vox populi* is at the same time the present dread of the saint and the philosopher, and their hope for the future. If they dare, in the interest of moral and rational progress, to defy it, they become heroes and martyrs; but in the hour of their martyrdom, they are sustained by the knowledge that at some distant day the power which now seems to be their conqueror will bow before their prophetic insight.

Public opinion is then the strongest available force which can be invoked in the cause of humanity, and of all the graces, charities, and sanctities of life. It is permanently powerful when enlisted on the moral side; but only then. Its weakness lies in the fact that it represents not only the deep moral feelings of the community, but its superficial notions. Its dictates are nearly as imperative in the one sphere as in the other. It crushes the weak; it worships success, strength, and riches, the symbol of strength; its golden calves are conspicuous in every market-place. It affects to set up its laws in the higher regions of speculation, with the result that the great pioneers of progress are generally its enemies. It attempts to make every question a social question; to render its notions fashionable, to get them represented in high places, and adopted by the powerful. It says to the philosopher, 'Think as we do;' to the artist, 'Give up your high aspirations, and paint or sing as we like.'

(4) There is, however, a power, which in the long run proves itself stronger even than that of public opinion, and which public opinion is constantly, though in vain, endeavouring to crush—that of great men, the leaders of moral feeling and intellectual activity. It is curious to observe what concessions it is at all times tacitly making to their direction. The history of religious opinion in England during the last thirty years affords some striking examples. English society as a whole professes to be Christian in the sense of orthodox Protestantism, but it does not like the alteration of any of its formulae. The influence of many leading moralists and religious teachers has, however, done much during the last century to create a hatred of cruelty; and accordingly many religious persons dislike the damnatory clauses of the Athanasian Creed. If they do not openly revolt against them they say to themselves that the framers of those clauses, whatever they said, could not have meant it. Leading men of science, again, have succeeded in making public opinion uneasy on the subject of miracles, or at least unwilling to think about

them.   Habits of intellectual compromise have thus grown up with regard to this question, which are probably spreading, and occasionally find expression in remarkable theories ; such, for instance, as that the Almighty has throughout history taught mankind by 'illusions,' and that while particular events, which two thousand years ago were regarded as miraculous, may really have occurred, thcy need not be regarded as miraculous any longer.

It seems at first impossible to indicate any element of permanence in the influence of great men.   And yet no fact in every-day life is commoner than devotion to some leader, than hero-worship of some kind or other.

Great or leading men are always distinguished by general power and insight, by a force which in the mind seems analogous to physical force in the body, a force which imposes itself at once, the faculty of command.   This superiority may be manifested in an exceptional group of facts, or in an exceptional insight into human action, the human heart, and human motives ; or in an exceptional tenderness and power of sympathy ; or in all these combined.

Difficult as the subject is, it seems possible to distinguish a permanent and a transitory element in the influence or authority of great men.

The influence of a great man is permanent in direct proportion to the extent of its beneficence ; or, in other words, it is the more or less lasting according as it tends more or less to improve and consolidate society.   Frederick II made Prussia a nation and a power in Europe.   Napoleon Bonaparte, if we may believe M. Taine and others, founded the modern French polity ; modern Italy owes its existence to Cavour and Garibaldi.   The private weaknesses or vices of these men are forgotten in the memory of their public services.   The names of great scientific men are remembered in virtue of the permanent effect produced by their discoveries upon the life of mankind.   The foibles and littlenesses of Voltaire we pass over, remembering his great services to the causes of mercy and truth.

It may safely be said that, however unjust posterity may be (and unjust it very often is) to the memory of good men, the name of no great man will live as a centre of authority whose efforts have been anti-social, or in so far as they have been anti-social. It is not merely personal ascendency, or strong passions, or intellectual power which has assured the great men their permanent position. Their influence depends on the intensity of their unselfish effort, the greatness of their social achievement, the width of the social interests which their effort and achievement embraces. Hence it happens, as a rule, that intellectual greatness alone, even where it is not crippled by moral defects, obtains tardier recognition than the greatness of the statesman or the saint.

The progress of knowledge, and intellectual advance in general, seems at first sight to be the least moral of all great tendencies, and hence the jealousy of them so often shown by society at large. But it should be remembered that every new piece of knowledge gained, whether positive or negative, marks the starting-point of a new duty. 'This is true; therefore this must be believed, or this must be done : this is false ; therefore it must be disbelieved or avoided.' In no case can the *savant* or scholar escape the moral relation. Sooner or later it becomes his duty to proclaim the truth that is in him, and no one can exaggerate the danger which he may have to incur, or the height of moral effort which may be implied in encountering it. The martyr's death may be necessary, but it is the birth-throe of a new life for the community, who give him his reward in their acknowledgment that it is for them and for their higher humanity that he dares and suffers.

Indeed, in the constitution of authority the services of great men are by far the most important element. We are apt to think of great things as done by the consent of the masses ; and no doubt the *momentum* of this consent is of enormous weight. But there is seldom any permanent unanimity among men without a leader to embody and emphasize their aspirations. Seldom, too, does it happen that these aspirations are not first anticipated and expressed by a great man.   The most fatal error which any community can commit is to crush its men of genius.   It is in their insight and anticipations that the future of society lies in the germ.

The position and authority of a great man is the absolute reverse of that which belongs to law and to general opinion. The man goes forward, and represents the future ; law, and to a great extent social opinion, represent the past.   The man is in peril ; law and society are, or think themselves, safe.   The man seems to die and to be forgotten, but lives ; law and social opinion seem to be alive, though they may be dead.

As I said at the beginning of this article, four kinds of existing authority may for the sake of convenience be distinguished, but they are, in fact, organically connected.   I have tried to argue that every kind of authority, where permanent, rests on a moral or a social basis, and that where it rests on any other foundation, it sooner or later crumbles away.   It is not necessary in this place to attempt a complete definition of a moral act, or to inquire what is the origin of moral ideas. One may fairly appeal to the acknowledged fact that mankind tends to recognize certain acts, or conditions, as absolutely desirable, and certain others as absolutely intolerable.   The real aim of society, the goal of progress where progress is desired, is the development of the moral sense as the safeguard of humanity.   It is not material prosperity, nor even freedom from pain.   A particular movement in the history of mankind may appear to have material prosperity, or freedom from pain, as its object ; but no one would admit that these are the absolute object of the general movement of human feeling.   What men aim at in reality is not a merely negative freedom from restraint or from trouble, but the constitution of freedom for spontaneous moral action, or (in other words) for healthy social action.

Where, then, at any given time, is the seat of authority in conduct and intellect to be found ?

For each individual the absolute guide can, in the long run, be no other than his own conscience. By conscience I mean moral feeling. The individual conscience generally, to a great extent, reflects the common conscience of society; but it is, of course, equally true that every individual has a peculiar conscience of his own, that moral feeling does not exist in every one to the same extent, and that, consequently, there is never a time when a conflict is not going on, both between good men individually, and between different bodies of men in the same society. It may be urged, on the other hand, that the conflict between one good man and another is due not to the better, but to the worse, part in each. In every man there is a dead and a living part, so to speak, of the moral self. The conflict between good men is a conflict of the worser elements in their being. Again, the conflict between great men—saints or philosophers—and society is due to the fact that the conscience of the saint or philosopher is far more alive than that of the society in which he lives, and is therefore in advance of it. The conflict between different bodies in the same society may be, and often is, in great measure a conflict of material interests, in which case it does not concern our inquiry. If it is anything better, the same may be said of it as of the conflicts between good men, that it is due to imperfect moral apprehension on one side or on both.

When the individual conscience is in doubt, recourse is generally had to some external authority. This ought to be the recorded moral experience of the past, as summed up by the great moral pioneers of all ages and countries. It should be looked for, not in the laws set up by any one body of men, but, so far as possible, in the actual moral tradition and practice of mankind, interpreted according to the circumstances of the inquirer.

In the sphere of intellect, on the other hand, authority is generally to be looked for in the utterances of the living leaders of intellectual life ; I say the living leaders, because the conclusions and discoveries of the past are generally embodied in record and practice, and the demand for fresh light can only be met by the men who are actually engaged in the intellectual labours of the age.

New intellectual results are more readily accepted than new moral results, because a change in thought may easily take place without any serious social displacement, while a change in conduct, if hastily adopted, cannot possibly do so. And, in any case, the final moral consummation can only be realized by a series of conflicts, perhaps deadly and tragical. But these conflicts are, after all, healthy and natural, for the *odium morale*, like the *odium theologicum*, is only an evidence of the seriousness with which the combatants realize their object.

XI.

THE RELATIONS BETWEEN NATURAL SCIENCE AND LITERATURE [1].

————•••————

WHEN asked to lecture for your Society, I felt, for a short time, a difficulty in hitting upon a topic which, while in itself interesting and important, should at the same time admit of being handled with any profit in an hour's address. Many of you may perhaps have smiled when you saw so vast a subject put down on your programme as that which I eventually selected; and, if so, I must feel that the smile was justified. Yet, even in so short a time, I hope that I may be able, not, of course, to exhaust the subject, or even to do it moderate justice, but to indicate one or two points of view from which it may be considered in its most general bearings.

I do not propose to touch on any question of detail such as the title of this lecture might seem naturally to suggest— such as, for instance, how far it is possible for one man to combine the studies of natural science and literature, or how far literary style and handling is necessary to the proper exposition of scientific problems, or whether the influence of natural science upon literature, either in regard to the views of life which it has suggested, or in regard to literary style

[¹ A lecture delivered before the Newcastle Sunday Society in December, 1886, and since published by Mr. Walter Scott (London, n. d.) with other similar lectures by Mr. Romanes, Professor Moseley, and others.]

and execution, is, on the whole, a healthy one; or whether methods borrowed from natural science can be applied to the historical sciences.   I wish rather to speak of natural science and literature as two great branches of national culture and intellectual progress, and to ask what, in this point of view, is the real relation between them.   Are they two unconnected and in reality hostile departments of knowledge, one of which is destined, sooner or later, to extinguish the other, or are they both the offspring of the same moral and mental impulse, and therefore connected by the strongest ties of kinship and natural alliance ?

Some thirty years ago it was the quarrel between natural science and religion—that is, between natural science and a particular form of religion—which occupied public attention in this country.   Much of the dust raised by that controversy has now been laid.   But we now find ourselves involved in another, and perhaps a more serious, misunderstanding. We are all familiar with the opposition between natural science and literature which has in late years made itself felt in the field of education.   It was, I think, some twenty or twenty-five years ago when the general public in England began to demand that something at least of natural science should be taught in the high English schools.   I say the general public, for Mr. Herbert Spencer had, I think, for-mulated the extreme demands of natural science some time before.   He went as far as to claim that natural science and not literature should form the basis of general education. I do not know how far Mr. Spencer's views are now shared by the educational public of this country; whether there is a really considerable number of thinking persons who would seriously wish, if not to exclude literature altogether from our higher education, at least to subordinate it to natural science. But I am not wrong in saying that such a view is by no means extinct either in England or on the Continent, and that it has, and will long continue to have, representatives whose character and abilities claim every consideration for their theories.

There is no doubt that we have to look forward to a dispute, more or less, between natural science and literature in the field of education. The question has, in this country at least, only entered upon its first stage. Literature, the study of which is based mainly upon the study of the Greek and Latin classics, still holds the educational field. I, of course, should be the last person to complain of the well-established tradition which founds literary study upon the mastery of the Greek and Latin classics. They lie at the foundation of all subsequent literature, and the nation that ignores them altogether does so at its peril. But the nation that altogether ignores the educational claims of natural science also does so at its peril. No one can say that those claims have been adequately satisfied, or anything like it. Sooner or later, supposing peace and prosperity to be for a long time the lot of this country, we shall, after, maybe, much opposition, see a number of well-organized scientific schools spring up in England ; schools in which mathematics and some branch of physical science will form the staple of the training, while literature will be represented by its modern, not its ancient, branches. Only in this way, so far as I can judge, can the problem be solved. The two systems cannot be combined ;—to give a boy, in the years between ten and eighteen, such a general education as shall ground him thoroughly in the elements both of literature and of natural science seems to me an impossibility. This would involve a strain on the growing organization of youth which it would not be able to bear, and which, in the majority of instances (I am not speaking of the exceptionally strong intellects , would lead to enfeeblement in manhood. We should not be anxious to communicate to a growing boy everything that is worth knowing. Education, in those eight critical years, will always, in spite of the dreams of theorists, remain in great part a gymnastic exercise for the muscles of the mind ; a general strengthening of the frame for the future need of life. So far as it attempts to exceed this its province, so far as it aims at becoming, not a method of training for the future, but a device for cramming as much knowledge as possible into the head in a given period, it will defeat its own object, will weaken instead of strengthening, and will break down in lamentable failure.

It may well seem presumptuous in me to be speaking at all on the position and claims of natural science. On this subject I have indeed no claim to say anything at first hand. My life has been entirely devoted, and will, so far as I know, continue to be devoted, to one branch of ancient literature. But I cannot, nor can any one who keeps his eyes open, fail to notice the swiftness with which natural science has made its advances in late years, and the growing probability, I might say the certainty, that it will continue to advance, and will end by profoundly modifying the character and relations of human society. No one who has any knowledge of any branch of literature, still less any one who has a real interest in literature as a whole, can refuse his sympathy to any important movement in the great march of progressive civilization. Nay, it is the duty of all such persons to keep their eyes upon everything of importance which appears to further this progress. I may say for myself, as a student of Latin literature, that I look forward with eagerness to the day when scientific education shall be constituted on some such basis as that which I have attempted to indicate, or, at least, on some satisfactory basis.

But this opposition between natural science and literature in the field of education, does it not, you will say, point to something more serious than a mere dispute between two sets of educationists? Are there not wider interests involved? It there not at present in the minds of many eminent literary men a real dislike of natural science, of its methods, of the constant inroads which it seems to be making daily upon the various provinces of human life, of the points of view which it seems to be continually forcing upon us? On the other hand, is there not, on the part of scientific men, a distrust and suspicion of literature, its methods, and the habits of mind which are engendered by the study of it? I might answer that such an opposition does not seem to be inherent in the nature of the case ; that literary men, for one thing, have not always been antagonistic to science. The fact is very much the reverse. Some of the greatest men who have adorned the world of literature by their works, or encouraged men of letters by their sympathy, have found room for the strongest interest in the progress of science. I need only mention Voltaire, Frederick the Second of Prussia, and the great poet Goethe. These men, however, belong to the end of the eighteenth and the beginning of the nineteenth century, a time when human progress was viewed as a whole ; when the modern division, a false and baneful one, I think, but now so popular, between the intellect and the emotions was unknown ; when no leading writer would have ventured to hint that what was true for the reason was false for the emotions, or what was true for the emotions was false for the reason.

This peculiar attitude, not often, it is true, distinctly avowed, but still very prevalent among us, is partly due, no doubt, to that general slackening of the thinking power which any one, who takes the trouble to observe, may note as a characteristic of this generation. But it has also, to a certain extent, been encouraged by the position taken up by some of our greatest literary men. I suppose that the greatest name among English men of letters during the last fifty years has been that of Thomas Carlyle. Who else has been gifted with such insight into the human heart, such depth of passion, such sympathy, such splendour of imagination, such sincerity, such burning penetration, such a power of seizing and presenting facts? Yet Carlyle was, if not hostile, at least indifferent to science. If we may believe Mr. Froude, he regarded the great hypothesis of Darwin with something like contempt. And Carlyle, be it remembered, was a disciple of Goethe. But the greatest lesson which Goethe has to teach, the lesson of patience, Carlyle, it would seem, never learned. *Ohne Hast, ohne Rast*—without hasting, without resting—should be the motto of all who presume to put their hand to the highest moral and intellectual work. Carlyle was too much in a hurry. His personal prejudices and caprices were too strong to allow of his forming temperate views of the great problems of human life. He lacked the power, which, if not the whole, is certainly a large part of greatness, of waiting for the light, of remembering that Nature does not ask what man likes. And if this impatience was the failing of Carlyle, what must be said of Ruskin? On the part of this tender and beautiful writer, whose courageous protest against greed and all sorts of moral uncomeliness has brought strength to so many souls, and whose exquisite style is the delight of so many readers, we find the most violent aversion to physical science.

The position is plainly a false one. We seem to be engaged in an irritating family quarrel. Two great forces which should be co-operating for the benefit of the human race are found to be in mutual opposition. On which side does the fault lie? or is there fault on both sides? One knows, at any rate, what each party thinks of the other. The scientific man thinks the literary man a being devoid of the power of observation, whose interest is centred, if not in an unreal, at least in a partial view of things, in a study not of facts but of words and forms, or at the best of unfruitful abstractions. His mind is in the past, not in the present; he is the victim of memory and tradition and imagination and sympathy, not the pioneer of steady advance. The man of letters on his side complains, with the hero of Tennyson's *Maud*, that

'The man of science himself is fonder of glory, and vain,
   An eye well practised in Nature, a spirit bounded and poor.'

He thinks him shallow, without interest for the past, apt to encourage, if not to hold, low views of life. There is a literary fanaticism as well as a scientific fanaticism. One would make natural science the sole engine of human progress; the other would almost limit the intellectual life to the contemplation of the past, and the development of the imaginative faculty. But I am not concerned this evening with the extreme opinions of individuals, but with the facts of the case. And I would ask whether natural science and literature are naturally enemies, or whether they are not rather helpmates necessary to each other in the work of the world.

Perhaps it will be easier to answer this question if we first attempt to define what are the respective spheres of natural science and literature.

It is hardly necessary to insist that with regard to all the outward mechanism of life our debt to scientific investigation is incalculable. There is no need to repeat what every one knows, that for the means of easy communication between city and city, nation and nation, and for the preservation of human life against disease and death, we are indebted to scientific research, and to scientific research alone. Social life has been transformed by it, and the course of history altered. Take only the case of new routes opened to commerce. What changes have been brought about by the opening of the Suez Canal! What further changes may not be expected should the Panama Canal ever be completed! The facilities of communication have done much, and are every day doing more, to substitute one form of civilization for many. Unless some great natural convulsion should destroy at a stroke the civilizations of Europe and America, the nations of the world can never again live in solitude. Thousands can now travel with ease, and every day, where one adventurous explorer hardly dared to penetrate in a generation.

Consider, again, the region of medical science and art, and observe how the hand of the physician is already on the throat of disease. What a promise for the future is there! Indeed, I have an enthusiastic scientific friend who believes that political power will one day gravitate to the medical profession, such power does he think they will acquire over the whole conditions of human life.

But I will not weary you by repeating what you all know; for I am anxious to call your attention to another aspect of the question which is perhaps less obvious. It is this. Science has a moral function. It does more than merely ameliorate the physical condition of mankind. Its office is not limited to making communication easy and diminishing bodily suffering. The processes and the labour by which great discoveries are made involve in themselves a devotion at all times intense, and sometimes heroic, to the cause of truth and the good of mankind. Science, we should remember, has its heroes and its martyrs ; men who have forgotten themselves for the great object of serving their fellow-creatures. The mere fact that such immense demands on human courage and industry and patience are made by Nature upon those who would interrogate her secrets, is of the utmost moral importance. It renders infinitely more necessary than ever before the cultivation of the love of truth, and of the courage to utter it. These qualities are now seen to be as essential to the humblest scientific explorer as to the greatest philosopher. And the moral fibre of society in general is braced and strengthened by this necessity to an extent which it is impossible fully to estimate.

This is the moral function, or at least the moral result, of active scientific research. But again, philosophy itself, the highest effort of the human reason ; what does it not owe to these investigations ? Some of the philosophic systems which have most deeply influenced Europe, which have framed men's thoughts, and brought into them harmony and order where chaos reigned before, have to a large extent been based upon physical science. It was the philosophy of Aristotle, in great part founded upon the investigation of natural phenomena, which dominated the theology of the Middle Ages ; it was the philosophy of Leibnitz, a man who left his mark on several sciences, that gave its form to theological speculation in the eighteenth century ; it is the theory of Evolution, first hit upon by hypothesis, and more recently confirmed by extended observations, which now promises to recast our whole view of Nature and of human life. Such are the three great services of natural science to mankind, material, moral, and intellectual.

If so much is to be conceded to natural science by mere on-lookers, what, it may be asked, is left to literature except to record the progress of knowledge? M. Renan, perhaps the greatest man of letters now alive in Europe, has expressed more than a misgiving on this subject. The historical sciences, he says, are always being reconstructed. They admit of no advance and no certainty. Natural science, on the other hand, has an assured and certain progress; it has the future in its hands.

Must literature, then, throw up the cards? The answer to this question depends on the answer to another, What is literature?

Literature is not, as is sometimes supposed, a mere intellectual plaything, a recreation or means of enjoyment for an idle mind. I should, indeed, be inclined to go the length of saying that there ought to be no such thing as learned leisure or lettered ease, if by such terms is implied no more than a refined form of self-indulgence. Literary leisure, if it is to be worth anything, should be the devotion of the whole powers to a great branch of human advancement. For literature is the living record of the life of humanity. Can any pains spent upon the improvement and amplification of this record be adequate to such an object? We look forward to the future, and in the future, it is true, lies the realization of those hopes which hold men's heads erect, and make them bright and brave to face the problems of life. But if our life would gain depth and strength as well as brightness, it must rest on the memories of the past. Man is a being 'of large discourse, looking before and after.' If it is natural to love parents, children, kinsmen, and friends, shall not our heart go out also to our fellows who have gone before us? Should we not welcome as the faces of our brothers the faces of all men in whose deeds and sufferings the ever old, ever new story of human life has wrought itself out ? The theme of all history, fiction, and poetry is the same ; it is man and his story. The variations are the changes of time and surrounding. Just as in a great musical composition one conception is dominant, but set off and illustrated as it develops by a thousand subsidiary ideas which seem to grow out of, and again return to, the central thought ; so through all literature runs the story of humanity, so stern, so tragical, yet so tender, full of tears and smiles, of great achievement, and great events brought about by great achievement ; the spiritual unity of the human soul discerned amid the confused detail of individual character, battered and shaped by the strokes of circumstance.

Literature is (1) the record of facts, (2) the record of feeling and imagination, or (3) the record of thoughts.

(1) The record of facts. This branch of literature includes history and all written work subsidiary to history. Of the serious parts of literature it is this last, the written work subsidiary to history, which is most plentifully represented in our generation. The same thirty or forty years which have seen such strides made in the natural sciences, have witnessed also a reawakening of the passion for knowledge throughout the whole intellectual world. In every department of knowledge the scholar is busy. The language, the customs, the religion, the laws, the fables, the oldest writings of all peoples on the earth are now being submitted to a scrutiny such as they have never known before. The newly-born science of Anthropology demands the assistance of every form of literary research ; all is fish that comes to its net. Here, at any rate, is a direct link between natural science and literature. The spirit and its method of both forms of research is the same. Hypotheses, wild and rash, or probable and full of promise, may, nay must, be thrown out on all hands ; but in the long run the unerring touchstone of fact must be applied to them, and only that will survive which endures the application.

Not, of course, that research is the only form of historical literature. History is much more than a mere collection of facts ; it is the record of facts in their organic connexion. The historian is not only a lover of truth, not only a chronicler of events. These, indeed, he must be at his peril, but how much more ! Insight into human nature—and this implies the rarest knowledge and finest sympathy of which man is capable ; the power of tracing the delicate relation between deed and motive, and the pressure of action upon circumstance and circumstance upon action ; knowledge of the world, in short, in the highest sense of that expression ; beyond all this, the grasp of mind which shall seize and unfold the hidden laws of the great movements in the opinions and desires of nations, the greatness of imagination to conceive, and the readiness of hand to present, the whole in a luminous picture. From this point of view the task of the historian may well seem to demand powers which, perhaps, have never been, and never will be, united in one individual. If I am not much mistaken, there is required in a great historian something of the same combination of powers as in a great student of Nature— patience in collecting facts, and the power of tracing relations between them. The sympathetic touch, the power of imaginative presentment, is not required—at least, not so imperatively required—in the physicist ; although imagination is necessary to form a great hypothesis. Before the theory is proved it must have been conceived as possible.

But, it may be asked, great as are the powers requisite to form a historian, will not large masses of history soon have found their final chronicler and be laid on the shelf, for men never to return to them ? Is not Renan right in saying that the historical sciences are always being reconstructed, that they never advance ? Yes, they are always being reconstructed, but they do advance. Of some portions of history it may perhaps be true that there is little to be added to our knowledge of them, though even this assertion would be hazardous when every year brings fresh discoveries in detail to throw light even on those periods which we think we know best.

But with regard to what I may perhaps call the wider relations of history, the bearings of one group of historical facts upon another, the connexion of the history of one nation with that of another, the progress of knowledge is constantly making momentous changes, and will continue to do so. There is hardly any line of investigation in any branch of physical science which may not, sooner or later, end by affecting, in some degree, our views of history; hardly any historical fact which may not ultimately have its use in assisting scientific investigation, or in confirming its results.

(2) Another great branch of letters is formed by what I may call the literature of imagination. In this I would include poetry, and all kinds of prose fiction.

Poetry is not bound, of course, to truth of fact. A poet may invent the story on which he founds his lyric, or his epic, or his drama; or he may take an existing story, and alter or modify its details at pleasure. But when this is said, the sphere of the poet's liberty is defined. He is not free to describe human feeling and action as other than what, according to the laws of human nature, they must be. He is not free to make characters inconsistent with themselves. He is not free to violate the truth of Nature in any of her manifestations. This, too, must be added, that the wider the sphere of his sympathies, and the deeper their roots, the greater, the truer, and the more representative of its age will his poetry be.

There are certain works which the world has agreed to call classical. These are the writings whose fame is absolutely assured so long as civilization exists; the writings which, whatever else is read, must always be read so long as there are people who care to read at all. Let us glance at some of these, and ask what is the secret of their great position. The elements which may always be discerned in such productions are grandeur of conception, width of view, force of passion and imagination, and industrious elaboration of form. The Homeric poems are a mirror of the ancient life which they describe, in all its aspects. Virgil's *Aeneid* is an imaginative presentment of the Roman world at the moment of its transition from a republican to an imperial constitution. In the *Divine Comedy* of Dante all the highest culture and thought of the Middle Ages is summed up; the modern world, with its infinity of individual feeling, its wide and lofty aspirations, its sensitiveness to every wave of emotion, its industrious working after real knowledge, finds its prophet in Goethe. All these writers, besides being representatives of the mental attitude of a whole age, show the power of their characters, by leaving their stamp indelibly on the language in which they wrote.

But what separates poetry from prose fiction?

First, a greater sensitiveness and depth of feeling, which is reflected in the poet's language and in the form of his composition. It is the duty of a prose writer to write well; it is the duty of a poet to write perfectly. Let him give all his time and pains to his language, and he will hardly have given enough. Poetical diction and metre, rhythm, and even rhyme and alliteration, are mere expressions of a hidden sympathy between sound and emotion, the laws of which we have not yet ascertained. That strong feeling will express itself in rhythmic as rhyming words is a law of nature. When was there ever an exciting election contest without its rhymes and its epigrams? Ascend the scale of emotion from its lowest to its highest point, and you arrive at last at the marvellous and subtle music of a Milton, which seems to echo the voices, not only of Nature, but of long generations of prophets and poets in its manifold and closely-wrought harmonies.

The novelist has a field for imagination wider than that which is open to the poet, though in his wider field he may be content with humbler flights. He is nearer to the actual facts of life. Indeed, the novelist and historian may to a certain extent claim the same ground. One thing, if no other, they must have in common, the knowledge and love of mankind, and the perception of the laws which regulate the play of human conduct. The greatest novelists are those who, to a deep and delicate sympathy with the phases of human action and passion have added a comprehensive view of history; an appreciation of its greatness. Such writers are Fielding in the last century, Balzac and Thackeray in our own. These great novelists are in full contact with history and politics; they have an eye for great situations wherever they are to be found. At the same time they move on the whole in the sphere of simple ideas and feelings; ideas and feelings which, nevertheless, are those out of which is born all that is sublime and all that is degraded in life. Balzac has such a vivid sense of the power of those natural intuitions, that in his imagination they flame up to a height unfamiliar to our soberer English perceptions. In Fielding and Thackeray, under the veil of a simple yet eminently beautiful style, and a rigidly accurate and unambitious style of drawing, you feel the seriousness and meaning of human life. You see the narrow and difficult path of goodness climbing to the sun-lit heights, and the bottomless abyss of destruction on either hand. Prediction is always dangerous; but I cannot help believing that the works of these three writers, owing to their combination of depth of feeling with comprehensiveness of view, will last as long as literature itself.

Between poetry and novels on the one hand, and physical science on the other, there is, I need not say, no more relation than the general unity of spirit which links all great work together; a unity of spirit based partly on the desire to see and to record things as they are, partly on the exciting influence which the mere contemplation of facts in their harmonious unity has on the imagination. The mind is always restless and progressive. Give it a set of facts, the laws of which are completely ascertained, enable it even to trace all facts whatever to their ultimate origin, and to analyse the network of laws which connect them, still it will not be satisfied. The imagination and the love of beauty are awakened in the same proportion as the understanding is informed; the whole being is absorbed in a rapture which transcends the limits of pleasure and pain.

(3) The highest form of literature is philosophy, which is the summing up of the whole moral and intellectual effort of the age with which it deals. The philosopher aims at penetrating to the laws or final principles, not of any one set of phenomena, but of all phenomena. As the centuries roll on, and knowledge is increased, old systems of philosophy are thrown off and new ones formed. But a great philosophic system has always the same characteristics. It seeks to elicit their meaning out of all known facts ; to bring facts under law, and to bring many laws under one law. For the sake of convenience I have called philosophy a branch of literature. It is rather science and literature in their ultimate unity.

Let us now return a little upon our path, and having stated, very barely and meagrely, what are the respective spheres of literature and natural science, let us ask again whether there is any natural antagonism between them. The moral and intellectual impulse from which both literature and natural science have sprung is one and the same. It is no more and no less than the forward movement of the human spirit. Natural science is not, in spite of appearances, often mis- understood, materialistic. Concerned with matter it is, but science is mind concerned with matter, mind working for its own satisfaction. On the other hand, literature is not all fancy, nor its pursuit all enjoyment. Even in its most imagi- native phases, as I have tried to show, it would starve without a basis of fact ; and, however little it may be concerned with fact, it demands the whole mental and moral powers of its followers, as the condition of rewarding them and the world. Let men of letters and men of science forget themselves and think only of their work, how to do it, if possible, to perfection, and all disagreement will vanish. If there is a quarrel between literature and natural science, it is because the representatives of one side or the other have formed an inadequate idea of their duty. I am bound to say that for some time past, at least in England, there has been more of manly effort, more of patient self-renunciation, among the students of natural science than among the students of literature. I am not speaking of a past generation, of such men as John Stuart Mill or Herbert Spencer. But in the present generation it seems to me that a kind of paralysis has seized upon the thinking power which should produce good literature in this country. One cannot but notice, side by side with a restless desire to produce, a curious impatience of the labour of learning, of thinking, and even of writing well. Emotion, sentiment, a newly awakened interest in a subject, are taken as ample justification for writing about it. We have swarms of novels, but no great novelist; much poetry, but very little which combines the two essential requisites of perfection in form with singleness of aim, and indirect interest in modern problems.

What are the causes of this phenomenon I do not venture to say. But it is well to remember that the same cause has in times past virtually undermined the foundations of good literature, and that it may do so again. We are apt to assume, from the experience of the last three hundred years, that a supply of good literature will never be wanting. But there have been very long periods of history when the creative power seemed to have become extinct. At the beginning of the second century A.D. the spirit of the ancient Greek and Latin literature, the determination to think and to know, to live in the light of day, to write adequately to one's best ideas, sickened and died. A long period of barrenness followed, which lasted more than a thousand years. During that time many great men were born, but very few great books. If anything is to save literature at the present time, it is the spirit which inspires the best scientific work. Even the most imaginative work, even lyric poetry itself, suffers when put out of a healthy relation to fact. Imagination and fancy, without the courageous determination to face things as they are, to be straight and right with the world as it is, are like plants severed from their roots. Their mother earth gives them life no longer.

To combat the encroachment of emotion and sentiment upon the domain of reason (and I think there is a real danger now of such encroachment) a powerful intellectual movement is required, such as shall be adequate to draw forth the whole power of those leading spirits who ought to aim at asserting their influence in shaping the course of future events. Such a movement was wanting in the ancient world, but may be kept alive in the modern world by the spirit of scientific investigation. Again and again it must be urged that it is the love of truth, the determination to penetrate to things as they are, which is the spring and principle of moral life. The devotion to this great end purifies and elevates every part of our existence, clothing it in the austere grace of virtue. And it is this devotion which in honest scientific investigations is, so to speak, organized and concentrated.

There is a unity in all moral and intellectual effort, which is felt at once by those seriously concerned in furthering such effort, whether the sphere of their studies be the same or not. It is in the present age more than ever important that all should join hands who have the great cause at heart; who care that men should be led in the steep and narrow path of advance; for follow they always will, in the long run, those who will call 'Forward' to them in such a cause. In the present age, I say, it is most important, for literature and science are no longer now, as they once were, the property of a comparatively small and privileged class. The tendency—the inexorable tendency—of things is towards destruction of privilege and diffusion of knowledge. Yet even in the most democratic state of society and politics there must be leaders; nay, let us hope, and do all we can to realize the hope, that a democratic society may choose its leaders better than an aristocratic society. It is sometimes hinted that a democracy is jealous of superior merit. I hope not; I shall not believe this until I see it. The danger to which democracy is liable seems to me to be not that it will naturally dislike superior merit—that I believe to be a shallow and ill-tempered calumny—but that the demand made by the people upon their leaders' individual efforts may be too much for the healthy development of their leaders' powers. The peril to the intellect in a large popular community is that it should become relaxed in quality; that reflection should take the place of thought, and sentiment of passion ; that men should write before they think, and think before they learn. Every one in any way marked out as capable of serving his fellows is now called upon to give them, and that visibly and audibly, a large part of his time. It is right that every one's heart should be with his fellow-men. But the interests of the nation will not be well served if its superior men are prevented from concentrating their powers upon the great task of elevating the level of existence.

It is, on the contrary, in the highest interests of the nation that every motive should be set before its intellectual leaders which may inspire them to the love of intellectual toil, and that they should in the same proportion be discouraged from allowing anything to weaken or dissipate their intellectual force. Literature and natural science represent two of the most important factors in the higher life of a country. Neither can subsist in a healthy state without the other. In face of the gigantic growth of science there is a visible danger lest literary men should feel their interests overborne, and started into antagonism against an intellectual force which is, in reality, identical with that which has inspired the best work of their own predecessors.

To English literature, with its memories of Shakespeare, Milton, Locke, Hume, Gibbon, Fielding, Byron, Macaulay, Carlyle, the voice of its greatest representative seems to say—

> ' To thine own self be true,
> And it will follow as the night the day,
> Thou canst not then be false to any man.'

Without the spirit that animates the best scientific work literature will become emasculate and ultimately die. Imagine, if such a thing be possible, a society in which the whole of the best mental power and effort should be given to physical science. I almost think that a new literature would evolve itself from the mere sense of confinement. The mind must, after all, work upon itself and express itself. But of this I am sure, that the human race cannot afford to drop its connexion with its own past, nor to renounce its powers of imagination and its love of beauty. It is for the production of these and such-like qualities, after all, that civilization exists.

One sacred fire animates the frame of human history, bursting into flame and light in the great acts by which genius in discovery, or invention, or research, or imagination asserts itself. The extinction of this fire would be the destruction of humanity itself.

BIBLIOGRAPHY

———◆◆———

THE following list is intended to contain everything which Mr. Nettleship wrote, with the exception of a few—I believe, a very few—anonymous pieces. I have compiled it in the hope that it may be of use to scholars : incidentally it will be found to illustrate the history of Mr. Nettleship's studies, and his method of work by printing his material piecemeal. The dates are the years of publication : within each year the larger works and original contributions are given precedence of reviews. References are usually to volumes and pages.

1863.

Quibusnam praecipue de causis exortum sit Bellum Civile Americanum. Oratio Latina in theatro Sheldoniano habita die Junii 17, 1863. Oxonii, 8vo. [Chancellor's prize for Latin Essay.]

1869.

The Mostellaria of Plautus. Journal of Philology, ii. 229-234. [A review of Ramsay's Mostellaria.]
Review of Wagner's Terence. Academy, i. 55.
Review of Ribbeck's Beiträge zur Lehre von den lateinischen Partikeln. Ib. 87.

1870.

Sertum Carthusianum .. cura G. B. Brown. Cantabrigiae, 8vo. [This contains five pieces of Latin and Greek verse written at the Charterhouse by Mr. Nettleship while a schoolboy.]
Review of Ritschl's Neue Plautinische Excurse, i. Academy, i. 114.
Review of Schweizer-Sidler's Elementar- und Formenlehre der lateinischen Sprache für Schulen. Ib. 168.
Review of Ritschl's Opuscula, vol. ii. Ib. 275.

Review of Bergk's Beiträge zur lateinischen Grammatik. Ib. 301.
Review of Corssen's Aussprache, Vokalismus und Betonung der
lateinischen Sprache, i. (second edition). Ib. ii. 81.

1871.

P. Vergili Maronis Opera. The Works of Vergil, with a Commentary by John Conington. Vol. iii, containing the last six books
of the Aeneid. London, 8vo : part of the Bibliotheca Classica.

[Conington published the first volume of his Vergil, Eclogues and
Georgics, in 1858 (second edition, 1865), and the second volume,
Aeneid i–vi, in 1863. In the same year he asked Mr. Nettleship
to assist him with the third volume by writing the notes to books
x–xii. In the end he wrote the notes on books vii–ix and xi ;
Mr. Nettleship wrote most of the notes on books x and xii, and
edited the whole volume, after Conington's death, in 1871. The
subsequent editions of all three volumes were supervised by
Mr. Nettleship : see under 1872, 1874, 1876, 1880, 1883.]

On the Lengthening of Short Final Syllables in Vergil. Journal
of Philology, iii. 95–102. [Reprinted with slight alterations in the
third volume of Conington's Vergil : excursus to book xii.]

Review of Keil's Plini Epistulae. Academy, ii. 147.

On the Pronunciation of the Letter *v* in Latin [a letter]. Ib. 253.

Review of Corssen's Aussprache, Vokalismus und Betonung der
lateinischen Sprache, ii. (second edition). Ib. 361.

Review of Biedermann's Christliche Dogmatik. Ib. 517, 534.

1872.

P. Vergili Maronis Opera . . . with a Commentary by John
Conington. Vol. ii, second edition, revised by Long and Nettleship.
[This did not differ much from the first edition, published in 1863.]

The Satires of A. Persius Flaccus, with a Translation and Commentary by J. Conington . . . edited by H. Nettleship. Oxford, 8vo.
[Second edition, 1874 ; third edition, 1893.]

On the Etymology of consul, exsul, insul, praesul. Journal of
Philology, iv. 272–274.

The True Aim of Classical Education, with a few practical suggestions as to the methods of teaching classes in the highest forms of
classical schools. Harrow. 8vo, pp. 16.

Review of Roby's Latin Grammar from Plautus to Suetonius,
i. Academy, iii. 98.

Review of Schweizer-Sidler's Taciti Germania. Ib. 155.

Review of Wagner's Trinummus. Ib. 298.

Review of Merguet's Entwickelung der lateinischen Formen-bildung. Ib. 358.

Review of Merguet's Ableitung der Verbalendungen aus Hilfsverben und die Entstehung der lateinischen -e Declination. Ib. 358.

Conington's Persius [reply to a review]. Ib. 419.

1873.

Review of Madvig's Adversaria, i. Academy, iv. 55.

Review of Naumann's Mélanges Philologiques. Ib. 257.

Review of Forbiger's Virgil (ed. 4), i. ii. Ib. 357.

1874.

P. Vergili Maronis Opera . . . with a Commentary by John Conington. Vol. iii, second edition, revised by Long and Nettleship. [This edition differs very slightly from the first.]

The Satires of A. Persius Flaccus, with a Translation and Commentary by J. Conington . . . edited by H. Nettleship. Second edition, revised.

On the word βουγάϊος. On vis (second person of volo), invitus, nvitare. On Thucydides, i. 37. Vergiliana [Ecl. iv. 5 ; Aen. ii. 615, iii. 525, vi. 126, 273.] Ovid, Fasti, ii. 676. Journal of Philology, v. 18-27.

Review of Pretor's Letters of Cicero to Atticus, i. Academy, v. 292.

Brief review of Prichard and Bernard's Selected Letters of Cicero. Ib. 292.

Brief review of Prichard and Bernard's Selected Letters of Pliny. Ib. 293.

Review of F. A. Paley's edition of Lycidas. Ib. 425.

Review of Jules Simon's la Réforme de l'enseignement sécondaire. Ib. 693.

Review of Lothar Meyer's Zukunft der deutschen Hochschulen und ihrer Vorbildungsanstalten. Ib. 693.

Review of Matthew Arnold's Higher Schools and Universities in Germany. Ib. 693.

Review of Kennedy's Public School Latin Grammar. Ib. vi. 486.

1875.

Suggestions Introductory to a Study of the Aeneid. Oxford, 8vo, pp. vi. and 47. [Reprinted in Essays in Latin Literature, pp. 97–142.]

Review of Roby's Latin Grammar from Plautus to Suetonius, ii. Academy, viii. 457.

Review of W. Morris' Aeneids of Vergil done into English Verse. Ib. 493.

Review of J. S. Reid's Academica of Cicero. Ib. 607.

1876.

P. Vergili Maronis Opera . . . with a Commentary by John Conington. Vol. ii, containing the first six books of the Aeneid. Third edition [a reprint of the second].

Essays on the Endowment of Research, by various writers. London, 8vo. [To this Mr. Nettleship contributed an article on the present relations between classical research and classical education in England (pp. 241–268), which is reprinted in the present volume.]

Duumviri, triumviri ; saeculum ; superstes, superstitio, superstitiosus. Journal of Philology, vi. 97–99.

Review of Ribbeck's Römische Tragödie im Zeitalter der Republik. Academy, ix. 612.

Review of Jebb's Attic Orators. Macmillan's Magazine, November.

1877.

Grandis ; laetus ; aura. Remarks on Passages in Varro, Cicero [pro Murena 42], Vergil [Aen. ix. 731.] Journal of Philology, vii. 169–176.

Review of Ussing's Plautus, i. Academy, xi. 34.

Review of Opuscula Philologica ad Io. Nic. Madvigium . . . a discipulis missa. Ib. 79.

Review of Ellis' Commentary on Catullus. Ib. 165.

Review of Gustavus Fischer's Latin Grammar, together with a systematic treatment of Latin composition, *and* Elements of Latin Grammar in connexion with a systematic and progressive Latin Reader. Ib. xii. 45.

1878.

The Roman Satura. Oxford, 8vo. pp. 20. [Reprinted above.]

Catullus. Fortnightly Review, May 1878. [Reprinted in Essays in Latin Literature, pp. 84–96.]

Review of Rudolf Hirzel's Untersuchungen zu Cicero's philosophischen Schriften. Academy, xiii. 13.

The Bodleian MS. of Catullus [letters]. Ib. 441, 465.

Two Oxford MSS. of the Life of Vergil attributed to Donatus [a letter]. Ib. xiv. 13.

1879.

Maurice Haupt. A public lecture delivered in the Hall of Corpus Christi College, Oxford, on May 24, 1879. [Reprinted in Essays in Latin Literature, pp. 1-22.]

Ancient Lives of Vergil, with an essay on the poems of Vergil in connexion with his life and times. Oxford, 8vo. pp. 70.

Vergil [part of 'Classical Writers,' edited by J. R. Green]. London, 8vo. pp. 106.

Notes on the Aeneid. Journal of Philology viii. 50-61.

On the pro Cluentio of Cicero. Ib. 233-248. [Reprinted in Essays in Latin Literature, pp. 67-83.]

Adfectus and Adfictus. Ib. 273-4.

A Harleian MS. of Servius [a letter]. Academy, xv. 11.

Review of J. E. B. Mayor's Thirteen Satires of Juvenal, ii. (second edition). Ib. 459.

1880.

Notes on the Graeci Annales of Fabius Pictor. Journal of Philology, ix. 51. [Reprinted in Essays in Latin Literature, p. 341.]

Verrius Flaccus [first article]. American Journal of Philology, i. 253-270. [Reprinted in Essays in Latin Literature, pp. 201-221.]

Review of Lewis and Short's Latin Dictionary. Academy, xvii. 199.

1881.

P. Vergili Maronis Opera . . . with a Commentary by John Conington. Vol. i, fourth edition, revised, with corrected orthography and additional notes and essays.

Verrius Flaccus [second article]. American Journal of Philology, ii. 1-19. [Reprinted in Essays in Latin Literature, pp. 222-247.]

Notes on Placidus. Ib. 342-4

Review of Wilkins' Cicero de Oratore, ii. Academy, xx. 241.

1882.

Sermons preached in the Chapel of Harrow School and elsewhere, by Thomas Henry Steel, with a prefatory memoir by H. Nettleship [pp. 63]. London, 8vo.

Thilo's Servius. Journal of Philology, x. 153–171. [Reprinted in Essays in Latin Literature, pp. 322–340.]

Dissignare. Ib. 206–8.

Lexicographical Notes. Ib. xi. 99–115.

Notes on the Glosses quoted in Hagen's Gradus ad Criticen. Ib. 116–8.

The Earliest Italian Literature, considered with especial reference to the evidence afforded on the subject by the Latin language. Ib. 175–194. [Public lecture, June 1882 ; reprinted in Essays in Latin Literature, pp. 45–66.]

Nonius Marcellus. American Journal of Philology, iii. 1–16, 170–192. [Reprinted in Essays in Latin Literature, pp. 277–321.]

Notes in Latin Lexicography : carina ; Dossennus ; lacuar and laquear ; plăga ; res summa [Aen. ii. 322, xi. 302]. Transactions of the Oxford Philological Society, 1882–3, 3–4.

Review of Anecdota Oxoniensia, Classical Series, i. 2. Nonius Marcellus : the Harleian MS. 2719, collated by J. H. Onions. Academy, xxii. 170.

Review of Ellis' Ibis. Philologische Wochenschrift, ii. 560.

1883.

P. Vergili Maronis Opera . . . with a Commentary by John Conington. Vol. iii. revised.

The de Arte Poetica of Horace. Journal of Philology, xii. 43–61. [Reprinted in Essays in Latin Literature, pp. 168–187.]

Notes in Latin Lexicography. Ib. 191–202.

The Bucolic Caesura. American Journal of Philology, iv. 75–76.

The Noctes Atticae of Aulus Gellius. Ib. 391–415 [Reprinted in Essays in Latin Literature, pp. 248–276.]

Horatian Chronology. Transactions of the Oxford Philological Society, 1882–3, 23–26.

Vergil in 1881 and 1882. Transactions of the Cambridge Philological Society, iii. 222–227.

Review of T. E. Page's Horatii Carminum libri iv. Academy, xxiv. 301.

Review of A. Palmer's Satires of Horace. Ib.

884.

P. Vergili Maronis Opera . . . with a Commentary by John Conington. Vol. ii, fourth edition, revised, with corrected orthography and additional notes and essays.

Biographisches Jahrbuch für Alterthumskunde, begründet von C. Bursian, vii. 47–52. Obituary Notice of Mark Pattison.

Reply to a Review of Notes on Latin Lexicography [Journal of Philology, 1883, xii. 191] in Wölfflin's Archiv, i. 312. Wölfflin's Archiv, i. 461.

Review of Hertz's Aulus Gellius, i. Academy, xxvi. 155.

1885.

Lectures and Essays on Subjects connected with Latin Literature and Scholarship. Oxford, 8vo. pp. xii. and 381.

Notes in Latin Lexicography. Journal of Philology, xiii. 67–80, 164–168; xiv. 29–34.

Cicero's Opinion of Lucretius [ad Q. F. ii. 11]. Ib. xiii. 85.

Notes on a few of the Glosses quoted in Hagen's Gradus ad Criticen. Ib. 168.

Ius Gentium. Ib. 169–181. [Reprinted in Contributions to Latin Lexicography.]

Notes on the Epinal Glossary. Ib. xiv. 34–39.

Review of Verrall's Studies in the Odes of Horace. Academy, xxvii. 47.

Review of Mark Pattison's Memoirs. Ib. 215.

Review of E. A. Sonnenschein's Mostellaria. Ib. 348.

Review of Wilkins' Epistles of Horace. Ib. xxviii. 258.

1886.

Coniectanea [Varro ap. Non. 543; Cicero pro Plancio, 95; Lucretius, iv. 418; Livy, ii. 23. 8; Quintilian, i. 6. 1, vi.1, x. 1. 83; Marius Victorinus, pp. 9, 11 Keil; Cledonius, p. 47 Keil; Servius in Donatum, p. 444 Keil; (Sergius) expl. ad Donatum, p. 532 Keil; Salvian de Gubern. Dei, i. 47]. Journal of Philology, xv. 21–23.

Notes in Latin Lexicography. Ib. 24–27.

Part of the Excerpta Charisii and the fragment de Idiomatibus Generum, printed in the fourth volume of Keil's Grammatici Latini. Ib. 27–28.

Notes on Vergil. Ib. 29–34.

The Historical Development of Classical Latin Prose. Ib. 35–56. [Reprinted in the present volume.]

Dierectus. Ib. 186–188. [See Contributions to Latin Lexicography, p. 437.]

The Study of Latin Grammar among the Romans in the first century A.D. Ib. 189-214. [Reprinted in the present volume.]

Coniectanea [Plautus, Poenulus, prol. 1, 586, 628; Bacchides, 440; Cicero pro Flacco, 18, 20; Charisius, Servius; the St. Gallen Glossary; the Epinal Glossary]. American Journal of Philology, vii. 496-499.

Latin Etymologies [averruncus, densus, obnoxius, obscenus, sentio, temerare]. Suggestions towards a Glossary of Technical Terms of ancient Latin Grammar. On varieties of form representing an older stage of vocalism [Avius, Ovidius; Bavius, Bovius; Pacuvius, pecu]. Transactions of the Oxford Philological Society, 1885-6, 10-16.

On the Latinity of the Epicedion Drusi [Consolatio ad Liviam]. Ib. 16-19.

Review of Krebs' Antibarbarus, re-edited by Schmalz (sixth edition), i. ii. Academy, xxx. 280.

Review of Beck's de M. Valerio Probo Berytio Quaestiones Novae. Ib.

1887.

Passages for Translation into Latin Prose, with an introduction. London, 8vo. pp. viii. and 135. Also a key to the same.

The Study of the Modern European Languages and Literature in the University of Oxford. Oxford, 8vo. pp. 20.

Dictionary of National Biography, xii. 13-17. Biography of John Conington.

The Relations between Natural Science and Literature. A lecture delivered before the Tyneside Sunday Lecture Society. London, 8vo. [Reprinted in the present volume.]

Recent Theories of the Saturnian Verse [Keller, Havet]. Transactions of the Oxford Philological Society, 1886-7, 23-25.

Evidence given by the Latin Grammarians on the Pronunciation of Latin. Ib. 1887-8, 9-20.

Saeculum, saecula [Epicedion Drusi, 45]. Wölfflin's Archiv, iv. 598-600.

The Composition of the de Verborum Significatu of Verrius Flaccus [a letter]. Academy, xxxii. 223.

The University Extension Scheme [a short letter]. Ib. 425.

Review of J. E. Mayor's Juvenal, vol. i, fourth edition, and vol. ii. third edition. Classical Review, i. 15-17.

Review of Boelte's de Artium Scriptoribus Latinis. Ib. 278-279.
Review of Haskins and Heitland's Lucan. Ib. 293-296.
Review of Reitzenstein's Verrianische Forschungen (Breslauer Philologische Abhandlungen, i. 4). Ib. 307-308.
Review of Gertz's L. Annaei Senecae Dialogorum libri xii. Academy, xxxi. 328.

1888.

Life and Poems of Juvenal. Journal of Philology, xvi. 41-66. [Reprinted in the present volume.]
Notes in Latin Lexicography. Ib. 67-70.
The Title of the Second Book of Nonius. Ib. 70.
Servius on Aeneid ix. 289. Ib. 160.
Adversaria [Cato Origines, ii. 27 Jordan ; Horace Odes, ii. 2. 5 ; Livy, ii. 21. 4, iii. 5. 14 ; Servius on Aen. x. 664, 705 ; Digest ii. 4. 20 ; Lucan, i. 314, iii. 558, vii. 139; Velius Longus, pp. 49, 52, 63 Keil; Sergius in Donatum, 520 Keil; Verg. Aen. xii. 158]. Ib. 189-192.
Coniectanea [Gellius, xviii. 4. 11 ; Nonius, 328, 9; Servius on Ecl. ii. 8, vi. 626, &c.; Orientius, i. 433, ii. 215, 219-222 ; Placidus, 8. 11 Deuerling; Glossae Nominum, p. 25, Löwe; Prodromus, p. 217 ; Eberhard of Bethune, viii. 242 Wrobel]. Ib. xvii. 117-119.
The Epinal Glossary. Ib. 120-124.
Lucan, iii. 559-560. Ib. 155-156.
Laedere numen. Ib. 157-158.
Angustator. Wolfflin's Archiv, v. 106.
Ambago, ambigio. Ib. 222.
Glossae Nominum (Löwe). Nonius, p. 127 Müller [perficus]. Ib. 414.
Sportula [Martial, ix. 72 ; Pliny, Epist. ii. 14. 4 ; Juvenal, x. 70]. Classical Review, ii. 37.
Review of Thilo and Hagen's Servius, iii. 1, In Bucolica et Georgica Commentarii. Ib. ii. 82.
Review of Fierville's Grammaire inédite du xiii. siècle. Ib. 214-215.
Review of Rawlins and Inge's Eton Latin Grammar for use in the higher forms, Kennedy's Revised Latin Primer, Postgate and Vince's New Latin Primer, and Kennedy's Shorter Latin Primer. Ib. 279-283.

1889.

Contributions to Latin Lexicography. Oxford, 8vo. pp. xxiv and 624.

Essays by the late Mark Pattison . . . collected and arranged by H. Nettleship. Oxford. 8vo. 2 volumes.

Ad Glossas Latinograecas [Corpus Glossariorum ii]. Wölfflin's Archiv, vi. 149-150.

Ordium, exordium. Ib. 433.

The Sacrifice of Education to Examination . . . edited by Auberon Herbert. London, 8vo. Pp. 91-95. A letter by Mr. Nettleship.

Review of Ellis' Commentary on Catullus (second edition). Academy, xxxvi. 240.

Review of Goetz and Gundermann's Corpus Glossariorum latinorum, ii. Glossae graecolatinae et latinograecae. Classical Review, iii. 128, 181.

Brief Review of Georges' Lexicon der lateinischen Wortformen, A—H. Ib. 181.

Brief Review of Günther's Quaestiones Ammianeae Criticae. Ib.

Brief Review of Neue's Formenlehre, vol. i. (third edition), fascicule i. Ib. 181.

Brief Review of Schweizer-Sidler and Gruber's Grammatik der lateinischen Sprache. Ib. 275.

Brief Review of Gundermann's Frontinus. Ib. 311.

Brief Review of Kübler's Iulius Valerius. Ib.

1890.

The Moral Influence of Literature. Classical education in the past and at present. Two popular addresses. London, 8vo. [Reprinted in the present volume.]

Adversaria [Cicero de Oratore, i. 241, in Verrem, ii. 5. 119 and 125; de Legibus, i. 17; Scriptor belli Africi, 48; Horace Ars Poetica, 245; Frontinus Strateg. i. 5. 1; Tacitus Hist. ii. 77]. Journal of Philology, xviii. 140-1.

On the Pervigilium Veneris and Tiberianus, i. 7. Ib. 142.

Literary Criticism in Latin Antiquity. Ib. 225-270. [Reprinted in the present volume.]

Vergil Georgic i. 263. Ib. 328.

Brief Review of Hoffmann's Codex Mediceus plut. xxxix des Vergilius. Classical Review, iv. 45.

Brief Review of Noiret's Lettres inédites de Michel Apostolis. Ib.

Brief review of Goetz and Gundermann's Corpus Glossariorum Latinorum, iv. Ib. 255.

Review of De Ponor's Festus, pars i. Ib. 412-413.

1891.

A Dictionary of Classical Antiquities, Mythology, Religion, and Art. From the German of Dr. Oscar Seyffert, revised and edited with additions by H. Nettleship and J. E. Sandys. London, 8vo. [Mr. Nettleship translated the articles from Astrology to Heræa and wrote additional notes on Latin literature.]

Dictionary of Greek and Roman Antiquities, by William Smith. Third edition by W. Wayte and G. E. Marindin, 2 volumes. London, 8vo. Vol. ii. p. 597. Article on Satura.

Cognomen, cognomentum. Commentationes Wölfflinianae, 183-8.

Notes in Latin Lexicography. Journal of Philology, xix. 102-108.

Adversaria [Plautus Miles, 654 ; Rudens, 60, 468, 509, 533, 538, 566, 574, 663 ; Vergil, Aeneid v. 602 ; Tacitus Dialogus, 28, 31 ; J. E. B. Mayor's Latin Heptateuch]. Ib. 109-112.

Notes on the Vatican Glossary 3321 [Corpus Glossariorum iv]. Ib. 113-128, 184-192, 290-295.

Horace de Arte Poetica [90, 172]. Ib. 296.

Review of Ellis' Noctes Manilianae. Academy, xl. 97.

Review of Fisch's Lateinische Nomina Personalia auf -o, -onis. Classical Review, v. 61-62.

Review of Stowasser's Dunkle Wörter. Ib. 263-264.

Review of Hessel's Eighth-Century Latin-Anglosaxon Glossary, preserved in the Library of Corpus Christi College, Cambridge. Ib. 382-384.

Brief Review of Hild's Juvenalis Satira Septima. Ib. 429.

Review of Förster's de Apulei quae fertur Physiognomia recensenda et emendanda. Ib.

Brief Review of Georges' Lexicon der lateinischen Wortformen. Ib. 431.

Review of Keil's Catonis de Agricultura liber, Varronis Rerum Rusticarum libri tres, ii. 2 ; Commentarius in Varronis Rerum Rusticarum libros tres. Ib. 474-475.

1892.

Isaac Casaubon, by Mark Pattison. Oxford, 8vo. Second edition [edited by H. Nettleship].

Authority in the Sphere of Conduct and Intellect.   International Journal of Ethics, ii. (Jan. 1892), 217–231. [Reprinted in the present volume.]

Notes on the Vatican Glossary 3321.   Journal of Philology, xx. 53–62, 183–190.

Notes in Latin Lexicography.   Ib. 175–181.

Tonitralis in Lucretius ii. 1105.   Ib. 181.

Absanitas=insanitas [Varro ap. Non. i. 67 Müller].   Wölfflin's Archiv, vii. 578.

Review of G. C. Warr's translation of Teuffel and Schwabe's History of Roman Literature (fifth edition).   Classical Review, vi. 62‑63.

Review of Stowasser's Zweite Reihe dunkler Wörter.   Ib. 167–168.

Brief Review of van Wageningen's Persiana.   Ib.

Brief Review of Norden's In Varronis Saturas Menippeas Observationes selectae.   Ib. 226.

Review of Keller's Lateinische Volksetymologie und Verwandtes. Ib. 408–410.

Review of Bonnet's le Latin de Grégoire de Tours.   Ib. 451–453.

Brief Review of Leeper's Translation of Juvenal.   Ib. 461.

Brief Review of Harnack's Gospel of Peter [Sitzungsberichte der kgl. preuss. Akademie der Wissenschaften zu Berlin, Nov. 1892]. Ib. 462.

1893.

The Satires of A. Persius Flaccus, with a Translation and Commentary by J. Conington . . . edited by H. Nettleship.   Third edition revised.

Corpus Poetarum Latinorum . . . edidit Io. P. Postgate, Fasc. 1. Londini 4⁰. 106–203, text of Vergil by Mr. Nettleship. [The text was printed in 1890 ; for the introduction see p. viii.]

The Printed Editions of Nonius Marcellus   Journal of Philology, xxi. 211–232.

Notes on Nonius, Book i.   Ib. 233–234.

Notes in Latin Lexicography.   Ib. 235–239.

1894.

Scaliger's Unpublished Emendations in Nonius.   Ib. xxii. 74–83 [printed after Mr. Nettleship's death].

INDEX.

Quintilian, 55; as literary critic, 77; source of his criticisms on Greek writers, 79; compared with that of Dionysius, 80; his criticisms on Latin writers, 84; his admiration for Cicero, 85, 114; opinion of Sallust, 108; teacher of Pliny and Tacitus, 114 *n.*; as a grammarian used Verrius' *de Orthographia*, 152; used Pliny's *Dubii Sermonis*, 158; used Remmius Palaemon, 166.

Remmius Palaemon, grammarian, 149; his *Ars Grammatica*, 163; partly preserved in Quintilian, 166; its contents, 168.

Research contrasted with education, 173; divorce of the two in England, 174; results of the examination system, 180; isolation of learned men in England, 182; reforms, 186.

Rome in the first century A.D., 135; how far described fairly by Juvenal, 139.

Sallust as a writer of prose, 107; copied Cato, 107.

Satura, origin, 24; Ennius, 27; Lucilius, 28; Varro, 35; Horace, 36; Petronius, 38, 76; Juvenal, 38; general characteristics, 29; Greek elements, 41.

Scholarship, English conceptions of,

175; at schools, 177; at Universities, 178; ways of reform, 186.

Schools in England, 176, 187: suggested reforms in teaching scholarship, 186.

Science, conflict with literature in the present day, 236; place in education, 237.

Tacitus as a literary critic, the *Dialogus*, 86; compared with the *Brutus*, 90; style of the *Dialogus*, 114 *n.*; of his historical works, 115.

Terentius Scaurus, quotes largely from Verrius, 151.

Varro (Terentius), *saturae* of, 35, 52; as a literary critic, 51; his *de Poematis*, 53; disliked by Horace, 52, 72; his grammatical treatises, 147; whether used by Quintilian, 151, 157, 159; their character, 157; used by Pliny, 161.

Velius Longus, quotes largely from Verrius, 151.

Vergil, influence on literature of the empire, 73; influence on Juvenal, 153; the *Aeneid*, 247.

Verrius Flaccus, 148; part of his *de Orthographia* preserved by Terentius Scaurus, Velius Longus, and Quintilian, 151; character of that work, 157; used by Pliny. 161.

THE END

For EU product safety concerns, contact us at Calle de José Abascal, 56–1°,
28003 Madrid, Spain or eugpsr@cambridge.org.

www.ingramcontent.com/pod-product-compliance
Ingram Content Group UK Ltd.
Pitfield, Milton Keynes, MK11 3LW, UK
UKHW010349140625
459647UK00010B/941